Mathematical Economics of Multi-Level Optimisation

Contributions to Economics

Gerhard Gehrig/Wladyslaw Welfe (Eds.)
Economies in Transition
1993. ISBN 3-7908-0721-4

Christoph M. Schneider
Research and Development Management: From the Soviet Union to Russia
1994. ISBN 3-7908-0757-5

Bernhard Böhm/Lionello F. Punzo (Eds.)
Economic Performance
1994. ISBN 3-7908-0811-3

Lars Olof Persson/Ulf Wiberg
Microregional Fragmentation
1995. ISBN 3-7908-0855-5

Ernesto Felli/Furio C. Rosati/Giovanni Tria (Eds.)
The Service Sector: Productivity and Growth
1995. ISBN 3-7908-0875-X

Giuseppe Munda
Multicriteria Evaluation in Fuzzy Environment
1995. ISBN 3-7908-0892-X

Boris Maurer
R & D, Innovation and Industrial Structure
1996. ISBN 3-7908-0900-4

Giovanni Galizzi/Luciano Venturini (Eds.)
Economics of Innovation: The Case of Food Industry
1996. ISBN 3-7908-0911-X

David T. Johnson
Poverty, Inequality and Social Welfare in Australia
1996. ISBN 3-7908-0942-X

Rongxing Guo
Border-Regional Economics
1996. ISBN 3-7908-0943-8

Oliver Fratzscher
The Political Economy of Trade Integration
1996. ISBN 3-7908-0945-4

Ulrich Landwehr
Industrial Mobility and Public Policy
1996. ISBN 3-7908-0949-7

Arnold Picot/Ekkehard Schlicht (Eds.)
Firms, Markets, and Contracts
1996. Corr. 2nd printing 1997.
ISBN 3-7908-0947-0

Karin Peschel (Ed.)
Regional Growth and Regional Policy Within the Framework of European Integration
1997. ISBN 3-7908-0957-8

Thorsten Wichmann
Agricultural Technical Progress and the Development of a Dual Economy
1997. ISBN 3-7908-0960-8

Ulrich Woitek
Business Cycles
1997. ISBN 3-7908-0997-7

Michael Carlberg
International Economic Growth
1997. ISBN 3-7908-0995-0

Massimo Filippini
Elements of the Swiss Market for Electricity
1997. ISBN 3-7908-0996-9

Giuseppe Gaburro (Ed.)
Ethics and Economics
1997. ISBN 3-7908-0986-1

Frank Hoster/Heinz Welsch/Christoph Böhringer
CO_2 Abatement and Economic Structural Change in the European Internal Market
1997. ISBN 3-7908-1020-7

Christian M. Hafner
Nonlinear Time Series Analysis with Applications to Foreign Exchange Rate Volatility
1997. ISBN 3-7908-1041-X

Sardar M. N. Islam

Mathematical Economics of Multi-Level Optimisation

Theory and Application

With 6 Figures
and 39 Tables

Physica-Verlag
A Springer-Verlag Company

Series Editors
Werner A. Müller
Martina Bihn

Author
Dr. Sardar M. N. Islam
Director
Sustainable Economic Growth Program
Centre for Strategic Economic Studies
Victoria University of Technology
City Campus
P.O. Box 14428, MCMC
Melbourne, Vic., Australia 8001

ISBN 3-7908-1050-9 Physica-Verlag Heidelberg New York

Cataloging-in-Publication Data applied for
Die Deutsche Bibliothek – CIP-Einheitsaufnahme
Islam, Sardar M.N.: Mathematical economics of multi-level optimisation: theory and application; with 39 tables / Sardar M. N. Islam. – Heidelberg: Physica-Verl., 1998
(Contributions to economics)
ISBN 3-7908-1050-9

Softcover Design: Erich Kirchner, Heidelberg

SPIN 10631536 88/2202-5 4 3 2 1 0 – Printed on acid-free paper

Acknowledgment

I thank all who have assisted me in the preparation of this book and its earlier version (Islam 1994). Prof. P. Sheehan, Director, and Prof. B. Grewal, Deputy Director, Centre for Strategic Economic Studies, Victoria University have always encouraged me to complete the book. I am indebted to them. Thanks are also extended to the Victoria University of Technology for providing the facilities for preparing the final draft of the book and to other persons who assisted me in different forms at different stages of this study, especially to Dr. B. Felmingham, Fred Puno, Margarita Kumnick, Lucy Firth, Gordana Volkanovska, and Tammy Tam. I am very grateful to Shantanu, my son and my best research assistant for this book. Without his help, I could not publish this book.

Last, but not least, is my hearty gratitude to my family members, specially my two sons Milon and Shantanu and my mother, who had to bear an enormous amount of suffering caused by time allocated for undertaking the study. I am not sure whether anything can compensate their loss and forbearance due to my absence from them during this study. I am indebted to them for the rest of my life.

Sardar M.N. Islam
Centre for Strategic Economic Studies
Victoria University of Technology
Melbourne
Australia

May 1997

Foreword

The main hypothesis of this study by Sardar M N Islam is that since there exists a multi-level policy making system in the energy sector, with interacting processes of government and private sector decision making, in the formulation of energy plans and policies, choices of these two level decision makers should be considered explicitly. To accomplish this goal, an optimum energy plan should be developed within the framework of a multi-level optimisation approach and of a model the energy sector utilizing this framework.

To support the hypothesis, a theoretical energy planning approach is developed in this volume within the framework of the theory of economic policy planning, policy systems analysis and multi-level programming which is an operational multi-level optimisation method. The Parametric Programming Search algorithm has been developed in order to provide an alternative algorithm for solving the multi-level programming problems.

On the basis of this theoretical model, an Australian Energy Policy System Optimisation Model has been developed and is outlined.

The multi-level optimisation model is used to formulate an Australian multi-level energy plan. The results of this study suggest that a reformulation of existing Australian energy policies is needed. This study also draws a conclusion that a multi-level optimisation approach can provide an operational methodology and a framework for optimum multi-level energy planning.

This study overcomes the limitations of existing single level optimisation models, and therefore makes a significant contribution to the principles and methods for economic modelling in a market economy. This is evident from the fact that Dr Islam's work in this area has already gained international recognition.

This book shall be of great interest to researchers, academics, practitioners, policy makers and students (especially post graduate students), in the areas of mathematical economics, resource and environmental economics and planning and operational research.

The Centre for Strategic Economic Studies is proud to be associated with the publication of this volume in the Physica-Verlag's series titled Contributions to Economics.

Professor Peter J Sheehan
Director
Centre for Strategic Economic Studies
Victoria University of Technology
Melbourne
Australia

May 1997

Contents

List of Tables

List of Figures

1 Introduction

1.1 Introduction

A long standing result from classical economics is geared to the establishment of the thesis that a market economy, through competitive equilibrium, ensures the most efficient allocation of resources[1] (Debreu 1959) judged by the Pareto optimality criterion (Pareto 1971) that no one can be made better off without making some one worse off.

In reality markets may fail to allocate resources in an optimum manner (market failures). There are several reasons why market failure may occur (Bator 1958): externalities (economies and diseconomies), incomplete or non-existence of markets, existence of monopolistic elements, and public goods and merit goods, government ownership, and existence of a social contract for fair distribution of income and wealth (Webb and Ricketts 1980). These market failures provide an economic rationale for the formulation of economic policies at the sectorial level such as an energy plan.[2] Government intervention in these conditions is justified as a means for achieving the efficient allocation of resources among other societal objectives. However, major economic decisions in a market (mixed) economy are undertaken by individual economic agents, while government policy decisions

---

[1] An historical account of different views on the efficiency of different economic systems may be seen in Blaug (1985), and Oser and Brue (1988).

[2] Because of these market failures and the resultant problems in the energy sector, a number of issues and options has developed in the energy policy area. Some of these policy issues relate to short-term adjustments in the energy market (in the form of supply, demand, input and price controls), an appropriate pricing and depletion of energy resources, conservation of energy, inter-fuel substitution, energy import independence, determination of appropriate tax regime in the energy sector, long-term adjustment in the economy, etc. (A comprehensive discussion on these issues and options and their resolution will be provided in Chap. 7.) The development of these issues necessitates the formulation of an energy plan that can resolve these issues in the pursuit of solving energy problems.

decisions influence the behaviour of economic agents. Therefore, a market economy is characterised by the existence of a two-level hierarchical decision making system.

There are two types of decision makers: policy makers (the government) and the economic agents (producers and consumers). These decision makers attempt to optimise their goals (optimising behaviour) subject to constraints and their decisions are interrelated. The goals of individual decision makers at various levels are rarely consonant, and intervention is usually justified by this inconsistency. The policy makers can control the actions of the economic agents by some direct controls, such as import control, price fixation, etc., or indirect controls such as taxes and subsidies, and policies which encourage expenditures for research and development.

A multi-level optimisation (MLO) modelling approach is appropriate in representing a hierarchical multi-level policy formulation systems of a market economy, especially in a sectorial policy context such as energy planning.

Energy planning is a relatively new discipline. Events in the world energy[3] market since the beginning of the 1970s to the present time, including the Iranian oil embargo and the dramatic oil price increases, and the heavy dependence of modern economies on energy, have created an increased awareness of the economic consequences of energy problems such as imported inflation, unemployment, recession, the finite nature of fossil fuels, and national security (Mork 1981; Munasinghe and Schramm 1983; Webb and Ricketts 1980). It has been argued that these energy problems are the manifestations of market failures in ensuring the allocation of resources in a socially desirable pattern (Griffin and Steele 1980).

For either pragmatic or ideological reasons, almost every nation has initiated the formulation of energy plans to accommodate energy problems (Meier 1984; Stancescu 1985;

[3] Energy is the power to do things. In this study the following forms of energy: potential, kinetic, heat, chemical, electrical radiant, and nuclear which are produced from common sources such as crude oil, coal, natural gas, etc. are considered (Harder 1982). Energy from such sources as human and animal muscles are not included.

Munashinghe and Schramm 1983). An energy plan[4] may involve energy (systems) planning and/or policy (system) planning. Energy planning involving both energy systems and policy planning can be defined as multi-level (two-level) energy planning. The upper level of this plan involves the formulation of a set of government optimum energy policies (energy policy planning), while at lower level an optimum plan of the sector or economic agents is specified which is referred to as energy systems planning. Thus in a developed market economy context, multi-level energy planning generates both an energy policy plan of the government (a set of policies) and an optimum energy system reflecting the optimum decisions of economic agents.[5] MLO models have the structure required for representing the multi-level energy planning systems.

1.2 The MLO Approach

A multi-level optimisation approach is developed to formulate a multi-level plan that can resolve the underlying policy issues and options and can provide a set of comprehensive policies. The essential elements of the approach and its justifications are discussed below.

1.2.1 The MLO Approach

An MLO (bi-level) model can formally be represented as follows.[6]

Optimise $W = w(\pm T, X)$ (a) policy objective function

$\{T\}$

---

[4] Energy planning may be defined as a process of influencing the energy sector resource allocation, directly or indirectly, by manipulation of the coefficients and variables of the energy system or by using a set of instruments such as taxes and subsidies, so that the energy sector performs in the directions consistent with the preferences of the policy makers.

[5] Unless otherwise mentioned, energy planning will mean energy system planning or energy policy planning or both in this study.

[6] Detailed discussion about the constraints, variables and the optimisation problem in (1.1) will be provided in Chap. 3 and Chap. 4.

s.t.

$g_1(\pm T, X) \leq R_1$ (b) policy constrains

(1.1)

Optimise $C = c(\pm T, X)$ (c) behavioural/energy

$\{X \mid \pm T\}$ sectoral objective function

s.t.

$g_2(\pm T, X) \leq R_2$ (d) behavioural/energy sectoral constraints

$X \geq 0$ (e) non-negativity constraints

where

$\pm T$ = a vector of variables controlled by the upper level decision makers or policy makers,

X = a vector of variables controlled by the lower level decision makers or energy producers and consumers.

For the policy studies, in the context of a multi-level hierarchical policy system, policy system analysis[7] provides the conceptual framework, the theory of economic policy planning offers the analytical and operational framework and MLP provides a methodology. Therefore, a policy system study needs to be developed within the framework of policy systems analysis, the theory of economic policy planning and MLP (Chap. 4).

Within the above modelling framework, an optimum energy planning model for Australia (AEPSOM) is developed. AEPSOM is a price control[8] MLP energy sector model, which

[7] This study adopts a systems analysis/study of energy planning. The essential elements of this approach (Enthoven 1962) are:

... a cycle of definition of objectives, design of alternative systems to achieve those objectives, evaluation of alternatives in terms of their effectiveness and costs, a questioning of the objectives, a questioning of the other assumptions underlying the analysis, the opening of new alternatives, the establishment of new objectives.

[8] Different forms of MLP are defined in Chap. 3.

incorporates the underlying energy policy objectives and instruments, and reflects the economic and technical characteristics of the energy sector.

To solve AEPSOM, the Parametric Programming Search (PPS) algorithm is developed. In this algorithm, the lower level problem is solved as a parametric programming problem. Alternative solutions generated by the parametric programme are searched to find the solution which optimises the upper level objective function and satisfies the upper level constraints.

1.2.2 Justifications for an MLO Approach

It should first be stressed that the MLO approach is not the only methodology which can be adopted for energy planning. The MLO is proposed as an alternative approach to energy planning since it has several advantages as a methodology for formulating a particular type of multi-level energy plan which is discussed in Chap. 4. The main intention of this study is to stimulate further discussion about the suitability of various types of models and approaches for energy planning rather than to give a definite verdict.

The justifications for adopting the proposed MLO approach to energy planning are summarised in the following paragraphs.

(1) Representation of the underlying policy system: In order to specify an optimum government policy in a multi-level policy system, an MLO approach is necessary since an MLO model can represent the characteristics and elements of the multi-level hierarchical policy system (the multi-level policy making system can be defined as an MLO model).

This is illustrated as follows. In the model (1.1), there are two objective functions and two sets of constraints (two optimisation sub-models). These two optimisation sub-models (policy model (equations 1.1.a to 1.1.b) and behavioural model (equations 1.1.c to 1.1.d)) represent the optimum decision making systems of the policy makers and economic agents. The policy makers optimise the policy objective function (maximisation of social welfare, GDP, etc.) subject to the policy constraints (limits on taxes, budget deficit, etc.). The economic agents optimise the behavioural objective function (minimisation of total energy sector cost) subject to the energy sector constraints (demand, supply, and capacity constraints, etc.).

The MLO model also captures the simultaneous interdependence and interactions between these two types of decision makers. Goal interdependence implies that the attainment of the upper level objective is dependent on the achievement of the objective of the lower level, although the objectives of the two levels are generally different (conflicting objectives). In equation (1.1) the two objective functions (two sub-models) are interdependent through the variable ±T which links both. The intervention of the authorities at the upper level on the lower level is also represented in the model by the policy instrument variable ±T. The MLO model also clearly makes a distinction between the variables which are under control of the two types of decision makers: policy makers control ±T (taxes and subsidies) while the economic agents control X (energy supply and use).

The MLO model also represents the hierarchical structure of the policy system. In the MLO model, the upper level decision makers choose ±T and then the decision makers at the lower level adjust their behaviour to optimise their decisions.

(2) Generation of a multi-level plan: In summary, an MLO model can generate a multi-level energy plan involving both an energy system plan and an energy policy plan.

(3) Formulation of a comprehensive and consistent energy policy plan: A further attribute is that of coordination. It has been stated before that government energy policies are sometimes incompatible, so a set of energy policies should be formulated in a comprehensive and integrated framework to ensure the consistency of these policies. Existing practice in energy modelling is to use econometric models to study energy-economic policies such as taxes and subsidies policies, while mathematical programming models are primarily used to study technology policies for example conservation policy. The achievement of consistency between these receives a major emphasis here. For example, optimum energy resource allocation and technological patterns suggested by a single level mathematical programming model in a behavioural model of the energy sector may not remain optimum if government

taxes and subsidies are introduced into the policy system. Alternatively, the consideration of the detailed technical structure of the energy sector may provide a different set of taxes and subsidies from that suggested by a macro-econometric model. Therefore, to formulate an appropriate multi-level energy plan, a methodology is needed which can be adapted to the formulation of both types of policies simultaneously. As an MLO model contains both taxes and subsidies and technical details of the energy sector (represented by $\pm T$ and X respectively in model (1.1)), an MLO model can be used to formulate a set of energy policies embracing energy economic and technology policies.

(4) Applied welfare economic applications: An MLO model can also be used to study some welfare issues related to energy planning such as the desirability of government intervention.

1.3 Energy Planning: Multi-Level Energy Planning System

While previous multi-level planning studies have considered the interrelationships between macro and sectoral planning problems, the present multi-level planning approach recognises the existence of multi-level decision making within a sector. The relevance of previous multi-level procedures and the case for the present multi-level planning approach have been summarised as follows.

In most cases of policy planning in market economies, macro and sector policy deliberations are not linked closely enough to benefit from such procedures. But at the sector level itself there is a two-level problem. The two levels are the decentralised level of producer and consumer decisions and the policy choice level, at which decisions are made on policy instruments (Hazell and Norton 1986, p. 321).

The rationale for the formulation of multi-level energy planning follows from the real world market failures common in the energy sector, and the concern for the attainment of societal objectives. Government intervention in these conditions is justified as a means for achieving the efficient allocation of resources among other societal objectives. However major economic decisions in a market (mixed) economy are undertaken by individual economic agents, while government policy decisions influence the behaviour of economic agents. Therefore, an energy sector in a market economy is characterised by the existence of a two-level hierarchical decision making system. There are two types of decision makers: policy makers (the government) and the economic agents (producers and consumers). These decision makers attempt to optimise their goals (optimising behaviour) subject to constraints and their decisions are interrelated. The goals of individual decision makers at various levels are rarely consonant, and intervention is usually justified by this inconsistency. The policy makers can control the actions of the economic agents by some direct controls, such as import control, price fixation, etc., or indirect controls such as taxes and subsidies, and policies which encourage expenditures for research and development.

Decision making in the energy sector may be viewed as hierarchical. The policy makers (the upper level decision makers) announce their policy measures first. Then the economic agents in the energy sector (the lower level decision makers) choose their optimum actions. On the basis of the reactions of economic agents to policy announcements, the policy makers choose their optimum policy.

The overall performance of the energy sector (resource allocation and consumption) depends on the decisions of both these decision makers, and the achievement of the government's economic policy objectives depends on the reactions of the economic agents to the policy measures announced by the government. Therefore, decisions of the government and economic agents are interdependent in the following sense: optimum decisions of any of them cannot be formulated separately, and a multi-level energy plan is appropriate since such a plan can incorporate the interdependent plans of different decision makers at different levels in the multi-level hierarchical policy system.

Models help the coordination of data necessary for energy planning, the construction of future scenarios, and the formulation of efficient and effective policy instruments (James 1983, pp. 2-3). Because of the roles that models play in energy planning, it is now established practice to use a model to undertake any type of responsible energy planning study.

1.4 Objectives of the Book

The objective of this book, which is a revised version of Islam (1994), is to develop and extend the theory of MLO and to apply the extended MLO approach to formulate a multi-level (quantitative) optimum energy plan. In the process, this study will endeavour to achieve the following sub-objectives:

(1) To evaluate the suitability of existing energy planning approaches/models for multi-level energy planning;

(2) To formulate a multi-level energy plan by adopting a multi-level optimisation (MLO)[9] approach to energy planning (based on the structure of multi-level programming (MLP),[10] the theory of economic policy planning (Tinbergen 1952) and of policy system analysis (Mesarovic, Sanders, and Sprogue 1973), and

(3) To explore the implication of this energy plan for a market economy.

1.5 Plan of the Book

The book is organised in the following manner.[11] Chapter 2 presents a discussion of the theory and methodology of MLP and the mathematical and economic properties of an MLP model.

---

[9] For a definition of optimisation see Skrapek, Korkie, and Daniel (1976). MLO may be defined as a process of obtaining the optimum (choosing the best alternative/option) solution (maximum social welfare, minimum cost, etc.) to a problem involving several decision making sub-problems at different levels of decision making and represented by a mathematical model consisting of several sub-models related to different sub-problems.

[10] The term 'MLO' relates to the general model structure, while MLP is a mathematical programming problem (emphasis is on solution algorithm) and multi-level planning refers to a plan which is the output of an MLO model. These different terms have been used to indicate different aspects of energy planning and modelling (Candler and Norton 1977).

[11] Like any other optimisation study, this study follows the different phases of an optimisation study (Taha 1976):

(a) definition of the problem under study/the objective of the study (Chap. 1 and 2),
(b) development of the relevant model (Chap. 4),
(c) solution of the model (Chap. 3 and 6),
(d) validation of the model (Chap. 6), and
(e) application of the model results (Chap. 7).

Chapter 3 presents a discussion of the algorithmic approach adopted in this study (PPS algorithm) and the mathematical properties and evaluation of the PPS algorithm solution of an MLP model.

Chapter 4 contains a survey of literature on existing overseas and Australian energy policy models. In addition, a discussion of the theoretical and conceptual foundations of an MLO energy planning model is provided and an approach to such energy planning is developed.

Chapter 5 consists of a discussion of the specification of AEPSOM for 1979-80 (while Appendix B discusses AEPSOM 1989-90) as an illustrative application. The rationale for specifying the elements (as they are in the study) of AEPSOM and the sources of its data are also discussed in this chapter.

Chapter 6 reports the essential results generated by AEPSOM and provides tests for the reliability of these results. This chapter also highlights some essential characteristics of multi-level decision making.

Chapter 7 discusses the multi-level planning applications of the model. It forecasts an optimum energy system and it prescribes an energy policy plan in the form of a set of optimum energy policies for Australia.

Chapter 8 consists of an overview of the main aspects of the study and makes some conclusions.

2 Multi-Level Optimisation

2.1 Introduction

Multi-level optimisation (MLO) is a useful technique for mathematical analysis. Recently, multi-level programming (MLP)[1] has been developed as a mathematical programming technique for multi-level optimisation (Candler and Norton 1977). Although it is a powerful analytical technique for multi-level optimisation, experiments (mostly at academic levels) are continuing to develop the mathematical and economic theory of MLO and algorithms to solve an MLP. The objective of this chapter is to develop the theoretical foundations of an MLO model.

2.2 Definitions

Some definitions are provided in this section.[2]

2.2.1 Linear Programming

The following is a linear programme (LP):

$$\text{Max}\, C = cX_{22}$$

$$\{X_{22}\}$$

---

[1] In this chapter, only one special type of MLP which is bi-level programming, is considered.

[2] The main mathematical terms used in this chapter will be defined at the appropriate places. The mathematical dictionary of Skrapek et al. (1976) contains most other terms and concepts used in this chapter.

s.t. (2.1)

$A_2X_{22} \geq R$

$X_{22} \geq 0$

Assumptions:

(1) A is an (M X N) matrix ; rank of (A) = M < N ;

(2) c, $X_{22} \in E^N$, $R \in E^M$;

(3) $S_1 = \{A_2X_{22} \geq R, X_{22} \geq 0\}$ is a non-empty, convex and compact set;

(4) the objective function is linear and continuous, and

(5) the LP problem has a unique optimum solution.[3]

Definitions:

(1) Activities:

X_{22} is the vector of the activities of the model (2.1).

(2) Basic solution:

A basic solution to LP is a solution vector $X_{22} \in E^N$ (an extreme point) which is obtained through solving the LP for M variables by setting the remaining N-M variables equal to zero.

(3) Basic feasible solution and optimum solution:

A basic solution vector $X_{22} \in E^N$ that satisfies the constraints: $A_2X_{22} \geq R$ and $X_{22} \geq 0$ is defined as the basic feasible solution and the basic feasible vector that optimises (in the present case maximises) the objective function $C = cX_{22}$ is the optimum solution.

2.2.2 Multi-Level Programming (Price Control Bi-Level Programming)

The following is a non-linear price control MLP model:[4]

---

[3] In large scale numerical linear programming models, this assumption is generally correct (Candler and Norton 1977).

[4] This is an abridged version of the model (5.1) in Chap. 5. In this formulation, the lower level objective function is being perturbed by ±T. The upper level constraints on and preferences for ±T are reflected (i) in the policy and budgetary constraints (2.1.c) and (2.1.d), and (ii) in the upper level objective function in model (2.3.a).

$$\text{Min } WL = wX_{11} \quad (2.3.a)$$

$\{\pm T\}$ Policy/Upper level problem

s.t.

$$X_{11} = I^*X_{22} \quad (2.3.b)$$

$$T_l \leq \pm T \leq T_p \quad (2.3.c)$$

$$\{(+T)X_{22} - (-T)X_{22}\} \geq 0 \quad (2.3.d)$$

$$\text{Min } C = (c \pm T)\, X_{22} \quad (2.3.e)$$

$\{X_{22} \mid \pm T\}$ Behavioural/Lower level problem

s.t.

$$AX_{22} \leq R \quad (2.3.f)$$

$$X_{11}, X_{22} \geq 0 \quad (2.3.g)$$

Assumptions:

(1) The objective function (2.3.a) is linear and continuous;

(2) $S_1 = \{X \mid A\, X_{22} \geq R;\ X_{11} = I^*X_{22};\ X_{11}, X_{22} \geq 0\}$ a non-empty, convex and compact set;

(3) $S_2 = \{X \in S_1 \mid C = \text{Min}\ \{(c \pm T)X_{22}\text{:}\ (X_{22} \mid \pm T), X_{11} = I^*X_{22}, T_l \leq \pm T \leq T_p; \{(+T)X_{22} - (-T)X_{22}\} \geq 0\}\}$ is compact, but other properties are not known since S_2 is not explicit,[5] and

(4) LP in the lower level problem has a unique solution.

---

[5] For formulating an optimum policy, the relevant opportunity set (feasible region) is S_2 which we cannot define in a single level model. Therefore single level models generate wrong results/policies (Candler and Norton 1977).

Definitions:

Activities and Coefficients:

w = a vector of coefficients of the policy objective function (1 x e),

X_{11} = a vector of policy target variables (e x 1),

X_{22} = a vector of sectoral behavioural variables (m x l),

c, A = vector and matrix of cost and technological coefficients (1 x m) and (n x m), in the lower level problem,

$\pm T$ = a vector of taxes and subsidies ($t_l, t_2, .., t_m$) (if $T < 0$ are subsidies, and if $T > 0$ taxes),

I = a matrix of (e x m) coefficients for defining the target variables,

T_l, T_p = vectors of lower and upper limits of $\pm T$.

Multi-Level Programming Solution. The definition of an optimum MLP solution is as follows (Fortuny-Amat 1979; Bialas & Karwan 1980). A solution to an MLP will be considered as an optimum (local) solution to the MLP if the solution satisfies the following conditions:

(1) The solution is in the opportunity set of the behavioural problem/lower level problem (feasible solution to the behavioural problem, 2.3.e to 2.3.g);

(2) The solution is optimal for the lower level problem (the behavioural optimum);

(3) The solution satisfies the constraints on the policy problem: $T_l \leq \pm T \leq T_p$; $\{(+T)X_{22} - (-T)X_{22}\} \geq 0$, and

(4) The solution is optimum for the policy problem which is the optimum solution to the lower level problem that provides an optimum value for the objective function of the policy problem (2.3.a).

Optimum: Local and Global. An optimum over S may be defined as follows.

(1) Maximum:

$\tilde{\tilde{X}}_{11}$ is a maximum solution vector of X_{11}

so that

$f(\tilde{\tilde{X}}_{11}) \geq f(X_{11})$, for all $X_{11} \in S$.

(2) Minimum:

$\tilde{\tilde{X}}_{11}$ is a minimum solution vector of X_{22}

so that

$f(\tilde{\tilde{X}}_{11}) \leq f(X_{11})$, for all $X_{11} \in S$.

(3) Local optimum:

X_{11} is a local maximum or minimum solution vector of X_{11}

so that

$f(\tilde{\tilde{X}}_{11}) \geq f(X_{11})$, or $f(\tilde{\tilde{X}}_{11}) \leq f(X_{11})$ for all $X_{11} \in N$, where N is a neighbourhood in S.

(4) Global optimum:

Maximum (or minimum) defined in (a) or (b) above is a global optimum.

Feasible Regions. An MLP has the following three feasible regions.

(1) Behavioural feasible region: The behavioural feasible region (S_1) is defined by the values that can be taken by the variables of the lower level problem (X_{22}), given the values of $\pm T$.

(2) Policy feasible region: The region defined by the constraints 2.3.c and 2.3.d imposed by the underlying policy system and/or budgetary considerations.

(3) Policy-behavioural feasible region: This region (S_2) is defined by the attainable values of the policy target variables (X_{11} or X_{22} as $X_{11} = I * X_{22}$) under different values of the policy instrument variables ($\pm T$).

2.3 Existence and Uniqueness Problem

To demonstrate the general problems of non-existence and non-uniqueness of MLP, we specify a non-numerical model of an MLP, which is specified as follows:

$$\text{Max } W = x_1 \, x_2$$

$$\{t_1, \; t_2\}$$

s.t.

$$\text{Max} \quad Z = p_1x_1 + p_2x_2^2 - c_1x_1^2 - c_2x_2 - t_1x_1 - t_2x_2$$

$$\{x_1, x_2 \mid t_1, t_2\}$$

s.t. (2.4)

$$a_1x_1 + a_2x_2 = R$$

$$x_1, x_2 \geq 0$$

To find the optimum values of x_1, and x_2 for any given t_1 and t_2, it is required to differentiate partially the behavioural sub-problem's Lagrangean function and make it equal to zero:

$$L = p_1x_1 + p_2x_2 - c_1x_1^2 - c_2x_2^2 - t_1x_1 - t_2x_2 + \Gamma(a_1x_1 + a_2x_2 - R) \tag{2.5}$$

$$\frac{\partial L}{\partial x_1} = p_1 - 2c_1x_1 - t_1 + a_1\Gamma = 0$$

$$\frac{\partial L}{\partial x_2} = p_2 - 2c_2x_2 - t_2 + a_2\Gamma = 0 \tag{2.6}$$

$$\frac{\partial L}{\partial \Gamma} = a_1x_1 + a_2x_2 - R = 0$$

For solving this set of linear simultaneous equations, they are redefined in matrix form:

$$\begin{bmatrix} -2c_1 & 0 & a_1 \\ 0 & -2c_2 & a_2 \\ a_1 & a_2 & 0 \end{bmatrix} \begin{bmatrix} x_1 \\ x_2 \\ \Gamma \end{bmatrix} = \begin{bmatrix} t_1 - p_1 \\ t_2 - p_2 \\ R \end{bmatrix} \tag{2.7}$$

Solving the set of simultaneous equations by the Cramer's rule, the values of x_1 and x_2 are found:

$$x_1 = \frac{a_2^2(p_1 - t_1) + a_1 a_2 (t_2 - p_2) + 2c_2 a_1 R}{2(c_1 a_2^2 + c_2 a_1^2)}$$

$$x_2 = \frac{2c_1 a_2 R + a_1[a_2(t_1 - p_1) - a_1(t_2 - p_2)]}{2(c_1 a_2^2 + c_2 a_1^2)} \tag{2.8}$$

The values of x_1 and x_2 are substituted in the policy objective function to find the optimum values of t_1 and t_2. First, the policy objective function is differentiated with respect to t_1 and t_2, and the values are set equal to zero:

$$\frac{\partial W}{\partial t_1} = x_1 \frac{\partial x_2}{\partial t_1} + x_2 \frac{\partial x_1}{\partial t_1} = 0$$

$$\frac{\partial W}{\partial t_2} = x_1 \frac{\partial x_2}{\partial t_1} + x_2 \frac{\partial x_1}{\partial t_2} = 0 \tag{2.9}$$

By substituting the values of x_1 and x_2, we get:

$$\frac{\partial W}{\partial t_1} = \frac{a_1 a_2[a_2^2(p_1 - t_1) + a_1 a_2(t_2 - p_2) + 2c_2 a_1 R]}{4(c_1 a_2^2 + c_2 a_1^2)^2} - \frac{a_2^2[2c_1 a_2 R + a_1 a_2(t_1 - p_1) - a_1^2(t_2 - p_2)]}{4(c_1 a_2^2 + c_2 a_1^2)^2} \tag{2.10}$$

$$\frac{\partial W}{\partial t_2} = \frac{-a_1^2[a_2^2(p_1 - t_1) + a_1 a_2(t_1 - p_2) + 2c_2 a_1 R]}{4(c_1 a_2^2 + c_2 a_1^2)^2} + \frac{a_1 a_2[2c_1 a_2 R + a_1 a_2(t_1 - p_1) - a_1^2(t_2 - p_2)]}{4(c_1 a_2^2 + c_2 a_1^2)^2}$$

To solve for t_1 and t_2 the two equations are rearranged as:

$$\begin{bmatrix} 2a_1^2a_2^2 & -2a_1^3a_2 \\ -2a_1a_2^3 & 2a_1^2a_2^2 \end{bmatrix} \begin{bmatrix} t_1 \\ t_2 \end{bmatrix} = \begin{bmatrix} \underbrace{2a_1^2a_2^2p_1 - 2a_1^3a_2p_2 + 2c_2a_1^3R - 2c_1a_1a_2^2R}_{F_1} \\ \underbrace{2a_1^2a_2^2p_2 + 2c_1a_2^3R - 2a_1a_2^3p_1 - 2c_2a_1^2a_2R}_{F_2} \end{bmatrix} \tag{2.11}$$

If the right hand side expressions are defined as F_1 and F_2 and the two simultaneous equations are solved, the results are:

$$t_1 = \frac{2a_1a_2^2F_1 + F_2(a_1^3a_2 + a_1a_2^3)}{2a_1^4a_2^4 + 2a_1^2a_2^6 - 2a_1^4a_2^4 - 2a_1^2a_2^6}$$

$$t_2 = \frac{2a_1a_2^3F_1 + F_2(a_1^2a_2^2 + a_2^4)}{2a_1^4a_2^4 + 2a_1^2a_2^6 - 2a_1^4a_2^4 - 2a_1^2a_2^6} \tag{2.12}$$

In either case, the values of the denominators are zero, because the determinant of the coefficient matrix is zero. So, we can not find any unique solution to the policy sub-model.

However, it is possible to impose the restrictions that may help us find a solution to the multi-level programming problem (Islam,1994-96 (8)). For example, one simple restriction which solves the problem is that either one of t_1 and t_2 is zero. Then we can find the values of the others.

2.4 Current State of MLP Developments

Since the development of MLP in 1977 (Candler and Norton 1977), there has been a considerable number of studies on MLP. These studies have been done in two areas of MLP: (1) model development and application, and (2) solution algorithm, with the main emphasis on the specification of an appropriate solution algorithm.

2.4.1 Model Development and Application

MLP models have been developed to represent and study the multi-level hierarchical decision making system, particularly at the sector levels. These model specification studies may be broadly grouped into two type: illustrative models and actual real world models.

Illustrative Models. These models are specified to demonstrate examples of MLP for developing algorithms to solve those types of models. Some of these models are very small, consisting of three or four variables. Other models have a dozen or so variables and equations. Although these models represent underlying systems, they are not large enough to capture the salient features of the underlying systems with their necessary details (for example Fortuny-Amat and McCarl 1981).

Real World Models. Some of the MLP studies have been undertaken to develop real world models of the underlying systems, for example Candler and Norton (1977), Bisschop, Chandeler, Duloy, and O'Mara (1982), Sparrow, Pilati, and Marcuse (1979), and Ballenger (1984).

Candler and Norton (1977) have specified a price control MLP model for the Mexican agricultural sector formed of 309 variables and 46 constraints. The policy target variables in the model are employment, income, the levels of maize and wheat productions, and the size of the government budget. The policy instruments which are included in the model are water taxation, subsidy, government expenditure, prices and a share of crop purchased by the government. Ballenger's (1984) study is similar to that of Candler and Norton, since both of these models are used mainly for tracing out the policy feasible space.

The model of Bisschop et al. (1982) is much larger than the Candler and Norton model. It is a price and resource control MLP model, with the maximisation of net farm income being the objective of the government and the public sector, while taxes, subsidies and the allocation of water resources are the available policy instruments.

The model of Sparrow et al. (1979) is a public-private sector interactive model for the formulation of a conservation policy in the iron and steel industry. The objective of the public sector is to maximise real benefits, measured in terms of the energy saved while the objective of the private sector is to minimise cost of production in the industry. The model solution provides the mix of research and development expenditures, both public and private, and the taxes and subsidies that optimise the policy objective function.

2.4.2 Solution Algorithms

Because of space limitations, a brief survey of the existing algorithms for solving MLP is provided here. More elaborated surveys are done in Candler, Fortuny-Amat and McCarl (1981) and Wen (1981), among others.

The Replacement Method: In the first approach, which is termed the Replacement Method, the lower level problem is replaced by its Kuhn-Tucher conditions (Bard and Falk 1982; Bialas, Karwan and Shaw 1980; Fortuny-Amat and McCarl 1981). The transformed MLP problem thus becomes a single-level mathematical programming problem although a non-convex one. This is caused by the complementary slackness conditions of the lower level problem.

Fortuny-Amat and McCarl (1981) solve this non-convex programming problem as a mixed integer programming problem by replacing the complementary slackness conditions by zero one integer constraints. Bard and Falk (1982) solve the transformed MLP by an algorithm which is based on branch and bound methods. Another method termed as the parametric complementary pivot approach is developed by Shaw (1980). In this approach, the objective function of the upper level problem is placed in the set of constraints which includes the complementary slackness conditions. A restricted basis entry simplex procedure is used to obtain a solution to the resultant problem. The objective function of the upper level problem is varied parametrically until all the feasible complementary basis are enumerated.

In the Bisschop et al. (1982) model, the objectives of both levels of the two level programme are the same i.e., minimisation of the cost of the agricultural sector. The principle of the algorithm in this model has been to determine the shadow prices and optimum values of the activities from the model ignoring the lower level objective followed by the placement of these values to the lower level problem to solve the optimum values of the lower level activities.

In the Candler and Townsley (1982) approach, the dual behavioural problem of resource control MLP is solved as a parametric programme to explore all the feasible basis to find the global optimum of the policy problem.

Other Solution Algorithms: The most important of the other remaining approaches is based on the Sequential Unconstrained Minimisation Technique (SUMT). With this approach, the constraints of the lower level problem of MLP are replaced by their penalty functions and the problem is transformed to an unconstrained optimisation problem. The lower level problem can be optimised by the INSUMT algorithm (SUMT in the lower problem), and the simultaneous optimisation of the two problems can be performed by a combined program, SUMT-INSUMT.

Another approach is to solve multi-level programmes iteratively. The basic principles of the iterative algorithm have been stated by Fortuny-Amat (1979). In this approach, 'some reasonable levels' of the policy instruments are exogenously determined and the lower level problem is then solved for all these levels of policy instruments. That level of policy instrument is chosen which produces the optimum value for the upper level objective function.

The essence of the algorithm is the exogenous selection of a finite number of values within a finite range of intervals of the policy instruments by adopting one of the methods for explicating the preferences of policy makers. Then, it is necessary to solve the behavioural model for each combination of the values of the policy instruments and to consider the value of the policy objective function for each set of values of policy instruments and to choose the one with the optimum value.

From the above discussion of the MLP algorithms, it appears that some sort of transformation of the original problem is necessary in most of the algorithms. This makes the solution of MLP relatively difficult. Also, in most cases the size of the transformed MLP becomes large in comparison with the original problem. Again, the algorithms are not usually commercially available. APEX III is the only commercially available software for MLP that requires easy transformation of an MLP model to be solved by it.

Therefore, there is a general need for developing both algorithms and software that are easily operational and readily available.

The development of an alternative algorithm in the present study was motivated by the general necessity for development of a new algorithm as well as by the hitherto non-availability of software for the problem under study.

2.5 Critical Evaluation and Directions for Further Research

The limitations of existing MLP studies are as follows.

(1) The illustrative MLP models cannot be used for any real policy studies since these models are not capable of representing the necessary details of the systems under study.

(2) The limitations of the large scale models are that (i) the policy planning problem characterised by the classification of variables as targets and instruments is not included in these models, and (ii) in some studies, the emphasis has been on the analysis of the reactions of economic agents to the changes in the public policies rather than on the formulation of a set of optimum policies that can achieve the government objectives.

(3) The general difficulty with some of the existing algorithms is that they can find only an approximate solution to MLP through an iterative process. In these cases, it is not possible to determine the global optimality of the solution.

The algorithms which find the exact MLP solution by simultaneous solution of a complete MLP, can not be used to solve large scale MLP models due to several reasons including the computer space and memory problem.

The needed directions for further research are as follows.

(1) Large MLP models should be developed representing the details of the underlying systems for undertaking useful policy studies.

(2) Algorithms need also be developed that can solve large MLP models exactly, preferably not iteratively, with minimum computer space and memory and CPU time requirements and those should be available commercially.

In view of this needed research in MLP, attempts are made in this study to develop an approach that can overcome some of the limitations of existing MLP models.

3 Multi-Level Programming

3.1 Introduction

It was stated in Chap. 2 that multi-level programming[1] is a recently developed mathematical programming technique (Candler and Norton 1977) and that experiments are still going on to develop an algorithm to solve an MLP. In most of the existing MLP algorithms, some sort of transformation of the original problem is necessary. This makes the MLP solution relatively difficult, because the size of the transformed MLP becomes large in comparison with the original problem. Existing algorithms are usually not commercially available.

Therefore, as it was argued in Chap. 2, there is a general need for developing both MLP algorithm and software that are easily operational and readily available. The objective of this chapter is to develop an algorithm of that type to solve an MLP.

The present chapter is structured as follows: Section 3.2 discusses the PPS approach. Section 3.3 demonstrates how the present algorithm can solve an MLP, while an alternative specification of an MLP (including ±T in the upper level policy objective function) is given in Section 3.4. Some issues in the application of this algorithm are discussed in Section 3.5. Section 3.6 contains a brief summary of the steps of the algorithm. Computer algorithms in different types of policy studies are discussed in Section 3.7. Section 3.8 identifies the alternative types of policy planning studies that can be undertaken by solving an MLP model using the PPS algorithm. Section 3.9 discusses the advantages and limitations of the proposed algorithm. Section 3.10 summarises the discussions in this chapter, and tries to point out the usefulness of the proposed search method for solving MLP. The uses of the PPS algorithm to

[1] In this Chapter, only one special type of MLP, bi-level programming, is considered.

solve different other types of MLP such as resource control, dynamic, and non-linear (behavioural model) MLP are discussed in other sections of this chapter.

3.2 Parametric Programming Search Algorithm

In the parametric programming search algorithm, the lower level sub-model (2.3.e to 2.3.g) is solved as a parametric programming problem (involving a variation of a scalar (θ) in the cost coefficients). The parametric programme generates alternative optimum solutions to the lower level sub-model for different levels of parametric variations. Then the solution to the complete multi-level programming problem (2.3.a to 2.3.g) involves finding that parametric solution to the lower level problem which yields the optimum value for the policy objective function (2.3.a) and satisfies the policy and budgetary constraints (2.3.c) and (2.3.d).

To elaborate the PPS approach the MLP in (2.3) is reformulated[2] as:

$\text{Min } WL = wX_{11}$

$\{X_{11}\}$

s.t.

$X_{11} = I^{*}X_{22}$

$\theta_1 \leq \theta \leq \theta_p$

$\{(+\theta U)X_{22} - (-\theta U)X_{22}\} \geq 0$

$$\text{Min} \quad C = (c \pm \theta U)X_{22} \qquad (3.1)$$

[2] In MLP (3.1), equating $\pm T = \pm\theta U$ needs some clarification. In the MLP model (3.1) $\pm T$ is a vector of variables, while $\pm\theta U$ is a vector of parameters. Since $\theta \pm T$ can be varied in a parametric programming along a ray generating different values of θU along that ray, similarly $\pm T = \pm\theta U$ is made in that sense. Adaptation of different values of U provides the possibility for varying θ along different rays $(U_1\theta, U_2\theta, \ldots, U_n\theta)$ and thus for considering a wide range of values (not all) of $\pm T$ $(T_1, T_2, \ldots T_n)$ for finding optimum $\pm T$. This correspondence between $\pm T = \pm\theta U$ is maintained through the whole study.

$\{X_{22} \mid \pm\theta U = \pm T\}$

s.t.

$A_2X_{22} \geq R$

$X_{11}, X_{22} \geq O$

The lower level problem of (3.1) is a parametric programming problem of the type shown in (2.3). Thus an MLP model can be reformulated as an MLP model with the lower level problem as a parametric programming problem.

Therefore, the steps of the PPS algorithm will be firstly, to solve the lower level problem as a parametric programme. This defines the policy behavioural-feasible region (S_2) byθU and X_{22} or X_{11}. Secondly, to find the value of ± U and corresponding X_{22} (a point in S_2) that yield the optimum value for the upper level objective function. It may however be mentioned that although in the algorithm the lower level objective function is being perturbed, the upper level is preferred. The above points are illustrated in Figure 3.1.

Figure 3.1 shows the different levels of parametric variations ($\theta_1 u_1$, $\theta_2 u_1$,..., $\theta_n u_1$) and the different values of the lower level objective function (optimum values) together with the values of the policy objective function. Evidently therefore, the policy objective function attains its optimum value at the 9th level of parametric variation. Consequently, the optimum values (the optimum MLP solution) of x_1 andθu_1, are $\tilde{\tilde{x}}_{1(9)}$ and $\tilde{\tilde{\theta}}_9 u_1$, and the optimum value of the policy objective function:

$\tilde{\tilde{W}}L = w(\tilde{\tilde{x}}_{1(9)})$.

To illustrate the algorithm, the following linear programming problem is used (Daellenbach, George, McNicle 1983, p. 43):

Max $\quad F = 24x_1 + 20x_1$

$\{x_1, x_2\}$

s.t.

Figure 3.1 Choice of an Optimum Parametric Variation Level

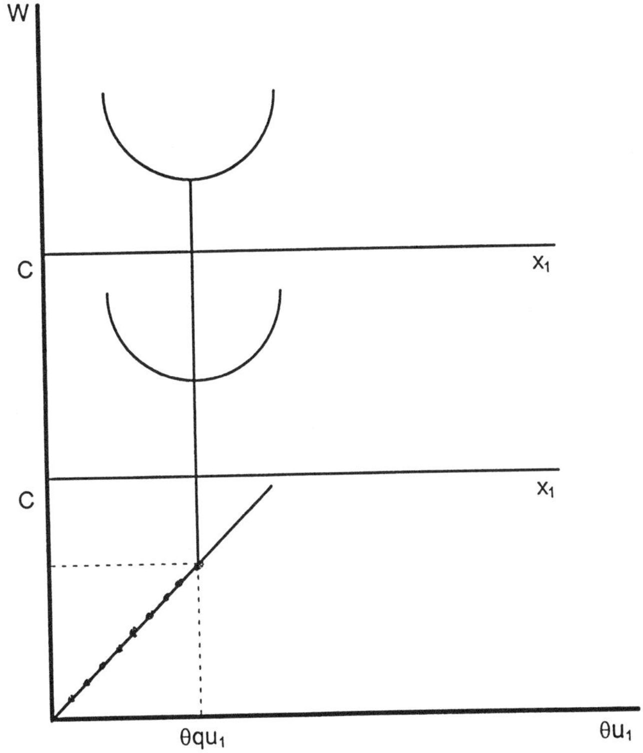

$0.5x_1 + x_2 \leq 12$

$x_1 + x_2 \leq 20$ (3.2)

$0.06x_1 + 0.04x_2 \leq 1$

$1200x_1 - 800x_2 \geq 0$

$x_1, x_2 \geq 0$

A parametric programming formulation of the above linear programming problem is as follows (Daellenbach et al. 1983, pp. 131-132):

$\text{Max } F = (24 + 24\theta)\, x_1 + 20\, x_2$ $\{-1 \leq \theta \leq 100\}$
$u_1 = 24$

s.t.

$0.5x_1 + x_2 \leq 12$

$x_1 + x_2 \leq 20$ (3.3)

$1.5x_1 + x_2 \leq 24$

$1200x_1 - 800x_2 \geq 0$

$x_1, x_2 \geq 0$

The following are the alternative solutions to the parametric programme within the θ range of -1 to 100.

1. $\theta = 0$ $x_1 = 12$ $x_2 = 6$ $F = 408$
2. $\theta = -1$ $x_1 = 6x_2 = 9$ $F = 324$
3. $\theta = -7/12$ $x_1 = 12$ $x_2 = 6$ $F = 240$
4. $\theta = 1/4$ $x_1 = 16$ $x_2 = 0$ $F = 384$

The initial solution with $\theta = 0$ is the usual solution to the linear programming problem (equation 3.5), in other words, it is the optimum solution to the linear programme in (equation 3.6). In the parametric programme, as the cost coefficient was varied parametrically by θ, the alternative optimum solutions 1 to 4 were found.

An MLP[3] can be defined by incorporating the linear programming of (3.2) in (3.1) as follows:

$$\text{Max } W = 2x_1 + x_2$$

s.t.

$$-24 \le t_1 \le 2400$$

$$\text{MaxF} = (24 + t_1)x_1 + 20x_2$$

s.t

$$0.5x_1 + x_2 \le 12 \qquad (3.4)$$

$$x_1 + x_2 \le 20$$

$$1.5x_1 + x_2 \le 24$$

$$1200x_1 - 800x_2 \ge 0$$

$$x_1, x_2 \ge 0$$

and by using its parametric programming reformulation (3.3) as:

$$\text{Max } W = 2x_1 + x_2$$

s.t.

[3] To keep the example simple, it is assumed in this MLP model that only one tax (t_1) is imposed by the policy makers, and that only the policy constraint exists.

$-24 \leq 24\theta \leq 2400 \quad \{t_1 = 24\theta\}$

$\text{Max } F = (24 + 24\theta)\, x_1 + 20x_2 \quad \{u_1 = 24\}$

s.t.

$$0.5x_1 + x_2 \leq 12 \tag{3.8}$$

$x_1 + x_2 \leq 20$

$1.5x_1 + x_2 \leq 24$

$1200x_1 - 800x_2 \geq 0$

$x_1, x_2 \geq 0$

In the PPS algorithm, the lower level problem in (3.5) is solved as a parametric programming problem in the same process as is used to solve model (3.2). In the present example, the alternative solutions were obtained: solution 1. $\theta = 0$; solution 2. $\theta = -1$; solution 3. $\theta = -7/12$, solution 4. $\theta = 1/4$.

The PPS algorithm searches these four alternative solutions to find the solution which provides the optimum value for the policy objective function, and satisfies the constraint that $-24 \leq 24\theta \leq 2400$. The different values of the policy objective function for various parametric solutions are:

(1) $W = 30$,

(2) $W = 21$,

(3) $W = 30$, and

(4) $W = 32$.

optimum solution to the MLP in (equation 3.3 or 3.4) satisfying the constraint $-24 \leq 24\theta = 6 \leq 2400$ and $t_1 x_1 = 96$.

The relevant optimum results are:

(1) Policy objective function: $W = 32$;

(2) Tax: $t_1 = \theta u_1 = (0.25 \times 24) = 6$; and

(3) Activities: $x_1 = 16$, $x_2 = 0$.

3.3 MLP Solution by the PPS Algorithm

3.3.1 MLP Solution and its Proof

The arguments stated so far become obvious looking at the structural similarities between a usual MLP (2.3) and a parametric programming embedded MLP (3.1).

A comparison of these models reveals that they are essentially similar. The only difference is in the objective functions of the lower level problems of these two models. In (3.1), the objective function is $C = (c \pm \theta U)X_{22}$, while in (2.3) it is $C = (c \pm T) X_{22}$. Since these two models are the same (for some values of $\pm T$ determined byθU), it therefore follows that $\theta U = \underline{+}T$. And a comparison of the structural similarities between the models in (2.3) and (2.4) shows that $\pm\theta U$ can be interpreted as the values of taxes and subsidies (changes in the costs of different activities) imposed by the policy makers along a ray determined by $\pm U$. Therefore, the parametric programme can define S_2 by relating $\pm\theta U$ and X_{22} or X_{11}.

In the MLP stated in (2.3), the programming problem is to find a point in S_2 (which is S_1) or the values of $\pm T$ and X_{22} or X_{11} (within a certain range of $\pm T$) that optimise the value of the policy objective function. The programming problem as in (3.1) can be solved to find the values of $\pm$ U and X_{22} or X_{11} (a point in S_2, which is also in S_1) (within a range of θ: $\theta_1 \leq \theta \leq \theta_p$) that optimises the policy objective function. Since the PPS algorithm can find $\pm \tilde{\tilde{\ }}_i U$ and $\tilde{\tilde{X}}_{22}$ (or $\tilde{\tilde{X}}_{11}$), which are the optimum values of taxes and subsidies, and the activities of the lower level problem (the optimum values of X_{11} can be obtained from the relationship $X_{11} = I^*X_{22}$), the PPS algorithm can solve an MLP.

The structural similarities between (2.3) and (2.4) help to formulate the following theorem.

Theorem. An MLP can be solved by solving the lower level sub-model as a parametric programming problem and by choosing the level of parametric variation (the level of policy instruments: $\pm T$) that optimises the policy objective function, and satisfies the constraints in the upper level problem.

Proof. Mathematical requirements of an MLP solution are satisfied by the solution obtained by the PPS algorithm. At this solution point, the lower level problem has an optimum solution, that solution satisfies the upper level constraints and that solution also provides optimum value for the policy objective function. Therefore, the PPS algorithm can find a solution of an MLP (a policy optimum).

To illustrate the above points, an MLP is stated as:

$$\text{Min } WL = wX$$

s.t.

$$X = (X_{11}, X_{22}) \in S_2 \tag{3.6}$$

where:

$$S_2 = \{X \in S_1 \mid C = \text{Min } \{(c \pm T)X_{22} : (X_{22} \mid \pm T),$$

$$T_1 \le \pm T \le T_p, \{(+T)X_{22} - (-T)X_{22}\} \ge 0\}\}$$

and

$$S_1 = \{X \mid A\, X_{22} \ge R;\, X_{11} = I^*X_{22}; X_{11}, X_{22} \ge 0\}$$

It was assumed that S_1 is a closed and bounded opportunity set of the lower level problem while the characteristics of S_2 cannot be determined.

The elements of the MLP solution may now be analysed with the framework of the MLP stated in (3.9). Condition (1) (Section 2.2.2) means that the solution to the lower level problem will be in S_1. Condition (2) implies that a solution will be at an extreme point of S_1. Condition (3) requires that the extreme point in S_1 will also be in the policy-behavioural opportunity set S_2. Condition (iv) implies that the extreme point in S_1 that the lower and upper level problems. This extreme point is the saddle point of MLP.

The implications for the solution of an MLP can now be analysed as follows. Since the lower level constraints are linear, S_1 is a convex set, and optimum solutions of the lower level problem will occur as one of the extreme points of S_1. The search for the optimum solution to an MLP can be directed and limited to the extreme points of S_1. Thus, to solve an MLP we need only make a search in S_1 to find out the extreme point in S_1 which will be in S_2 (the saddle point) that optimises simultaneously the objective functions of the optimization problems at both levels. Parametric programme can uncover extreme points in S_1 (given U) and the PPS algorithm can find the extreme point in S_1 which satisfies the upper level constraints and provides optimum value for the upper level objective function.

To show how a parametric search can solve MLP, a compressed MLP model with parametric programming at the lower level is formulated as:

$$\text{Min } WL = wX$$

s.t. (3.7)

$$X = (X11, X22) \in S2$$

where:

$$S2 = \{X \in S1 \mid C = \text{Min } \{(c \pm \theta U)X22 : (X22 \mid \pm\theta U),$$

$$\theta_1 \le \theta \le \theta p, \{(+\theta U)X22 - (-\theta U)X22\} \ge 0\}\}$$

and

$$S1 = \{X \mid AX22 \ge R; X1 = I^*X22; X11, X22 \ge O\}$$

The PPS algorithm (a) parametrically perturbs the objective function of the lower level problem ($C = c \pm \theta U$) and uncovers extreme points of S_1 as θU ranges from θ_1 to θ_p (satisfies MLP solution conditions 1 and 2), and (b) searches these extreme points to find the extreme point in S_1 that yields the optimum value for the upper level objective function (condition 4), and that also meets the policy and budgetary constraints 2.3.c and 2.3.d: ($\theta_1 \leq \theta \leq \theta_p$); $\{(+\theta U)X_{22} - (-\theta U)X_{22}\} \geq 0$ (condition iii)(ie, the extreme point be in S_2).

The theorem is proved. It therefore follows that the PPS algorithm can find an MLP optimum solution.

A parametric programming solution approach to a dual behavioural problem has been developed by Candler and Townsley (1982), a study that supports the present algorithm.

3.3.2 Economic Interpretations of MLP Solution by the PPS Algorithm

Economically, an MLP solution involves the finding of the values of $\pm T$ and activities X_{22} that satisfy the policy constraints and provide optimum value for the policy objective function. The policy makers have the choice of varying the value of $\pm T$ within a certain range (subject to some constraints) until a set of activities X_{22} is found which can generate an optimum value of the policy objective function.

The mathematical process of the PPS algorithm used to find the MLP solution is exactly the same as the economic principle discussed above. The parametric programme generates all the possible values of $\pm\theta U$ ($\pm T$) and the corresponding optimum solutions X_{22}s (on the ray determined by θU). These optimum solutions are the ones which can be obtained by the policy makers by adopting different values of $\pm T$. In other words, these alternative parametric solutions show the alternative outcomes of pursuing different levels of $\pm T$. The PPS algorithm searches these optimum solutions for choosing the level of $\pm T$ and finding the corresponding optimum solution X_{22} which generate the optimum value for the upper level objective function (satisfying constraints in the upper level).

The PPS algorithm ensures the interdependence between the two sub-optimisation problems (the upper and lower level problems) in the following way: ±T (±θU) introduced by policy makers intervenes in the decision making of economic agents, the result of which is a set of alternative parametric solutions to the lower level problem (X_{22}). Therefore decisions of economic agents X_{22} are subject to interventions from the upper level (±θ). These alternative optimum decisions of economic agents are judged in terms of the criteria embedded in the policy objective function and that decision of economic agents would be desirable to policy makers which will generate an optimum value of the policy objective function. Therefore, policy makers' choice of ±T (±θU) as the optimum policy is constrained by economic agents' reactions (X_{22}) to ±θU. Thus, the choice of ±T (±θU) by policy makers is constrained by the upper level constraints and the reactions of economic agents (X_{22}) to such interventions and the decisions of economic agents (X_{22}) are also constrained by ±T (± θU) and other behavioural constraints. Therefore, in the PPS algorithmic representation of MLP, interdependence between two level decision makers is established. In other words, in the PPS algorithm, an MLP is solved interdependently (any sub-optimisation problem is not solved independently).

3.3.3 Mathematical Properties of the MLP Solution

Existence, Uniqueness, and Global Optimality of MLP Solution. The properties of the PPS algorithm solution need to be discussed at this point. Generally, the problems of existence, uniqueness and global optimality of MLP are still not resolved. For a discussion of the properties of an MLP model solution, we refer to the MLP representation given above.

The properties of S_2 are not known since it is not explicit (algebraically nor numerically). S_2 will only be known when S_1 is known, which in turn will depend on the optimum decision of the lower level decision makers (economic agents). The undesirable possibilities are that S_2 may be empty, disjoint, and even non-convex. In the first two cases, there will be are that S_2 may be empty, disjoint, and even non-convex. In the first two cases, there will be a solution existence problem; and in the third case, there is the problem of the determination of uniqueness and global optimum (shown in Chap. 2.).

Accepted views regarding these problems of policy existence, uniqueness and global optimality are as follows (Candler and Norton 1977):

(1) In a large-scale real world problem, the problem of policy existence may not be encountered; and

(2) Appropriate algorithms can be adopted to overcome the policy uniqueness problem and to find the global optimum of an MLP policy model.

Existence, Uniqueness, and Global Optimality of MLP Solution In the Case of the PPS Algorithm. The PPS algorithm can find an optimum on the ray determined byθU if S_1 is bounded, closed and convex (i.e., if a solution to the lower level problem exists).

It should be mentioned that the existence of an MLP solution (the validity of the theorem) depends on how the parametric programming of the lower level problem is terminated. There are three ways (Murtagh 1981) for parametric programming to be terminated and there are three alternative conditions of existence in the above theorem. In the first case,θ will increase until the MLP problem becomes unfeasible (for the values ofθ above a certain value, the linear programming solution is unbounded). The optimum solution to MLP in this case may be within the range of θ_l to θ_f of the value of θ, where θ_f is the upper value of θ beyond which the solution to the problem becomes unfeasible. If that is the case, then there will be no MLP solution existence problem. The second case is where θ increases infinitely without changing the most recently found optimum solution to the parametric programming. Here, a solution to an MLP will exist but imposing an upper limit on θ will be necessary. In the third case, θ increases up to its pre-specified upper limit, if any, and an optimum solution will be found within the range θ_l to θ_p of the value of θ where θ_l and θ_p are the lower and upper limits and determined exogenously. In the present form of specification of MLP as in (3.1), the existence problem, which can be caused by different forms of the parametric search

And the optimum solution will be within that range. Therefore, in all these situations, the PPS algorithm will not encounter the solution existence problem.

However, as the algorithm only searches along the ray determined by ± U and finds an optimum in this ray, there is no guarantee that the PPS algorithm can find a global optimum.

The parametric search can be extended by changing the units, directions and range of the parametric variation and many alternative optima (on the rays determined by the parametric variations) can be examined to form an idea about the plausibility of the MLP solution obtained. Of course, it may be suggested to continue the search until further improvement in the policy objective function is not possible, but it may not be practical in real situations due to time and resource constraints. However, the non-determination of a global optimum may not be a very serious limitation of an algorithm if the algorithm finds some improved results (Candler and Norton 1977, p. 37)[4] since:

(a) There is question whether real world market equilibrium sometimes leads to local optimum,

(b) These results provide an improved plan over the base or original plan,

(c) Improvement rather than optimality is sometimes considered as an objective of policy analysis (Kornai 1969).

3.4 An Alternative Specification of an MLP Model

To make an MLP problem economically more meaningful and non-trivial, the MLP in (3.1) can be specified again including ± T in the policy objective function as[5] follows:

$\text{Min WL} = awX_{11} \pm b(\pm T)X_{22}$[6]

[4] Views of others on the usefulness of search methods, specially of the ones that cannot provide a guarantee for finding the global optimum, will be stated in the Conclusion (Sect. 3.11).
[5] A similar version of AEPSOM is specified in Chap. 5 and will be reproduced in Chap. 6, model (6.2).
[6] This alternative policy objective function is similar to the ones in Equations (5.6) in Chap. 5 and (6.2.a) in Chap. 6.

$\{\pm T\}$

s.t.

$X_{11} = I^{*}X_{22}$

$$T_l \leq \pm T \leq T_p \qquad (3.8)$$

Min $\quad C = (c \pm T)X_{22}$

$\{X_{22} \mid \pm T\}$

s.t.

$AX_{22} \leq R$

$T, X_{11}, X_{22} \geq 0$

This model is different to the original formulation in (3.1) because of a different specification of the policy objective function.

The PPS algorithm can be applied to this specification of MLP as well. The same algorithmic principle applies, however, in model (3.8) alternative parametric solutions will be searched to find the optimum value of the new policy objective function.

3.5 Some Issues in Using the PPS Algorithm

The PPS algorithm searches the policy-behavioural region along a line determined by (1) the units, (2) the signs and (3) the direction and ranges of the parametric variation.

Therefore, discussions on the determination of the units, signs, and direction and range of the parametric variation is necessary.

3.5.1 Units of Parametric Variation

The determination of the appropriate units of parametric variations (including its sign) ±U is important in the PPS algorithm. ± U makes a search along a line in n-space. Therefore, one particular ±U uncovers all the extreme point optima along the line determined by ±θU. The application of the PPS algorithm with a particular set of ±U can find global optima on a thin line. By choosing another set of ±U, another global optima on another line can be generated. Therefore, generation of the MLP optimum solution depends on the determination of the appropriate unit of parametric variation (±U). Therefore, considerable attention needs to be given to the question of the choice of the units of parametric variation in the PPS algorithm since the units determine the range and direction of the search done by the PPS algorithm.

The question remains, how to find the appropriate ±U? In single level parametric programming, the units of parametric variation are generally obtained from the information of the system or environment under study. For example, if a = production cost of a product in the base period, and θ time, then the cost equation for any future period can be presented as $c = a + u\theta$. A numerical example of the cost equation is as follows: $c = 5 + 0.4\theta$. The unit of parametric variation $u = 0.4$ can be obtained from market surveys, econometric estimates, trend analysis, etc.

Therefore, in many single level parametric programming studies, finding the units of parametric variations may not be a problem. But that is not the case in parametric programs in MLP in the PPS algorithm.

In the present formulation of MLP, the following $\pm u_j$ is appropriate since this vector provides a direction of search towards the preference direction of the upper level objective function:[7]

$\pm u_j = \pm h_j = - c_j \pm wI_j$, $j = 1,2,\ldots,n$ (I_j = jth elements of the matrix I. The elements of this matrix are either 1 or 0.)

[7] Suggested by an anonymous referee.

The selection of $\pm u_j$ in the above procedures does not give any guarantee for the generation of global or even local MLP solution, since the search is along a line. There is a need, therefore, for trying other alternative units to make search along other lines in S_2. Generally, it will be prudent to vary the units (U) as much as possible starting with the units $\pm u_j = \pm h_j$. The following alternatives were tried in the present study :

(1) To choose U so that its elements are either +1, 0, Or -1.

(2) To choose the units to equal $\pm c_j$ or 0 (c_j = cost coefficients; j = 1,2,...,n).

There is, of course, a general problem of multiple optima in the case of small variations in U. The problem is illustrated in Figure 3.2.

Figure 3.2 shows that changing the units of parametric variations of the behavioural objective function coefficients, which will move it as shown by $c(U_1)$, $c(U_2)$, $c(U_3)$, and $c(U_4)$, may not change the optimum solution to the lower level problem. Therefore, the optimum solution to the upper level problem will not change. So, in this case, we will find a range of values of the policy instruments (different values of parametric variations), not a set of unique values of the policy instruments, that will provide the same value for the policy objective function.

3.5.2 Signs of the Direction of the Coefficients Subject to Parametric Variations

The signs of the parametric variation of different cost coefficients (±) depend on the choice of taxes or subsidies applicable to different activities. If a tax is imposed on an activity, then the sign of the parametric variation of its cost coefficients will be +, in the case of a subsidy it will be -.

It may, however, be mentioned that the signs of parametric variations will be different in two types of policy studies:

(1) The policy study involving the determination of the optimum levels of existing taxes and subsidies and prices (if any price is under control); and

(2) The policy study that involves the determination of the optimum mix and levels of taxes and subsidies and prices.

Existing Taxes and Subsidies. In the first case, the lower level problem is solved by making the coefficients of the lower level objective function, which are subject to existing taxes and subsidies, to vary parametrically (ie. the lower level problem is solved as a parametric programming problem). The optimum solution to the complete multi-level programme provides a set of optimum values for existing taxes and subsidies.

Optimum Mix of Taxes and Subsidies. In this case, at first the lower level sub-model should be solved as a linear programming problem with the lower level objective function contained within it (as a normal behavioural model):

$$\text{Min } C = cX_{22}$$

$$\{X_{22}\}$$

$$\text{s.t.} \qquad (3.9)$$

$$A_2X_{22} \geq R$$

$$X_{11}, X_{22} \geq 0$$

The vector of the level of optimum activities is defined as X^{B}_{22}. Then the lower level sub-model should be solved with the policy objective function in it as follows:

$$\text{Min } WL = wX_{11}$$

$$\{X_{11}\}$$

$$\text{s.t.} \qquad (3.10)$$

$$X_{11} = I^{*}X_{22}$$

$$A_2X_{22} \geq R$$

$$X_{11}, X_{22} \geq 0$$

Figure 3.2 Changes in the Units of Parametric Variations

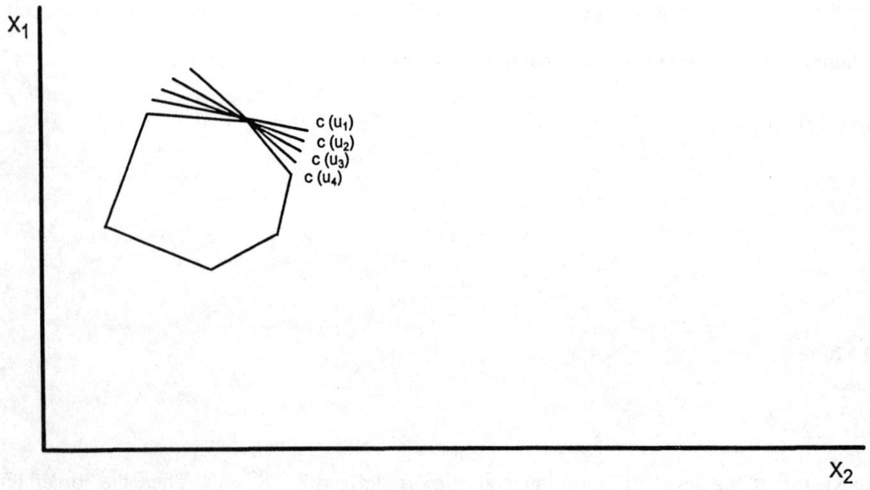

This model is termed a central control policy model. The solution to the central control policy model determines the optimum value of the policy objective function and the optimum set of activities. Let us define this vector of the activities as $X^P{}_{22}$.

The next step involves a comparison between the two sets of activities to identify the differences between the choices of the individual economic agents and the choices of the policy makers. So, the differences can be used as an indication for the mix and the direction of the policy instruments, taxes and subsidies, necessary to influence the activities of individual economic agents. So the vector:

$\pm u_j = -x^P{}_{22(j)} + x^B{}_{22(j)}$

or, $\pm u_j = -x^P{}_{22(j)} + x^B{}_{22(j)}$

can be used to determine, signs and mix of the parametric variations in the following way:

$$u_j < 0 \text{ if } x^P{}_{22(j)} > x^B{}_{22(j)};$$
$$u_j > 0 \text{ if } x^P{}_{22(j)} < x^B{}_{22(j)}; \quad (3.11)$$
$$u_j = 0 \text{ if } x^P{}_{22(j)} = x^B{}_{22(j)};$$
$$j = 1, 2, .., n$$

Table 3.1. Determination of Optimum Mix of Taxes and Subsidies

Activities	$X^P{}_{22}$	$X^B{}_{22}$	U	±
$x_{22(1)}$	20	10	10	–
$x_{22(2)}$	15	26	11	+
$x_{22(3)}$	21	21	0	0

For applying the PPS algorithm, cost coefficients c_1 and c_2 should be subject to parametric variations and the signs should be - and + respectively.

The numbers in Table 3.1. imply that a mix of tax on $x_{22(2)}$, subsidy on $x_{22(1)}$, and nothing on $x_{22(3)}$ is the optimum mix of tax and subsidy in this example.

3.5.3 Direction and Range of Parametric Variation

The direction of the parametric variation depends on the units and signs of the parametric variation which have been discussed above. There are other factors that will also have effects on the direction of the parametric variation. In an MLP model, if $\pm T$ is entered in the upper level objective function, this will provide the desired direction for the parametric variation. The policy constraint, determined on the basis of the underlying government policy environment, will determine the range of parametric variation. For example, if the policy feasible region is specified as $T_l \leq \pm T \leq T_p$, then the desired parametric variation will be restricted only within this specified region.

3.6 A Summary of the Algorithmic Steps

(1) Choose a set of the units (U) of the parametric variations (θ). There are several alternatives for that:

(a) Units equal to $\pm c_j$, ($j = 1,2,\ldots,n$) or 0;

(b) Units equal to +1, 0, or -1; and

(c) Units (u_j) as close as possible to ($-c_j \pm w_2 I_j$), $j = 1,2,\ldots,n$.

(2) Determine which units will be equal to 0 and the directions ($\pm$) of the variations of the remaining parameters. The following are the alternatives:

(a) Existing tax and subsidy regime. Identify the existing taxes and subsidies. If a tax is imposed on a particular activity (fuel or energy), then the direction of the parametric variation of that activity should be positive; and if subsidy is given then it should be negative (for example if tax is imposed on x_{22j}, then the coefficient of the lower level objective function c_j, should be subject to parametric variation in the positive direction $+u_j$, otherwise (for subsidy) in the negative direction $-u_j$). The activities on which taxes and subsidies are imposed are the ones of which the cost coefficients are subject to parametric variation.

(b) Optimum tax and subsidy choice. Solve the lower level sub-model in model (3.1) twice.

(i) Firstly as a linear programme, as in model (3.9)

(ii) Secondly, with the inclusion of the upper level objective function as in model (3.10) to find two alternative sets of optimum activities: X^B_{22} and X^P_{22}.

(iii) Find the differences between these two sets of activities as $X^B_{22} - X^P_{22}$ and choose the signs of the units ($\pm U$) to equal the sign of $\pm(X^B_{22} - X^P_{22})$ or set $U = 0$ if the difference is equal to 0. (iv) Choose the signs according to $\pm U$.

(3) Determine the range of the parametric variation by studying the underlying policy system.

(4) Solve the lower level problem of an MLP as the parametric programming problem specified following Steps 1 and 3.

(5) Search the alternative (parametric) solutions to the lower level problem generated in Steps 1 to 4 to find out the solution which provides the optimum value for the upper level objective function and satisfy the policy and budgetary constraints.

(6) Continue Steps 1 to 5 until no further improvement in the upper level objective function is possible.

(7) In the case that all the possible combinations of the units and directions of parametric variations can not be tried to solve an MLP, any solution to an MLP will be a reasonable approximate solution to an MLP if (i) it generates a value of the upper level objective function fairly close (as close as possible) to the value of the policy objective function of the central control model specified from an MLP (in the same way as in model (3.10)), and if (ii) the value of the policy objective function of MLP is lower then the value of the policy objective function calculated from the values of X^B_{22} determined by the behavioural model (3.9). In this case, the MLP solution provides an improved plan over the original plan or no plan.

3.7 Software

The main software for implementing the PPS algorithm in this study was the linear programming package (with parametric programming facility) of Pearse and Hardaker (1984). The software can solve the lower level problem as a parametric programming problem. Two alternatives for searching these parametric solutions to find an optimum MLP solution are as follows. (1) For an MLP as in (2.3) without (2.3.c) and (2.3.d), two sub-programmes were developed by Gatenby (1986) in consultation with the present author to find the MLP solution. The first sub-programme searches the alternative parametric solutions to find the MLP solution. The second sub-programme changes the units of parametric variations. The combined package, consisting of the above three programmes and named POLICY PROGRAMME, was used to solve an MLP.

(2) In the case of MLP as in (2.3) including (2.3.c) and (2.3.d) and as in the alternative specification in Section 2.5, the Policy Search Programme as in (ii) below is to be replaced by Lotus 1-2-3. Lotus 1-2-3 can be used to calculate the values of the policy objective function in (3.8) and the constraints (2.3.c) and (2.3.d) to find the optimum value (maximum or minimum) through an iterative procedure from the results of the parametric solutions to the lower level problem. The POLICY PROGRAMME has the following operation sequence:

(a) Parametric Linear Programming package yields ($X_{22(1)}, X_{22(2)}, \ldots, X_{22(n)}$) and ($\theta_1 U, \theta_2 U, \ldots, \theta_n U$) ;

(b) Policy Search Programme (two sub-programmes/ Lotus 1-2-3) searches the outputs of (a) and finds $W = w(\tilde{\tilde{X}}_{22})$, $\tilde{\tilde{X}}_{22}$ and $\tilde{\tilde{\theta}}U$, the optimum values of the upper level objective function, activities, and taxes and subsidies ;

(c) Output of (a) should be checked on whether ($\theta_1 U, \theta_2 U, \ldots \theta U$) are within the range of $\theta_l \leq \theta \leq \theta_p$.

(4) Lotus 1-2-3 can calculate the values of the budgetary constraints from the output of (i) to determine the solutions ($X_{22(1)}$, $X_{22(2)}$,..., $X_{22(n)}$) which satisfy these constraints.

3.8 Use of the PPS Algorithm in Different Types of Policy Studies

The PPS algorithm can be used in two types of policy studies, which is already evident from the previous discussion on the units of parametric variations. Firstly, the policy study involving the determination of the optimum values of existing taxes and subsidies (and prices if any price is under control) along with other energy policies. Secondly, the policy study that involves the determination of the optimum mix and level of taxes and subsidies and prices along with other energy policies.[8]

3.9 Application of the PPS Algorithm to Different Types of MLP

In this sub-section, it will be demonstrated that the PPS algorithm can also be applied to other types of MLP, such as resource control, price and resource control, dynamic, and non-linear (behaviour model) MLP.

In a parametric programming problem, there can be three types of parametric variations: variations in the cost coefficients; variations in the right hand side parameters; and a simultaneous variation in both. The case of variations of coefficients of the objective function is already dealt with (price control MLP). A parametric programme with variations in the right-hand-side parameters can be used to solve a resource control MLP, and a parametric programme with both types of variations can be used to solve a price and resource control MLP.

[8] In Chap. 6, further discussion on these two types of policy studies will be provided.

3.9.1 Solution to a Resource Control MLP

Resource Control MLP. A resource control MLP (bi-level programming) is usually defined as:

$$
\begin{aligned}
&\text{Min} \quad Wl = wX_{11} \\
&\{X_{11}, X_{21}\} \\
&\text{s.t.} \\
&\text{Min } C = c_1X_{21} + c_2X_{22} \\
&\{X_{22} \mid X_{21}\} \qquad\qquad (3.12) \\
&\text{s.t.} \\
&A_1X_{21} + A_2X_{22} \geq R \\
&X_{11} = I_1{}^*X_{21} + I_2{}^*X_{22} \\
&X_{11}, X_{21}, X_{22} \geq 0
\end{aligned}
$$

Here X_{11} and X_{21}; and X_{22} are the energy target and behavioural variables respectively.

It would be more appropriate to redefine the above MLP as an activity control MLP, since the upper level controls the activities (production and consumption) of the lower level, but not the supply (domestic production or import) of resources.

If the above MLP is called an activity control MLP, then another type of MLP can be defined as a resource control MLP in the case where supplies of resources are controlled by the upper level decision makers. A resource control MLP can be stated as:

$$
\begin{aligned}
&\text{Min} \quad Wl = wX_{11} \\
&\{X_{11}, X_{21}\}
\end{aligned}
$$

s.t.

$$\text{Min} \quad C = c_2X_{22}$$

$$\{X_{22} \mid X_{21}\} \tag{3.13}$$

s.t.

$$A_2X_{22} \geq R + A_1X_{21}$$

$$X_{11} = I_2{}^*X_{22}$$

$$X_{11}, X_{21}, X_{22} \geq 0$$

For solving this resource control problem, the parametric programming of the behavioural sub-model may be represented as:

$$\text{Min } C = c_2X_{22}$$

$$\{X_{22}\}$$

s.t. (3.14)

$$A_2X_{22} \geq R \pm \theta B \qquad (\theta B = -A_1X_{21})$$

$$X_{22} \geq 0$$

where B = a vector of the units of parametric variations $(b_1, b_2, \ldots, b_n)$, and θ = parametric variation.

The complete resource control MLP, with the parametric programme in the lower level problem, may be stated as:

$$\text{Min } Wl = wX_{11}$$

$$\{X_{11}, \pm\theta B = \pm X_{21}\}$$

s.t.

$$\text{Min } C = c_2X_{22}$$

$$\{X_{22} \mid \pm X_{21} = \pm\theta B\} \quad (3.15)$$

s.t.

$$A_2X_{22} \geq R \pm \theta B$$

$$X_{11} = I^*X_{21}$$

$$X_{11}, X_{22} \geq 0$$

Here $\theta_1, \ldots, \theta_n$ are the marginal rates of substitution between the optimum value of the behavioural objective function and the changes in the level of supply of resources. The reaction function $X_{22}\ \phi\ (R \pm \theta B)$ shows the changes in optimum responses of individual economic agents due to changes in levels of resource supplies or control of resources. Like a price control MLP, the solution to resource control MLP requires finding the value of B (additional supplies of resources) and the corresponding values of X_{22} that provide the optimum values of the policy objective function.

The solution to a resource control MLP using parametric programming is illustrated in Figure 3.3. In this case, the resource level varies with the different levels of parametric variations (shown in Figure 3.3.c). Optimum solution to MLP occurs at the 9th level of parametric variation.

An Example. To demonstrate the applicability of the PPS algorithm to a resource control MLP, we refer to the following example:

The RHS parametric programming formulation of the linear programming problem in (3.2) is as follows (Daellenbach et al. 1983, p. 140).

$$\text{Max } C = 24x_1 + 20x_2$$

s.t.

Figure 3.3. PPS Algorithm Solution of Resource Control MLP

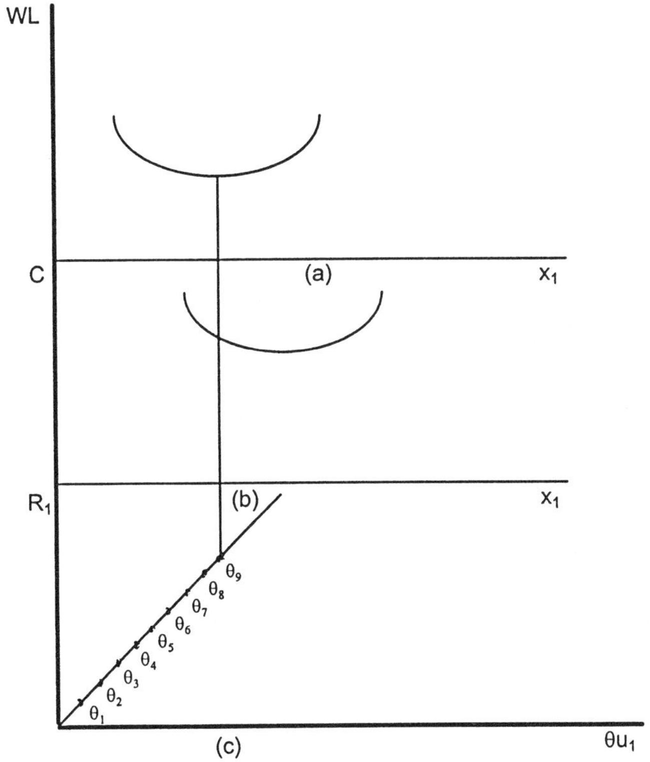

$0.5x_1 + x_2 \leq 12$

$x_1 + x_2 \leq 20$ (3.16)

$0.06x_1 + 0.04x_2 \leq 1 + \theta \ \{-1 \leq \theta \leq +\infty\}$

$1200x_1 - 800x_2 \geq 0$

$x_1, x_2 \geq 0$

In this example only one constraint is subject to the parametric variation, but all the constraints can be subject to parametric variations. The following are the results of the parametric solutions:

Solution 1: $\theta = 0 \quad x_1 = 12 \quad x_2 = 6 \quad C = 408$

Solution 2: $\theta = 1 \quad x_1 = 0 \quad x_2 = 0 \quad C = 0$

Solution 3: $\theta = 0.25 \quad x_1 = 6 \quad x_2 = 9 \quad C = 324$

Solution 4: $\theta = 0.17 \quad x_1 = 16 \quad x_2 = 4 \quad C = 464$

Solution 5: $\theta = 0.25 \quad x_1 = 20 \quad x_2 = 0 \quad C = 480$

A resource control MLP formulation consisting of the above right hand side parametric programme is as follows:

Max $W = 2x_1 + x_2$

s.t.

Max $C = 24x_1 + 20x_2$

s.t.

$0.5x_1 + x_2 \leq 12$ (3.17)

$x_1 + x_2 \leq 20$

$0.06x_1 + 0.04x_2 \leq 1 + \theta \quad \{-1 \leq \theta \leq +\infty\}$

$1200x_1 - 800x_2 \geq 0$

$x_1, x_2 \geq 0$

The application of the PPS algorithm involves searching of those five solutions and finding the one which provides the optimum value of the upper level objective function. The following is an illustration of how the PPS algorithm finds the optimum solution. The five parametric solutions to the programming problem provide the following values of the upper level objective function: Solution 1: W = 30; Solution 2: W = 0; Solution 3: W = 21; Solution 4: W = 36; Solution 5: W = 40. The PPS algorithm searches all these solutions and finds Solution 5 as the optimum solution to the above resource control MLP. The optimum solution results are:

(1) Upper level objective function W = 40.

(2) Parametric variations: $\theta = 0.25$.

(3) Activities: $x_1 = 20$, $x_2 = 0$.

Signs, Units, Direction and Range of Parametric Variations. If there exists a resource control policy environment, the signs, directions and range of the parametric variations can be determined by studying the underlying policy system. For example, if the government policy is to increase the use of a resource, then the sign of the parametric variation would be + and if the policy is to decrease the supply then it would be -. Also the direction of the parametric variations can be determined by including the resource control variables in the policy objective function. The range of variations will certainly be specified from the information about the underlying policy system.

The units can be adopted in the following process. The policy and behavioural models are specified as:

$$\underset{\{X_{21}\}}{\text{Min}} \quad W = wX_{11}$$

s.t. (3.18)

$$A_1X_{12} + A_2X_{22} \geq R$$

$$X_{11} = I_1{}^*X_{22} + I_2{}^*X_{22}$$

$$X_{11}, X_{12}, X_{22} \geq 0$$

and

$$\underset{\{X_{22}\}}{\text{Min}} \quad C = cX_{22}$$

s.t. (3.19)

$$A_2X_{22} \geq R$$

$$X_{22} \geq O.$$

Let optimum activity vectors of the models (3.13) and (3.14) be $\tilde{\tilde{X}}^{P}{}_{22}$ and $\tilde{\tilde{X}}^{B}{}_{22}$ respectively. The units of parametric variation then can be determined as:

$$U = \tilde{\tilde{X}}^{P}{}_{22} - \tilde{\tilde{X}}^{B}{}_{22}$$

If it is necessary to identify which activities are controlled, then the signs and units of the parametric variations should be as follows:

$$u_j > 0 \text{ if } \tilde{\tilde{x}}^{P}{}_{22(j)} > \tilde{\tilde{x}}^{B}{}_{22(j)}$$

$$u_j < 0 \text{ if } \tilde{\tilde{x}}^{P}{}_{22(j)} < \tilde{\tilde{x}}^{B}{}_{22(j)} \qquad j = 1,2,\ldots,n.$$

$$u_J = 0 \text{ if } \tilde{\tilde{x}}^{P}{}_{22(j)} = \tilde{\tilde{x}}^{B}{}_{22(j)}$$

Algorithmic Steps. When the signs, units, and range of parametric variations in a resource control MLP have been specified, steps 5 to 7 of the price control MLP solution algorithm in Section 3.5 can be followed to find an optimum solution.

3.9.2 Solution of a Price Control and Resource Control MLP

A price and resource control MLP (bi-level programming) can be defined as follows:

$$\text{Min} \quad Wl = wX_{11}$$

$$\{\pm T, X_{21}\}$$

s.t.

$$\text{Min} \quad C = (c_2 \pm T)X_{22}$$

$$\{X_{22} \mid \pm T, X_{21}\} \qquad (3.20)$$

s.t.

$$A_2X_{22} \geq R - X_{21}$$

$$X_{11} = I_1{*}X_{21} + I_2{*}X_{22}$$

$$X_{11}, X_{21}, X_{22} \geq 0$$

The above MLP can be stated as an MLP problem with a parametric programming problem in the lower level :

$$\text{Min} \; Wl = wX_{11}$$

$$\{\pm T, X_{21}\}$$

s.t.

$$\text{Min} \quad C = (c_2 \pm \theta U)X_{22}$$

$\{X_{22} \mid \pm T = \pm\theta U; X_{21} = \theta B\}$ (3.21)

s.t.

$A_2X_{22} \geq R \pm \theta B$

$X_{11} = I_1{}^*(\pm\theta B) + I_2{}^*X_{22}$

$X_{11}, X_{22} \geq 0$

A comparison of the behavioural problem in (3.15) with the parametric programming problem in (3.16) reveals that they are similar (subject to the conditions discussed for the price control MLP). The behavioural problem in (3.16) is a parametric programming problem the main difference from the behavioural problem in (3.15) being that R- X_{21} has been replaced by R ± θB and ±T has been replaced by ±θU.

The algorithm for solving the MLP in (3.15) will be the same as it was in the previous cases.

3.9.3 Solution to a Dynamic MLP

To demonstrate the applicability of the PPS algorithm in solving a dynamic MLP (bi-level programming), the following dynamic MLP is specified:

$$\text{Min} \qquad W = \sum_{i=1}^{T} \frac{w_i G_i}{(1+d)^i}$$

$\{\pm T_{1i}, \pm T_{2i}, \pm T_{3i}, Y_{pi}\}$

s.t.

$G_i = I_1 Y_i + I_2 X_i + I_3 Z_i$

$Yp_i = Yc_i$

$T_l \leq \{\pm T_1, \pm T_2, \pm T_3\} \leq T_p$

$$\text{Min} \quad C = \sum_{i=1}^{T} \frac{(c_{1i} \pm T_{1i})Y_i}{(1+r)^i} + \sum_{i=1}^{T} \frac{(c_{2i} \pm T_{2i})X_i}{(1+r)^i} + \sum_{i=1}^{T} \frac{(c_{3i} \pm T_{3i})Z_i}{(1+r)^i}$$

$\{X_i, Y_i, Z_i\}$

s.t. (3.22)

$Z_i \geq \overline{X}_i$

$Z_i = a_i X_i \quad i = 1,2,\ldots,$

$X_i = b_i Y_i$

$Y_i + Yp_i \leq \overline{Y}_i$

$\sum_{i=1}^{T} X_i \geq \overline{X}_1$

$G_i, Yp_i, Y_i, X_i, Z_i \geq 0$

where:

d = social discount rate,

r = market rate of interest rate,

w = vector of the coefficients of the policy objective functions $(1 \times m_1)$ $(1 \times k)$,

G = energy target variable vector (k x 1),

Y,X,Z = vectors of primary energy, secondary energy and end-uses of energy: (l x 1), (n x 1), and (p x 1),

I_1, I_2, I_3= matrices elements of which are either 1 or 0,

$\pm T_1, \pm T_2, \pm T_3$ = vectors of tax and subsidy related to Y, X, and Z: (l x 1), (n x 1), and (p x 1),

Yp = amount of Y that is directly controlled,

Yc, $\overline{Z}$, $\overline{Y}$, $\overline{X}$ = the right hand side constants of Yp, Z, Y, X,

i = time period 1,2, ..., n.

The above model can be condensed for convenience to the following two period model:

$$\text{Min } WL = w_{1b}X_{11b} + wd\, w_{1p}\, X_{11p} \tag{a}$$

$$\{\pm T_b, \pm T_p\}$$

s.t.

$$\text{Min } C = (c_b \pm T_b)X_{22b} + (cd\ c_p \pm T_p)X_{22p} \tag{b}$$

$$\{X_{22b}, X_{22p} \mid \pm T_b, \pm T_p\}$$

s.t. (3.23)

$$X_{22b}^1 + A_{11b}X_{22b} \geq R_b \tag{c}$$

$$X_{22p}^1 + A_{11p}X_{22p} \geq R_p \tag{d}$$

$$B_{11b}X_{22b} + B_{11p}X_{22p} \geq R_d \tag{e}$$

$$X_{11b} + X_{11p} = I_1{}^*X_{22b} + I_2{}^*X_{22p} \tag{f}$$

$$X_{11b}, X_{11p}, X_{22b}^1, X_{22p}^1, X_{22b}, X_{22p} \geq 0 \tag{g}$$

The b and p subscripts define the variables in the base year and the planning year respectively. wd and cd are discount factors, while X_{22b}^1 and X_{22p}^1 are the resource control variables.

A statement of the above dynamic MLP with a parametric programming version of the lower level problem is as follows :

$$\text{Min } WL = w_{1b}X_{11b} + wd\, w_{1p}X_{11p} \tag{a}$$

$$\{\pm T_b, \pm T_p, X_{22p}^1, X_{22p}^1\}$$

s.t.

$$\text{Min} \quad C = (c_b \pm \theta U_1)X_{22b} + (cd\ c_p \pm \theta U_2)X_{22p} \qquad \text{(b)}$$

$$\{X_{22b}, X_{22p} \mid \pm\theta U_1 = \pm T_b, \pm\theta U_2 = \pm T_p, \pm\theta B_1 = X_{22b}{}^1, \pm\theta B_2 = X_{22p}{}^1\}$$

s.t. (3.24)

$$A_{11b}X_{22b} \geq R_b \pm B_1 \qquad \text{(c)}$$

$$A_{11p}X_{22p} \geq R_p \pm B_2 \qquad \text{(d)}$$

$$B_{11b}X_{22b} + B_{11p}X_{22p} \geq R_T \qquad \text{(e)}$$

$$X_{11b} + X_{11p} = I_1{}^*X_{22b} + I_2{}^*X_{22p} \qquad \text{(f)}$$

$$X_{11b}, X_{11p}, X_{22b}{}^1, X_{22p}{}^1, X_{22b}, X_{22p} \geq 0 \qquad \text{(g)}$$

By applying the PPS algorithm, the optimum solution to the dynamic MLP can be obtained.

3.9.4 Solution to an MLP Having a Non-Linear Behavioral Model

A non-linear MLP (bi-level programming) is specified as:

$$\text{Min} \qquad Wl = wX_{11}$$

$$\{\pm T, X_{11}\}$$

$$\text{Min } C = (c \pm T)X_{22}{}^2$$

$$\{X_{22} \mid \pm T\}$$

s.t. (3.25)

$$A_2X_{22}{}^2 \geq R$$

$$X_{11} = I^*X_{22}$$

$$X_{11}, X_{22} \geq 0$$

A parametric programming version of the above non-linear MLP is as follows:

$$\text{Min} \quad Wl = wX_{11}$$

$$\{\pm T, X_{11}\}$$

$$\text{Min } C = (c \pm \theta U)X_{22}^2$$

$$\{X_{22} \mid \pm\theta U = \pm T\}$$

s.t. (3.26)

$$A_2X_{22}^2 \geq R$$

$$X_{11} = I^*X_{22}$$

$$X_{11}, X_{22} \geq 0$$

The linearised form of the above model is as follows:

$$\text{Min} \quad Wl = wX_{11}$$

$$\{\pm T_1, \pm T_2, \pm T_3\}$$

s.t.

$$\text{Min} \quad C = (f_1 \pm \theta U_1)r_1 + (f_2 \pm \theta U_2)r_2 + (f_3 \pm \theta U_3)r_3$$

$$\{r_1, r_2, r_3 \mid \pm\theta U_1 = \pm T_1, \pm\theta U_2 = \pm T_2, \pm\theta U_3 = \pm T_3\}$$

s.t. (3.27)

$$a_1r_1 + a_2r_2 + a_3r_3 \geq R$$

$$X_{11} = I_1^*r_1 + I_2^*r_2 + I_3^*r_3$$

$$X_{11}, r_1, r_2, r_3 \geq 0$$

where the r's are the different grid points for linearisation of the non-linear MLP. Notice that the model (3.27) and the linearization conditions on the grid points form a linear MLP which can be solved by the PPS algorithm. It may be mentioned here that non-linear parametric programming (Brosowski and Deutsch 1985) can also be used to solve a non-linear lower level problem, and the PPS algorithm can be used to find the parametric solution that yields the optimum value for the upper level objective function.

3.10 Advantages and Limitations of the PPS Algorithm

3.10.1 Advantages

(1) To solve MLP with the PPS algorithm, it is not necessary to make a transformation in the original MLP. The sise of the transformed MLP in some existing algorithms may become a problem, as discussed previously.

(2) Parametric programming software is commercially available (Pearse and Hardakar 1984). Lotus 1-2-3 is also commercially available. The additional sub-programmes required to solve an MLP can easily be developed.

(3) The PPS algorithm can be used to solve large scale MLP models.

(4) The algorithm has favourable operational characteristics. These relate to the accuracy and efficiency of the algorithm, and to the cost and efficiency in extending and transferring it.

(a) Accuracy: As no other algorithms or models were available to test the accuracy of the results provided by the PPS algorithm, results obtained in this study were used to make a judgment. It can be seen in Chap. 6 that the value of the policy objective function in MLP solution is 8.2% different to that of a central control policy model,[9] and an improvement by 44.46% over the behavioural model.

[9] If it is accepted that the central control policy model solution is an ideal basis for the determination of policy directions, then a solution which is only 8.2% different to the ideal situation may be considered reasonably accurate. By increasing the range of search it would be possible to obtain better results.

(b) Efficiency: Since different models were solved by the PPS algorithm, there were different CPU times in cases of different models. However, the CPU time needed for solving AEPSOM (with existing taxes and subsidies) was 40 seconds.

(c) Cost and Efficiency in Extension and Transfer: For implementing the PPS algorithm the major computer programme needed is parametric programming software. The other two sub-programmes are relatively smaller. The alternative programme Lotus 1-2-3 is commercially available. The whole computer programme can easily be transferred. If parametric programming software is available then the other two sub-programmes can be written by somebody having reasonable knowledge of computer programming or Lotus 1-2-3 can be used. Therefore, the complete computer software for solving an MLP model, is relatively simple to obtain, develop, or transfer.

3.10.2 Limitations

(1) One limitation of the PPS algorithm discussed above is that the parametric search is limited to a single line, determined by the units and signs of the parametric variations (±U). Therefore, it is not possible to guarantee that the algorithm can find a global optimum. But, as it was stated before, the units of the parametric variations can be changed to extend the search in the policy-behavioural set.

(2) An important methodological issue is whether or not macro-economic constraints can be included in an MLP model, if a solution is sought by the PPS algorithm. For analysing the issue, let us give a condensed statement of an MLP model with macro-economic constraints as:

$$\text{Min} \quad Wl = w_1X_{11} + w_2X_{22}$$

$$\{\pm T\}$$

s.t.

$$p_1X_{11} + p_2X_{22} = R_1$$

$$\text{Min } C = (c \pm \theta U)X_{22} \tag{3.28}$$

$$\{X_{22} \mid \pm\theta U = \pm T\}$$

s.t.

$$A_2X_{22} \geq R_2$$

$$X_{11}, X_{22} \geq 0$$

where:

X_{11} = a vector of macroeconomic variables (m x 1),

X_{22} = a vector of energy variables (n x 1),

w_1, w_2 = vectors of the policy objective function coefficients,

c = a vector of the behavioural objective function coefficients,

R_1, R_2 = vectors of the RHS constants.

A statement of the above problem with macroeconomic constraints in the lower level of the MLP problem is as follows:

$$\text{Min} \quad Wl = w_1X_{11} + w_2X_{22}$$

$$\{\pm T\}$$

s.t.

$$\text{Min} \qquad C = (c \pm \theta U)X_{22}$$

$$\{X_{22} \mid \pm\theta U = \pm T\}$$

s.t. (3.29)

$$A_2X_{22} \geq R_1$$

$$p_1X_{11} + p_2X_{22} = R_2$$

$$X_{21}, X_{22} \geq 0$$

The question is whether the above problems are similar. If they are similar, then Model (3.12) can be solved by the PPS algorithm. Experiments may be undertaken to test the problem in future work. However, the author's view is that the above two specifications will give the same values as the optimum solution, even though these two specifications are structurally distinct.

3.11 Summary and Conclusion

In the PPS algorithm, the lower level problem of a complete MLP problem is solved as a parametric programming problem. Alternative optimum (basic) solutions to the lower level problem are searched to find the one which is optimum for the upper level problem. The algorithm can be used to solve different types of MLP problems including a dynamic MLP. There are some unresolved methodological issues which may be investigated in further studies.

The PPS algorithm is a heuristic search method. Like any other heuristic method for solving an MLP, it has the disadvantage that it can not be guaranteed that a global optimum is found. The real evaluation of the usefulness of an iterative procedure, specially in the context of the problems of solving MLP (see Candler, Fortuny-Amat and McCarl 1981), has been stated as follows (Hazell and Norton 1986, p. 323):

> Conceptually the main drawback of the iterative procedure is that the determination of the true optimum solution can not be guaranteed. However, in practice, large numbers of solutions may provide the analyst with reasonable confidence that the true optimum solution is found.

McCarl and Spreen (1980) have also emphasised the usefulness of search methods as: 'these algorithms[10] are rather cumbersome and demanding in terms of computer capacity. Informal iterative or search methods also may be used in the quest for optimum policy.'

Having developed an algorithm to solve an MLP, the next task is to apply this algorithm for solving AEPSOM to undertake the desired Australian policy studies. This will be done in the next three chapters.

[10] The MLP non-search algorithms discussed in Chap. 2 (the present author's note).

4 A Multi-Level Optimisation Approach to Multi-Level Energy Planning

4.1 Introduction

The objectives of this chapter are as follows: (1) to discuss the suitability of existing national sector-wide optimisation models for the formulation of an optimum multi-level energy plan; and (2) to develop an alternative approach which will, possibly, be free from the limitations of existing models.

The chapter is organised as follows. In Section 4.2, there is a discussion of the standard model validation criteria. Section 4.3 discusses existing energy planning models, while Section 4.4 evaluates existing models by some commonly used model validation criteria. Section 4.5 discusses the foundations of the new modelling approach and in Section 4.6, an MLO model of energy planning is developed. Additional information on the characteristics of the proposed MLO approach and some analytical principles of a decentralised energy-economic policy that the model can help formulate are given in Section 4.7 and 4.8.

4.2 Model Evaluation Criteria

In order to be able to investigate whether existing energy models are capable of providing an appropriate modelling framework for multi-level energy planning, a critical survey of existing energy models in terms of some standard model validation criteria is necessary. However, it needs to be stated that the choice of a method is dependent on the uses of the model i.e. the objective of the modelling exercise. No method can be judged superior without reference to the underlying problems for which it is developed. For example, econometric methods are primarily used for quantitative estimation, analysis or prediction of some economic variables, while mathematical programming models are used mainly for optimum planning or forecasting. Econometric studies are based on historical data, while programming models use cross-sectional data and depend on equality and inequality constraints. In addition to the purpose (or use of the model) and nature of the study, several other factors such as the availability of data and computer programmes, and the size of information expected from the model after its implementation also influence the choice of an appropriate methodology.

In an optimisation model, validation of the model (the determination of exactness of a model in representing a system (Taha 1976, p.11)) is an important step. Validation tests are performed to determine the appropriateness of the model and the reliability of the model results. There are three levels of validation tests (Kresge 1980): descriptive, analytical and experimental. At the descriptive level, the following criteria are applied: (1) appropriateness of the model structure; (2) achievement of the objectives of the model; and (3) plausibility and usefulness of the results. At the analytical level some of the criteria which are applied are model documentation, implementation etc., while at the experimental level, audit by an independent group and in-depth assessment are performed by undertaking sensitivity analysis and replication of results.

In this section, the validation tests at the descriptive level will be discussed to evaluate existing energy models. Followings are the model evaluation criteria that are applied.

4.2.1 Appropriateness of the Model Structure in Representing the Underlying Systems

Multi-level energy planning requires modelling of the energy policy and energy system. As an energy policy system is characterised by a two-level optimum decision making or policy formulation process (discussed in Chap. 1), formulation of policies by the government in such a policy environment is dependent on the decisions of economic agents. Therefore, in this context, energy planning involves the determination of optimum decisions of economic agents and optimum policies of the government simultaneously. This necessitates a multi-level optimisation model representing two-level decision making for formulating an energy plan.

Further, the energy system involves many technological alternatives and capacity limitations. A methodology that can represent adequately the complex energy system operations is desirable. This requires that some of the constraints of an MLO energy model should reflect these types of relations of an energy system.

Finally, the present study is undertaken to address medium and long-term energy planning issues involving substantial structural changes in the energy system. Modelling of medium-term or long-term energy sector planning involving inequality constraints requires a mathematical programming methodology (if the study is an optimisation study) since mathematical programming models can capture structural changes in a system (Folie and Ulph 1977). The relationships in the multi-level optimisation model can be estimated either econometrically or they can be specified on the basis of the technical structure of the energy sector involving inequality and non-negative constraints (modelled as a mathematical programming specification of the energy sector). The reasons for not applying econometric methods for energy sector planning may be summarised as follows (Norton and Schiefer 1981; Shumway and Chang 1977): econometric methods can not be adopted in a multi-product/activity and/or multi-regional environment since the degrees of freedom are usually inadequate; they are not applicable for policy planning in a situation characterised by fundamental structural and policy changes compared to the past period of statistical series or historical variation; econometric methods cannot include inequality constraints, such as the capacity constraint, which are important in energy sector planning; econometric models usually cannot provide much complementary information on the behaviour of the variables of a system model; econometric models are generally used for dealing with short-term energy policy issues (Folie and Ulph 1977), and not for long-term energy planning problems.

For these reasons, a predominance of mathematical programming applied to energy planning is observed (Riaz 1984; Folie and Ulph 1977; Julius 1981).

4.2.2 Achievement of the Objectives of a Study by the Model

As stated previously, if the purpose of this study is the formulation of an optimum multi-level energy plan, both economic and technological, then an explicit statement of the policy planning problems should be made. This requires the specification of the policy objectives and constraints, and a classification of the policy variables as targets and instruments. Yotopoulas and Nugent (1976, pp. 421-422) have stressed the importance of an identification of the policy targets and instruments in the following way:

> Perhaps the greatest shortcoming in planning to date has not been internal inconsistency, infeasibility, or sub-optimality of the plans per se but rather the failure to link planning goals with practical and specific policy instruments, the utilisation of which would ensure fulfilment of the planning goals.

4.2.3 Plausibility, Usefulness and Adequacy of Model Results

A set of results generated by a model has to be plausible. Also a comprehensive set of information of the energy system is necessary for an appropriate energy planning work. An energy plan involves, among other things, (a) pricing policy; (b) tax and subsidy policy; (c) depletion policy; (d) exploration and development policy; (e) conservation policy; (f) education and information policy; (g) research and development policy; (h) an investment policy or plan; (i) technological policy; (j) equity policy; and (k) industrial policy. A methodology is required that generates information adequate for the formulation of a comprehensive set of energy policies containing as many of these elements as possible. Otherwise, consistencies cannot be tested.

In summary, the formulation of an energy plan with an emphasis on the economic and technical aspects of the energy sector in a mixed economy, requires a model that can represent a multi-level decision making process with inequality constraints and a comprehensive set of energy policies. The modelling approach should be developed within a framework in which the energy planning problem is explicitly described.

4.3 Existing Energy Sector Optimisation Models

Energy policy models can be classified on the basis of the methodology adopted in each type of model. These models can be classified as one of the following types: (1) Network/process models; (2) Mathematical programming models; (3) General equilibrium models; (4) Econometric models; (5) Dynamic optimisation models; (6) Simulation models, and (7) Coupled/hybrid models.

Since this study leads to the formulation of an optimum energy plan, and as optimising behaviour of decision makers is assumed in this study, only optimising models or models which can represent such behaviour will be relevant for this survey. Since not all of the above types of energy models can be, or have been used for optimum energy planning, only the ones which can be, or have been used for this purpose will be discussed here. For discussion, these models have been regrouped as static optimisation models, dynamic optimisation models, and hybrid models.

4.3.1 Static Optimisation Models

Mathematical Programming Models. Mathematical programming models are developed in order to identify an optimum energy system. The optimisation criteria are contained in the objective function of the mathematical programming problem as:

$$C = f(X) \tag{4.1.a}$$

where[1] X = a vector of instruments/activities in the model (n x 1), as $X = (x_1, x_2, \ldots, x_n)$.

[1] Symbols used in different chapters have been defined separately in each chapter.

The objectives of the problem are usually in the form of minimisation of pollution, imports; or, maximisation of output, employment, profit, net (social) surplus; or, sometimes, in forms which involve different objectives such as the minimisation of cost, pollution, and the maximisation of employment simultaneously.

Constraints in mathematical programming models are the structure of the energy system under study. A general representation of the structure of an energy system may be given as follows:

$$H(X) \geq R \tag{4.1.b}$$

where H(X) = vectors of constraint functions (m x 1);

R = vector of given constraint parameters (m x 1).

The constraints in a programming model are usually the demand, supply, resource, capacity and pollution constraints, and the intermediate energy balance equations in the present context.

The solution to mathematical programming models determines an optimum energy system - either in the normative or behavioural sense - and has been used to formulate an optimum energy policy and to analyse the sensitivity of the energy system to some changes in the economy. The result of mathematical programming models can be used to formulate energy policies of the (a), and (c) to (i) types stated in section 4.2.3.

Some well known mathematical programming models include: the Brookhaven model set (Kydes 1978), PILOT, DIES, EFOM, the Birmingham Energy Models, and CEC (see the following surveys: Hoffman and Wood 1976; Planco Inc. 1979; Julius 1981; Rath-Nagel and Voss 1981; Hildebrandt undated).

General Equilibrium (GE) Energy Models. These models are developed within the established tradition of general equilibrium analysis in economics. The modelling approach is based on the consideration of the simultaneous existence of equilibrium output and price in all sectors of an economy, which is achieved when demand and supply are equal in all the interdependent markets. GE models represent the relationships of demand and supply of primary inputs, intermediate products and final output in factor and commodity markets (Intriligator 1971).

Numerical GE models which are used for formulating an optimum economic policy can be classified into three groups:

(1) activity analysis general equilibrium models;

(2) computable General Equilibrium (CGE) models; and

(3) macroeconometric general equilibrium models.

Activity Analysis Models: An activity analysis GE model can be developed by specifying an input-output model in an optimisation framework (Intriligator 1971). In an activity GE model, the objective function is usually specified to constitute either a problem of maximisation of the output in different sectors of the economy or the final demand, or a problem of minimisation of input costs. A standard activity analysis GE model is as follows:

$$\text{Max}\,W = \text{In}F$$

$$\{X,F\}$$

s.t.

$$(I - A)X - F \geq 0$$

$$eX \leq L \tag{4.2}$$

$$kX \leq K$$

$$dX \leq R$$

where: In = a vector of 1's (1 x n) and I = identity matrix,

X = a vector of outputs in different sectors (n x 1),

F = a vector of final demands (n x 1),

A = a matrix of the input-output coefficients(n x n),

e, k & d = vectors of employment, capital, and energy coefficients (1 x n),

L, K & R = vectors of available working age population, capital and energy (n x 1) respectively.

A theoretical model in this line is Park and Kubursi (1983). As far as the author knows, no numerical model has yet been developed.

The solution to this model provides an optimum allocation of resources i.e. an optimum output level and structure, and optimum input use levels and structure. Therefore, this type of model can be used to determine or plan the optimum allocation of resources in the economy. For the energy sector, these models can provide information necessary for formulating energy policies of the types: (a), and (e) to (j) stated in section 4.2.3.

Computable General Equilibrium (CGE) Models: The tradition of computable general equilibrium modelling goes back to Johansen's path-breaking work (Johansen 1960). A general presentation of a CGE model is as follows:

$$
\begin{aligned}
&X = f(k, L) && \text{- Production function} \\
&K = f(Px, Pk, Pl) && \text{- Input demand function (capital)} \\
&L = f(Px, Pk, Pl) && \text{- Input demand function (labour)} \\
&C = f(Px, Pl) && \text{- Consumption function} \\
&X = AX + C && \text{- Input-output model}
\end{aligned}
\tag{4.3}
$$

where X = a vector of output in different sectors (n x 1)

K,L = vectors of input demands in each sector of the economy (n x 1) and (n x 1);

C = a vector of sectoral consumption (n x 1);

A = a matrix of the input-output coefficients (n x n);

Px = a vector of output prices (1 x n);

Pk, Pl = vectors of interest and wage rates (1 x n) and (1 x n).

The CGE model is represented by a set of simultaneous equations of demand and supply of inputs and outputs; inter-industry balances and aggregate macroeconomic relationships.

A CGE model in reduced form may be represented as:

$$Y = f(X) \tag{4.4}$$

where Y = a vector of endogenous macroeconomic variables

X = a vector of exogenous macroeconomic variables

It can be reformulated as an optimum policy model by plugging in a policy objective function such as :

$$\underset{\{X,Y\}}{\text{Max}}\, W = f(X,Y) \tag{4.5}$$

s.t.

$$Y = f(X)$$

Interpretation of the variables in this policy model is different from economic models. In a policy model, the endogenous and exogenous variables of an economic model are the instrument and target variables (Fox, Sengupta and Thorbecke 1973).

The model can provide an optimum set of values for policy instruments. It is important to note that no optimisation CGE model has yet been developed for the energy sector.

Macroeconometric General Equilibrium Energy Models: A macroeconometric GE energy model in reduced form may be represented as:

$$Y = f(X) \tag{4.6}$$

where Y = a vector of endogenous macroeconomic variables

X = a vector of exogenous macroeconomic variables.

These models are simple extensions of macroeconometric models. In macroeconometric models, relationships between economic aggregates such as GDP, investment, saving, consumption, price level, money supply, and government expenditure are specified. The coefficients of the models are estimated econometrically. In macroeconometric GE energy models, the variables are defined separately as energy and non-energy types. These models can be reformulated as optimum policy models as in (4.5).

Some examples of macroeconometric GE energy models are Sweeny (1981), Hogan and Manne (1977), and Allen et al. (1976).

Solution to an optimisation macroeconometric GE model provides a set of optimum values for energy policy instrument variables such as prices, taxes and subsidies, and investment.

4.3.2 Dynamic Optimisation Energy Models

Dynamic energy modelling involves the problem of optimisation of an energy system over a period of time (Intriligator 1971). The optimisation problem is evaluated in terms of an objective function (or performance index or integral), which is usually defined as:

$$J = \int_{t_0}^{t_T} I[X(t), U(t), t]\, dt \tag{4.7}$$

where $X(t)$ = a vector of state variables

$U(t)$ = a vector of control variables

t = time $t_0, t_1, \ldots, t_T$

Dynamic energy systems, which are to be optimised, may be represented by a set of state equations:

$$\dot{X} = \frac{dX}{dt} = f(X(t), U(t), t) \tag{4.8}$$

here $\frac{dX}{dt} = \frac{dx_1}{dt}, \frac{dx_2}{dt}, \ldots, \frac{dx_n}{dt}$ for each $t = t_0, t_1, ., t_T$.

The optimisation problem is also subject to some initial conditions and some terminal conditions on the state variables

$$X(t_0) = X_0 \text{ and } X(t_T) = X_T \tag{4.9}$$

The feasible region or the boundary conditions of the control variables are specified, and the decision problem is to choose the optimum control trajectory from this feasible set:

$$U(t) \in U^n \in E^n \quad (4.10)$$

Similarly the boundary conditions on the state variables are:

$$X(t) \in X^n \in R^n \quad (4.11)$$

The dynamic optimisation energy models can also be discrete time stepped. The discrete time stepped dynamic optimisation problem can be considered as a mathematical programming problem (Intriligator 1971, p. 303) of the following form:

$$\max J = \sum_{t_0}^{t_T} I(X_t, U_t)$$

$$\{X_t, U_t\} \quad (4.12)$$

s.t.

$$X_{t+1} - X_{t0} = f(X_t, U_t)$$

$$X_t = X_0, \text{ given } U_t = U^n \in E^n$$

Basu's (1981) model is an example of an optimum control continuous model for the energy sector.

Solution of a dynamic optimisation model mainly provides information regarding prices, taxes and subsidies, optimum depletion rate, investments, and technological pattern in the energy sector.

4.3.3 Hybrid Models

In most large scale energy modelling, different types of models have been coupled with optimisation models to formulate a comprehensive set of energy policies. When both the energy sectoral and macroeconomic interrelationships are included in a hybrid model, various types of models such as input-output, macroeconometric or linear programming models are included. In this hybrid model, the values of the macroeconomic variables from a macroeconometric model are used in a linear programming model as the exogenous parameters (Meier 1984).

Some of the hybrid models in the energy sector are: BEEM (Behling, Marcuse, Swift and Tessmer 1975, Hoffman and Jorgenson 1977); BES (DeLucia and Jacoby 1982), and PIES (Hogan and Weyant 1980).

The output of a hybrid model consists of the outputs of the models included in the model suite. But the main objective for which the modelling work is undertaken is the development of an optimum energy system. If macroeconomic energy models (macroeconometric models or CGE models), formulated in an optimisation framework, are combined with mathematical programming models, the hybrid model can provide a comprehensive set of energy policies.

Output of a hybrid model has also been used to formulate multi-level planning involving planning at the macroeconomic level and planning at the sectoral level (Chap. 1). Results of the macroeconomic model (economy-wide model) provide information for general economic planning, while the energy sector model provides information for an energy sectoral plan (energy system plan).

4.4 Evaluation of Existing Energy Modelling Approaches

The first point that needs to be made is that not all of the energy sectoral optimisation models mentioned above were developed for formulating optimum energy planning. Some of these models were developed for forecasting future energy systems or for analysing the impact of different energy policies or technologies. This evaluation of the energy models is directed to all optimisation models in the energy sector, since even the optimisation models which have not been used to formulate optimum energy planning are applicable to energy planning.

Further, the present survey is not exhaustive. As the number of existing energy models is fairly large, all of them cannot be discussed individually. Therefore, limitations of different types of models (instead of individual models) are discussed. The limitations of a particular type of model are, to a large extent, valid for each model in that group.

In addition, extensive work on the methodological issues in sectoral modelling already exists. Candler, Fortuny-Amat, and McCarl (1981), McCarl and Spreen (1980), and Norton and Schiefer (1980) have discussed the general limitations of sectoral single-level optimisation models.

4.4.1 Limitations of Existing Energy Planning Models/Approaches

Inappropriateness of the Methodologies (related to criterion 1). The first limitation of existing energy models is the inappropriateness of the methodologies adopted in these models in representing the underlying systems (energy system and energy policy system).

General Methodological Limitations of all Existing Models: Outcome of government policy is dependent on the reactions of economic agents to such policies i.e. government and economic agents decisions are interrelated. To formulate a multi-level energy plan in this policy environment, a model is needed which can represent decision making systems of both the government and economic agents simultaneously, and therefore, can generate both an energy system plan and an energy policy plan. Technically, an appropriate model should be a multi-level one for the reasons discussed in Chap. 1. As existing optimisation models contain one objective function and only one set of constraints, they are inappropriate in the representation of the two level decision making of the energy sector and in the formulation of a multi-level energy plan. Consequently, they will also generate results unsuited to this problem (policies or forecasts). Single-level energy models can not generate analytical and numerical results related to the characteristics of multi-level decision making. Examples of such results derived from an MLO model may be seen in Chap. 6. Therefore, existing models are not developed within the appropriate methodological framework for multi-level energy planning.

As a basis of discussion, energy models may be classified as either positive or normative. A positive model represents the actual behaviour of the economic agents whereas a normative model represents the behaviour of economic agents as they ought to be.

For example, the following is a positive model which shows the cost minimisation decision making of the energy suppliers:

$$\begin{aligned} &\underset{\{X\}}{\text{Min}}\ C = cX \qquad \text{Behavioural objective function} \\ &\text{s.t.} \qquad\qquad\qquad\qquad\qquad\qquad\qquad\qquad\qquad (4.13) \\ &S = \{\, X \mid AX \geq R;\ X \geq 0 \,\} \quad \text{Energy sectoral opportunity set} \end{aligned}$$

The variables and coefficients are the same as in (4.2). This type of energy model is frequently used in energy planning by conducting sensitivity analysis in investigating the impact of some changes in energy policies or technologies. It can also be used to investigate changes in demand and supply on the energy system. This information is then supplied to policy makers so that they can choose a set of energy policies which they perceive as consistent with their preferences.

As there is no policy objective function in these models, they cannot be used to formulate a set of optimum policies that provide the best strategy for policy makers considering all the possible alternatives. But when this type of model is used to formulate an energy policy, some criteria are applied implicitly by the policy makers to enable them to choose the one they think is consistent with their preferences. As preference criteria are neither made explicit nor part of the model, the optimum policy cannot be identified by these models. Candler, Fortuny-Amat and McCarl (1981, p. 521) state this limitation as follows:

> While models have been constructed to reflect the competitive behaviour of the decentralised decision makers ..., little attention has been given to a clear articulation of policy objectives or the acceptable range for policy variables...

Positive models can be changed to normative models by incorporating a policy objective function in a model, instead of a behavioural objective function as follows:

$$\underset{\{X\}}{\text{Max}}\, W = wX \quad \text{Policy objective function}$$

s.t. (4.14)

$$S = \{X \mid AX \geq R\,;\, X \geq 0\,\} \quad \text{Energy sectoral opportunity set.}$$

This type of policy model overlooks an important component of policy planning problems. Policy makers' decisions are not subject to the constraints of the energy sector. These constraints represent energy market equilibrium conditions and technological characteristics of the energy sector. Norton and Schiefer (1980, p. 207) also claim that such models do not represent adequately the policy problem (or even the descriptive problem).

In another type of normative use of optimisation methods, the objective function of the type shown in (4.14) is retained, but some additional constraints are included in the model. These additional constraints are specified to include the preferences of the policy makers. The following model is an example of such practice:

$$\underset{\{X\}}{\text{Min}}\; C = cX \quad \text{Behavioural objective function} \qquad (4.15)$$

s.t.

$$S = \{\, X \mid AX \geq R;\, L \leq Xp \leq P;\, X, Xp \geq 0\,\}$$

Energy sectoral opportunity set and policy constraints.

Xp is the vector of variables directly controlled by the policy makers, L and P are the lower and upper limits of the constraints on Xp. The same objections which have been raised in connection with normative models such as (4.14) are also valid for the present type of formulation. In addition, in this specification it is impossible to know a priori whether there exists any solution to the model satisfying the policy constraints.

Methodological Limitations of Individual Models. On the basis of the above general limitations of single level optimisation models, methodological limitations of each type of model can now be evaluated.

Mathematical Programming Energy Models: The limitations of mathematical programming models are evident from the discussion of the limitations of single level optimisation models, since existing mathematical programming models are of the single level type. But mathematical programming methodology has several advantages for energy planning. It is operational and can include inequality constraints. It can also capture multi-input, multi-activity, and multi-output economic and technological systems of the sector. Furthermore, it can capture future structural changes in the sector and also provide complementary information such as pollution levels produced in the energy sector.

General Equilibrium Models: All the methodological limitations of single level optimisation models discussed above apply broadly to all general equilibrium models. Usually, the reaction functions in general equilibrium models are not decomposed into their relevant components which are the objective function of economic agents and constraints faced by them. Therefore, the policy reaction functions can not model the decision making of economic agents with its constituent components. And consequently, general equilibrium models cannot generate energy system plans, although they are useful in formulating energy policy plans.

To demonstrate this point, the three types of general equilibrium models are separately evaluated below.

Firstly, activity analysis GE models do not and cannot contain the decision making problems of economic agents as well as full details of an energy system (i.e. the energy sector constraints). Decision making problems of economic agents are suppressed in the input-output model. Also the energy sectoral decisions are influenced by many non-economic factors such as technical convenience, safety and efficiency which are not included in an activity analysis GE model. The existence of such phenomena as peak and off-peak demand, excess capacity and reserve capacity requires the relationships to be represented in inequality form. This type of information is missing in an activity analysis GE model.

Secondly, In the case of CGE models, the coefficients of CGE models are estimated econometrically. In some cases, the coefficients are derived from the national accounts system including the input-output models. In both these cases, however, the methodological structures of CGE models are the same. The problem with this type of CGE model is that reactions of individual economic agents to policy initiatives are represented by equations, such as the demand function for energy. The limitation of this type of functional representation of individual reactions in an energy policy study is that the decision criteria of the economic agents which are represented by an objective function of an optimisation model are not explicitly shown in the policy model (CGE) structure. The decision problems of policy makers are shown explicitly, but decision principles of economic agents are shown by some equations without explicit representation of their decision making problem in the form of an optimisation problem. In brief, CGE modelling does not provide the required multi-level dimension.

The other limitation of the CGE model (4.5) in optimum energy policy studies is that econometrically estimated demand and supply functions emphasise economic arguments such as prices and incomes, whereas energy demands and supplies depend on many technological factors. In a similar way to activity analysis GE models, CGE models do not contain detailed energy sector constraints, particularly none of a technical character.

Thirdly, the limitations of macroeconometric GE models are the same as those of all other GE models; inability to present energy policy systems and details of the energy sector.

Since all the GE models are single level optimisation models, these models cannot represent the optimum energy policy formulation process. But, with regard to limitations imposed by a lack of detailed representation of the energy sector, it can be argued that some equations representing the energy system under study can be incorporated in a GE model by adding some additional relationships. For example if the following set of equations represent an energy system :

$$Ye - f(Xe) = 0 \tag{4.16}$$

then a detailed GE model can be represented as :

$$\text{Max} \quad W = f(X, Y, Xe, Ye)$$

$$\{X, Y, Xe, Ye\}$$

s.t.

$$Y = f(X) \tag{4.17}$$

$$Ye - f(Xe) = 0$$

$$X, Y, Xe, Ye \geq 0$$

where Ye, Xe are vectors of the energy sector endogenous and exogenous variables, and X and Y are defined in (4.5).

The problem with the above type of presentation of an energy policy formulation system in a GE is that the energy system is being specified as a part of a macroeconomic system and being evaluated (directly) in terms of the preference criteria of the policy makers. But, an energy system optimisation problem needs to be evaluated in terms of the preferences of the individual economic agents as well. Therefore, though societal objectives are included in GE models, 'there is no pretence of simulating the actual behaviour of economies' (Candler and Norton 1977, p. 11), thus the model in (4.17) does not portray the two level decision making problem at all.

Dynamic Optimisation Models: These limitations of CGE models are also present in optimum control (continuous) models. Discrete dynamic optimisation models possess the limitations of mathematical programming models. Candler and Norton (1977, p. 11) state the limitations of control models in the following way:

> Control theory utilises an explicit usual econometric description of the underlying economic structure (feasible behavioural set). With the econometric description, the choice of instrument values is limited to that range of values which has been experienced during the period of historical observations. This restriction may be a strong one.

Hybrid Models: Hybrid models are constituted by various aspects of the models discussed above, each component of a hybrid model would have the limitations of each method. Generally, in existing hybrid models, preferences of the policy makers are not explicated and policy variables are not classified (i.e. they fail to satisfy the second criterion). Again, hybrid models are not developed and solved as a single, integrated and interrelated MLO (policy model). Different levels of MLO problem are not treated simultaneously.

Non-specification of the energy policy planning problem (related to criterion two). There are conceptual problems in applying existing energy models for energy planning. First of all, preferences of policy makers are not made explicit and policy variables are not properly defined and classified to identify the underlying problems of policy planning. In some modelling studies, where the underlying energy policy targets and instruments have been stated, there is unprecise discussion of how these statements of policy problems relate to the preferences of policy makers. Also missing is a discussion of how some relevant quantitative information needed in a policy optimisation study such as the classification of the policy variables and the specification of the weights in the policy objective function are obtained. Secondly, the elements of existing energy policy systems, for example multi-level hierarchical decision making systems, is not sufficiently incorporated. Therefore, existing models are not developed within the relevant conceptual, analytical, and operational framework.

A more appropriate energy planning structure, therefore, is the one in which the energy planning model includes the underlying policy preferences involving a classification of policy variables as target and instrument variables to provide a clear presentation of the existing policy planning problem and embedded within it the relevant systems: economic, energy and policy.

Inadequate set of results (related to criteria three). The third limitation of existing models is the inadequate nature of the results provided by these models. Existing energy models cannot provide a comprehensive set of energy policies.

4.5 An Alternative Modelling Approach: Multi-Level Optimisation of Energy Systems and Energy Policy

The limitations of existing energy planning approaches can be overcome by adopting an MLO approach. The justifications and elements of this approach are discussed below.

4.5.1 Arguments for an MLO Approach

The main justification for the proposed MLO model is that such models represent underlying policy problems accurately. As the energy sector policy system is characterised by what is called a 'multi-level (multi-goal) hierarchical policy system', undertaking an optimum multi-level planning study in the energy sector requires the adoption of a model which can represent the characteristics of the multi-level policy system. Since there are two optimisation problems, an appropriate model should have two sub-optimisation problems embedded in it.

4.5.2 Elements of the MLO Approach

To overcome the limitations of the existing models, it is necessary to develop the MLO approach on appropriate theoretical, conceptual and methodological foundations which have been found to be lacking in existing models. This can be accomplished if the MLO approach is developed within the framework of the theory of economic policy planning, policy systems analysis and MLP.

It may, however, be mentioned that attempts for developing MLP models within an appropriate framework are not new. Fortuny-Amat (1979) has made clear the similarities between multi-level, multi-goal policy systems and MLP, although he did not integrate or analyse his model results, analytically or numerically, in terms of multi-level, multi-goal policy systems. Candler and Norton (1977) have made some reference to the theory of economic policy planning, although their studies have not been fully and explicitly undertaken within the framework of the theory of economic policy planning. With this background, the present study has attempted to integrate MLP, policy systems analysis and the theory of economic policy planning in the energy sectoral context so that the integrated MLO approach may provide an improved methodology for and understanding of the policy formulation problem in the energy sector.

The Theory of Economic Policy Planning

Analytical Framework: The first requirement of an appropriate modelling approach can be satisfied if an optimisation energy model is developed within the framework of the theory of economic policy planning (Tinbergen 1952). Fox, Sengupta, and Thorbecke (1973, p. 11) state that:

> The theory of economic policy is concerned with the analysis of decision situations and policy problems, using that part of general economic theory which can be quantitatively applied to economic data in some operational sense.

Therefore, the theory of economic policy planning provides an analytical and operational framework for economic policy analysis and planning. It provides an analytical and operational framework for policy planning since it deals with the following aspects of policy planning: (a) The policy characterisation problem (specification of a policy system model including the policy objective function, and a set of constraints of the system under study); (b) The policy selection problem (the classification of the variables of the policy model as the target and instrument variables), and (c) The policy steering problem (deviation of a set of optimum policies).[2]

There are three elements in the theory of economic policy planning: (i) a policy objective function, (ii) a policy model of the system under study (a set of policy constraints), and (iii) a classification of the variables, mainly as policy targets and instruments (Fox, Sengupta, and Thorbecke 1973). The basic structure of the theory of economic policy planning has been extended in many directions and has been applied to different areas. The basic theoretical framework has been extended to develop the theory of economic policy planning within the framework of mathematical programming and optimum control. It has been applied to various areas of economics involving the policy formulation problem such as growth, development planning, stabilisation, and sectoral policy and planning (Fox, Sengupta, and Thorbecke 1973). This study attempts to apply it to energy planning.

Analytical strength of the theory of economic policy planning lies: (a) in its emphasis on the explication of the preferences of the policy makers and the identification of target and instrument variables, (b) in it's analytical structure in which direct and casual relationships between the target and instrument variables are established and derived, both theoretically and numerically, and (c) in its ability to define and derive an optimum economic policy. Therefore, the theory of economic policy planning provides an appropriate analytical and operational framework for studying the underlying energy policy planning problem, and thus, for the formulation of an optimum energy plan.

Definition of an Optimum Economic Policy: An important reason for adopting the theory of economic policy planning is that it can define and help derive an optimum economic policy. At this point, therefore, it is needed to discuss the definition of an optimum policy and its derivation in the Tinbergen framework.

Generally an optimum policy is the 'best' policy. It can be interpreted in two alternative ways:

---

[2] In this study, the energy policy characterisation and selection problems will be discussed in Chap. 5, while the steering problem will be discussed in Chap. 6.

(1) Traditionally, an optimum policy is defined in terms of Pareto optimality criteria: a policy which can make no one better off without making someone worse off,[3] and

(2) Alternatively, an optimum policy may be defined as the policy which can attain the optimum value of the objectives of the policy makers. In terms of the Tinbergen approach, an optimum policy is the optimum value of a policy instrument (a set of instruments) which provide the optimum value of the policy objective function.

In the theory of economic policy planning, the problem of the formulation of the optimum economic policy[4] is stated as follows:

$$\underset{\{u\}}{\text{Min}}\ WL = W(x-\bar{x}, u-u^*) = (x-\bar{x})^T Q\,(x-x) + (u-u^*)^T R\,(u-u^*)$$

$Q \geq 0,\ R \geq 0$

s.t. $Ax + Cz = Bu + Dw$ - a macroeconomic model

where (4.18)

x : $N \times 1$; N endogenous target variables

x : $N \times 1$; N desired levels of the target variables

z : $R \times 1$; R endogenous non-target variables

u : $K \times 1$; K exogenous instruments

u^* : $K \times 1$; K desired levels of the instrument variables

---

[3] In terms of the results of the model (4.21), a set of policy instruments:

$(\tilde{\tilde{G}}, \pm\tilde{\tilde{T}}_1, \pm\tilde{\tilde{T}}_2, \pm\tilde{\tilde{T}}_3, \tilde{\tilde{Y}}_p)$

is Pareto efficient if:

(a) it is feasible,

(b) no other feasible states $(G, \pm T_1, \pm T_2, \pm T_3, Y_p)$ exist so that

$W(G, \pm T1, \pm T2, \pm T3, Y, X, Z) \geq W(\tilde{\tilde{G}}, \pm\tilde{\tilde{T}}1, \pm\tilde{\tilde{T}}2, \pm\tilde{\tilde{T}}3, \tilde{\tilde{Y}}p)$

(c) for at least one policy

$W(g_i, \pm t_{1j}, \pm t_{2j}, \pm t_{3j}, y_{pj}) \geq W(\tilde{\tilde{g}}_j, \tilde{\tilde{t}}_{1j}, \pm\tilde{\tilde{t}}_{2j}, \pm\tilde{\tilde{t}}_{3j}, \tilde{\tilde{y}}_{pj})$

[4] This section is adapted from Preston & Pegan (1983), Chap. 1 which shows the characterisation and selection problems.

W : J x 1 ; J exogenous data

and the dimensions of the coefficient matrix are:

A : (N + R) x N;

C : (N + R) x R;

B : (N + R) x K;

D : (N + R) x J;

In many applied works, the macroeconomic model is defined as follows:

$AX = Bu + D$

A set of optimum policies can be formulated by solving the model as a classical optimisation model (steering problem):

$$\tilde{\tilde{u}} = (M^TQM + R)^{-1} (Ru^* + M^TQY) \qquad (4.19)$$

where $M \equiv A^{-1} B$ and $Y \equiv X - A^{-1} D$

The classical optimisation model presented above is most commonly used in the theory of economic policy planning. However, as it was stated above, other forms are used in formulating optimum economic policy. In the present study, the theory of economic policy planning is embedded in MLP. In an MLP model, an optimum policy is identified by the optimum solution of MLP (characteristics of an MLP optimum solution are discussed in Chap. 3 (mathematical properties) and Chap. 6 (economic properties). Therefore, an optimum policy is defined in the present study as the policy (a set of instrument variables) which attains the optimum value of the policy objective function of the MLP model and corresponds to the optimum solution of the MLP model.

Policy Systems Analysis. Policy system analysis refers to the organisation and analysis of the various elements of the policy formulation process existing in an environment.

One important type of policy system is what is called a multi-level, multi-goal system, two characteristics of which are: goal interdependence or interactions among different levels of goal seeking, and intervention by one level on the other level (Mesarovic et al. 1973).

Interdependence or interaction between the different goals implies that achievement of one level's objective is dependent on the achievement of one of the other level's objectives.

Two types of interdependence exist: direct and indirect. In the case of direct interdependence, '...goals of the higher as well as the lower level units depend explicitly upon the outputs and behaviour of the casual systems...' (Mesarovic et al. p. 301).

In the case of indirect interdependence, '...goals of a given higher level unit may explicitly depend only upon the goals of the lower level units and implicitly upon the performance of the basic casual system...' (Mesarovic et al. p. 301).

Intervention is another characteristic of the multi-goal, multi-level policy system. The authorities of the upper level usually intervene on the lower level. Two types of intervention exist: direct and indirect. In the case of direct intervention, the casual sub-system is partly controlled by the upper level along with the control of the lower level. In case of indirect intervention, the upper level cannot directly control the decision of the lower level but can modify the behaviour of the lower level by adopting a set of appropriate instruments. In this case, the decision making on the part of the upper level is to choose the best method of modifying or influencing the behaviour of the lower level decision makers.

The justification for developing an MLO approach within the framework of policy systems analysis is that it provides a conceptual framework for policy planning studies. The adoption of the conceptual framework is useful since it will allow extensive use of formal concepts and analytical or quantitative techniques in policy planning studies (Mesarovic et al. 1973, p. 294). It is revealed that the development of the MLO approach within the framework of policy systems analysis helps systematic and improved study of the policy making system in the energy sector. Generally, policy system analysis is developed theoretically or conceptually. This study develops a numerical policy system analysis for the energy sector (see Chap. 6).

Multi-level Programming. Since a multi-level, multi-goal policy system exists in the energy sector, a methodology that can represent that policy system is required. This methodological requirement is satisfied by multi-level programming (MLP). The following discussion demonstrates this point.

MLP consists of a series of nested optimisation problems at different levels (Candler and Norton 1977; Bialas and Karwan 1980). An MLP model involving two levels of optimisation is represented[5] as follows:

Opt. $W = w(X_0, \pm T)$ Policy objective function[6]

$\{X_1, \pm T\}$

s.t.

$X_0 = g_0(X_1, X_2)$ Definitions of Target Variables

$g_1(X_0, X_1, \pm T) = R_1$ Policy constraints

Opt. $C = f(X_2, \pm T)$ Behavioural objective function

$\{X_2 \mid \pm T, X_1\}$ (4.20)

s.t.

$g_2(X_1, X_2) \geq R_2$ Behavioural constraints

$X_0, X_1, X_2 \geq 0$

where

X_0 = vector of policy target variables ($1 \times n_1$) such as energy conservation,

X_1 = vector of resource control policy instrument variables ($1 \times n_2$),

$\pm T$ = vector of price control policy instrument variables (taxes and subsidies) ($m \times 1$),

---

[5] This bi-level programming problem is a special case of MLP. In this study only bi-level programming problems (models and solution algorithms) have been considered. However, the term MLP has been used to represent bi-level programmes since some statements, arguments and conclusions made in this study have general MLP implications.

[6] The mathematical properties of the functions and feasible regions of an MLP model were discussed in Chap. 3.

X_2 = vector of behavioural variables (1 x n_2) such as supply, production, and end-uses of energy,

R_1 = vector of right hand side policy constraints (n_1 x 1) for example total sectoral budget allocation,

R_2 = vector of right hand side behavioural constraints (n_2 x 1) such as the exogenous supply of resources, demand for energy, capacity limits.

w = policy objective function containing policy objectives such as conservation of energy,

f = behavioural objective function representing criteria such as cost minimisation or social surplus maximisation,

g_0 = functions defining the policy target variables.

g_1 = policy constraints in the form of budget constraint, limits on the changes on taxes and subsidies, and import control,

g_2 = behavioural constraints such as energy supply and demand constraints,

$n = n_1 + n_2$.

The MLP given by (4.20) consists of two sub-optimisation problems: the policyproblem (upper level problem) and behavioural problem (lower level problem). The two sub-optimisation problems have two objective functions: the policy objective function and the behavioural objective function. There are two types of constraints: the policy constraints and the constraints on the behaviour of individual economic agents. There are three types of feasible regions which are searched to find the policy optimum. The feasible regions are: the policy feasible region generated by the policy constraints, and the policy target and instrument variables; the behavioural feasible region generated by the behavioural constraints; and the policy-behavioural feasible region generated by the reaction functions through the interactions of policy instruments, behavioural variables and policy target variables. The variables of an MLP model can be classified into three types: policy target variables; policy instrument variables and behavioural variables which are related to the behaviour of economic agents.

MLP can be of one of the following types: price control; resource control; and price and resource control. In a price control MLP model, the upper level decision makers control the behaviour of the lower level decision makers through ($\pm T$) prices, taxes, and subsidies while in a resource control MLP, the control is through the allocation of resources (X_1). In price and resource control MLP, both prices and resources are controlled by the policy makers.

Advantages of MLP for studying policy planning problems are made explicit in the following statement by Candler and Norton (1977, p. 40):

> The separation of the policy problem into two components, the policy sub-problem proper and the behavioural (or 'forecasting') sub-problem, has long been accepted as a rational approach. However, this approach has not often been implemented systematically. We hope that multi-level programming is a step in this direction.

An MLP problem has two objective functions and two sets of constraints. So, MLP can represent exactly the features of multi-goal, multi-level, hierarchical policy systems. The MLP model in (4.20) resembles a multi-goal, multi-level policy system. This has been discussed by Fortuny-Amat (1979, Section 4.5, pp. 34-39). In the MLP model, the policy makers have some targets or goals (X_0) which they try to achieve by directly or indirectly controlling the decisions of economic agents (producers and consumers of energy) through the instrument variables ($\pm T$, X_1). These two types of decision makers optimise their respective objectives f_1 and f_2, therefore, there are two separate domains of control which are interrelated by the reaction functions (g_0). While policy makers control $\pm T$, X_1, economic agents control X_2. The MLP model, therefore, represents the multi-goal, multi(two)-level policy making system, and thus, can fit within the conceptual framework of policy systems analysis. Consequently, an MLP model can provide some useful information regarding the characteristics of the multi-level decision making both analytical (this chapter) and numerical (as shown in Section 6.3). An MLP model also can represent the technical characteristics of an energy system since the constraints of an MLP model can be in inequality form. Consequently, an MLP model which satisfies the validation criterion (1) can represent the system under study. Moreover, the elements of the theory of economic policy planning can be incorporated in an MLP model. In the above MLP modelling framework, there is a policy objective function. The variables can be classified as: X_0 = the target variables, ±T, X_1 = the instrument variables, and X_2 = irrelevant variables (behavioural variables, in this study); and a model is (4.20). Therefore, MLP can represent and incorporate the elements of energy policy systems, and can also accommodate the elements of the theory of economic policy planning and can thus incorporate the underlying policy planning problem adequately and appropriately. So an MLO model satisfies the validation criteria 2. Since MLP is an optimisation technique developed within a mathematical programming framework containing economic variables such as taxes and subsidies and a detailed technical structure of the energy sector, MLP can provide information adequate for formulating a comprehensive set of energy policies (Chap. 6). As MLP is an operational method, it satisfies the model validation criterion (3) and it can be used for a comprehensive and integrated quantitative energy planning study of a country.

4.5.3 Justifications for an MLO Approach : A Summary

To summarise, an MLO energy plan developed within the above mentioned framework can overcome the limitations of existing energy planning approaches. It can represent the underlying energy policy system and therefore, generate an energy system plan and an energy policy plan simultaneously, can contain an explicit statement of the energy policy planning problem and can provide a comprehensive set of energy policies. Therefore, an MLO approach can be considered an appropriate modelling framework for multi-level energy planning. Although MLP has been applied to other areas and sectors of the economy (Candler, Fortuny-Amat, and McCarl 1981), MLP has not yet been applied for energy planning. So the present study is, probably, the first multi-level optimisation study in the energy sector.

It may, however, be mentioned that this study in its process of developing an energy sector MLP model will attempt to make some extensions in the MLP literature in model specification (Chap. 5), policy applications (Chap. 7) and solutions algorithm (Chap. 3).

Justifications for making efforts for these extensions may be revealed from the survey of the current state of MLP models provided earlier.

4.6 A Multi-Level Optimisation Energy Model

4.6.1 An Illustrative Representation of the Model

Within the conceptual, analytical and methodological framework proposed above, and considering the current level of development of MLP, the following abstract and illustrative representation of an multi-level energy planning model is specified:

Max $W = wG$ (a) Policy objective function[7]

$\{G, \pm T_1, \pm T_2, \pm T_3, Yp\}$

s.t. (4.21)

$T_l \leq \{\pm T_1, \pm T_2, \pm T_3\} \leq T_p$ (b) Policy constraints (price control)

$G = I_1 Y + I_2 X + I_3 Z$ (c) Equations defining energy targets

$Yp \leq Yc$ (d) Policy constraints: resource control

Min $C = (c_1 \pm T_1)Y + (c_2 \pm T_2)X + (c_3 \pm T_3)Z$

$\{Y, X, Z \mid G, \pm T_1, \pm T_2, \pm T_3, Yp\}$ (e) Behavioural objective function

s.t.

$Z \geq \overline{D}$ (f) Energy demand constraints

---

[7] In this specification of the policy objective function, the policy instruments have not been included. However policy instruments (±T) are included in the policy objective function in other specifications of MLO models.

$Z = aX$ (g) Intermediate energy balances

$X = bY$ (h) Supply balances

$Y + Yp \leq \overline{Y}$ (i) Supply constraints

$X \leq \overline{X}$ (j) Capacity constraints

$G, Y, X, Z, Yp \geq 0$ (k) Non-negative constraints

where[8]

w = vector of the coefficients of the policy objective functions $(1 \times m_1)$,

G = energy target variable vector $(k \times 1)$,

Y, X, Z = vectors of primary energy, secondary energy and end-uses of energy: $(l \times 1)$, $(n \times 1)$, and $(p \times 1)$,

I_1, I_2, I_3 = matrices the elements of which are either 1 or 0,

$\pm T_1, \pm T_2, \pm T_3$ = vectors of tax and subsidy related to Y, X, and Z: $(l \times 1)$, $(n \times 1)$, and $(p \times 1)$,

Yp = amount of Y that is directly controlled by the policy makers (sub-vector of Y),

T_l, T_p = lower and upper limits on $\pm T$,

$\overline{D}$ = the vector of given end-uses of energy $(p \times 1)$,

$\overline{Y}, \overline{X}$ = total supplies and capacities of fuels $(l \times 1)$ and $(n \times 1)$,

a, b = matrices of technical coefficients $(l \times n)$ and $(n \times l)$.

The above model is a partial equilibrium energy sectoral MLO model which should be used for formulating medium or long term energy plans. The characteristics of the modelling approach and the analytical characteristics that the model (4.21) can demonstrate are stated in Section 4.8.

[8] A description of the economic and analytical characteristics of this type of MLO energy planning model was given in Chap. 3.

4.6.2 A Discussion of the Model

In this model, the government's choice is to determine a set of policy instruments and strategies including taxes, subsidies, prices, government expenditures, etc. which will optimise the policy objective function involving the minimisation of the use of energy, crude oil and imported oil. The governments choice is constrained by the limits on the variation of taxes and subsidies and by the condition that net government revenue should be positive. The behavioural model represents the choice problem of economic agents in the form of the choice (for production and consumption) of the set of energy activities which can be provided at the minimum cost given the government choice of a set of energy policy instruments and strategies. The decisions of economic agents are subject to the energy resource supply, capacity and demand constraints.

4.7 Some Features of the Present Energy Planning Study/Approach

4.7.1 Applied Welfare Economic Study

The present approach is adoptable to applied welfare study since it deals with the principles of maximisation of social welfare in the energy sector. Therefore, this study is following the established steps of an applied welfare economic analysis: (i) to define a social welfare criterion; (ii) to identify the factors that may prohibit the achievement of the optimum level of welfare and, (iii) to suggest a set of policy actions, the adaptation of which will maximise social welfare (Oser and Brue 1988).

4.7.2 Multi-Level Optimisation Approach

As the objective of this study is to formulate an optimum energy plan, this requires an optimisation approach. The present multi-level energy planning approach recognises the existence of and is explicitly based on the two-level decision making system existing in the energy sector the upper level decision maker (the government) and the lower level decision makers (producers and consumers). In this MLO approach, it is assumed that both the government and economic agents engage in optimising behaviour for making decisions (rational choice). The assumption that the government engages in optimising behaviour is implied by the theory of economic policy of Tinbergen (1952). The assumption of the optimising behaviour of economic agents is implied by the neoclassical economic theory. The government attempts to maximise social welfare, while economic agents optimise their well being (Oser and Brue 1988). Such a two-level decision making system requires a two-level optimisation approach for modelling the energy sector planning problem.

4.7.3 Multi-Disciplinary Character

The present approach is multi-disciplinary in character. Energy planning and modelling (Meier 1984) involves the utilisation of the knowledge of mathematics, operations research, economics and energy engineering to develop computerised models to address energy planning and policy issues.

4.7.4 Partial Equilibrium Model

The energy sector planning may address only the energy sectoral issues and options (partial equilibrium approach) or it may incorporate energy macroeconomic interactions and policy issues (general equilibrium approach). Both of these approaches have advantages and disadvantages.

Economic planning is generally considered in a general, multi-market or multi-sectoral equilibrium context because of the welfare implications of general equilibrium analysis. As a result, a general equilibrium planning approach in which simultaneous interrelationships between different sectors of the economy are considered is usually to be preferred. The disadvantage of this approach is that in this type of models, the details of the energy sector, specially the technical details, can not be incorporated, and computational difficulties may arise.

However, the partial equilibrium approach to energy sector planning is well established and accepted in the profession following the Marshallian approach to partial equilibrium analysis (Marshall 1920). It is true that such an approach can not capture the secondary benefits and losses of the interrelated markets. But the partial equilibrium approach is justified by arguing that the optimum welfare in a partial equilibrium setting will also result in optimum welfare in a general equilibrium framework (Griffin and Steele 1980). The theory of second-best (Lipsey and Lancaster 1956-1957), however, advocates a different view. In a situation where some markets are not perfect, achievement of optimum conditions in one market may lead to overall welfare loss in the economy, rather than welfare gain. This theory may be true under some restrictive situations such as the strong substitutability and complementarity of goods, and markets characterised by implacable distortion. Generally, these conditions are not met and the partial equilibrium analysis is considered to have optimum welfare implications (Harberger 1971; Griffin and Steele 1980).

There are several other advantages of partial equilibrium analysis of the energy sector or energy sector planning: it allows consideration of special characteristics of each industry within the sector; it is computationally simple; it requires minimum data; and it provides an aggregated viewpoint in the appraisal of individual projects by presenting detailed information about the processes etc. (Riaz 1984, p. 26).

The real choice of the scope for energy sector planning hinges on some factors such as the objective and nature of the planning studies, adopted methodology, and computational facilities (availability of algorithm, software and hardware). Ignoring any computational problem, a partial equilibrium approach to energy planning will be found desirable if the objective of an energy planning study is to focus mainly on the detailed economic, technical and policy issues in the energy sector. The emphasis of such studies is on the '...detailed analysis of each sub-sector with special emphasis on interactions among them, substitution possibilities, and the resolution of any resulting policy conflicts...' (Munasinghe and Schramm 1983, p. 85).

As the emphasis of this study is on the detailed and comprehensive sectoral policy issues and options, the partial equilibrium approach (micro-energy planning) is adopted.

4.7.5 Multi-Level Energy Planning: Energy System and Policy Planning

The energy planning may involve the planning of the energy system (determination of the optimum energy demand-supply combination, technological pattern and activities), together with the formulation of a set of optimum energy policies or either of them separately. In the present study, energy planning refers to multi-level energy planning; the planning of the energy system and policy simultaneously.

4.7.6 Quantitative Energy Planning

Energy planning may refer to some qualitative energy policies such as the determination of the appropriate energy market regulation policy, institutional restructuring, control of ownership, etc. It also may refer to quantitative policies such as pricing policy, taxation policy, etc. In this study, only the quantitative energy policies are incorporated and studied.

4.7.7 Long-Term Energy Planning

Folie and Ulph (1977) have classified major energy policy issues in three groups: short, medium and long-term. The short-term energy policies are addressed to energy problems which arise from the instability in the energy market (supply, demand and price). The medium-term energy policy issues relate to the possibility of supply increases and inter-fuel substitution in energy supply, production and end uses within the structure of the existing energy system. The long-term energy policy issues deal with the problems of finding alternative, not readily adoptable, supplies of energy resources, and production and end-use technologies. This is only possible within a new structure of the energy system.

In the present study, the medium and long-term energy policy and planning issues involving substantial structural changes will be addressed. Therefore, these policy studies (Chap. 6) will have a time horizon of 10-15 years in terms of their implementation and implications.

4.7.8 Energy Sectoral Model

In any sector model, the energy sector is considered as an economic unit (Hazell and Norton 1986, Chap. 7) such as the household, firm or government. A sector model should have several elements such as: (1) descriptions of producers' and consumers' economic behaviour; (2) production conditions; (3) resource endowments; (4) market conditions (perfect competition in the present study), and (5) policy system. In the proposed MLO model, all these elements are present. The behavioural model represents the elements (1) to (4) and the complete MLO model represents (5).

4.8 Characteristics of Multi-Level Decision Making: Some Analytical Results

In this section, some analytical aspects of multi-level decision making embedded in the MLO model will be discussed. These analytical aspects are reflected in the processes of reactions and adjustments in various decision variables and relationships of different types of decision makers and the resultant equilibrium in the policy system in the model. Similar aspects of multi-level decision making revealed by AEPSOM results will be discussed in Chap. 6.

4.8.1 Optimum Policy in an MLO Model

In the theory of economic policy, developed on the basis of a single level optimisation model, the optimum values of the instruments are the policies that optimise the policy objective function. But in a multi-level optimum energy-economic policy framework, the optimum policy instruments are those for which the objective functions of different level policy makers attain their optimum values.

The optimum policies in the framework of MLP model can be provided by the complete MLP model with the Kuhn - Tucker conditions of the behavioural model (with ±T) as follows:

$$\text{Max } W = wG \quad \text{(a)}$$

$$\{G, \pm T_1, \pm T_2, \pm T_3, Yp\}$$

$$\text{s.t.} \quad (4.22)$$

$$T_l \leq \{\pm T_1, \pm T_2, \pm T_3\} \leq T_p \quad \text{(b)}$$

$$G = I_1 Y + I_2 X + I_3 Z \quad \text{(c)}$$

$$Y_p \leq Y_c \quad \text{(d)}$$

$$\{-(+T_1)Y - (+T_2)X - (+T_3)Z + (-T_1)Y + (-T_2)X + (-T_3)Z\} \geq 0 \quad \text{(e)}$$

$$c_1 \pm T_1 - b\mu - \Gamma \geq 0 \quad \text{(f)}$$

$$c_2 \pm T_2 - a\delta - \mu - \beta \geq 0 \quad \text{(g)}$$

$$c_3 \pm T_3 - \alpha - \delta \geq 0 \quad \text{(h)}$$

$$Z - D = 0 \quad \text{(i)}$$

$$Z - aX = 0 \quad \text{(j)}$$

$$X - bY = 0 \quad \text{(k)}$$

$$Y + Yp \leq Y \quad \text{(l)}$$

$$X \leq \overline{D} \quad \text{(m)}$$

$$(c_1 \pm T_1 - b\mu - \Gamma)Y = 0 \quad \text{(n)}$$

$$(c_2 \pm T_2 - a\delta - \mu - \beta)X = 0 \quad \text{(o)}$$

$$(c_3 \pm T_3 - \alpha - \delta)Z = 0 \quad \text{(p)}$$

$$(Z - \overline{D})\alpha = 0 \quad \text{(q)}$$

$$(Y + Yp - \overline{Y})\Gamma = 0 \quad \text{(r)}$$

$$(X - \overline{X})\beta = 0 \quad \text{(s)}$$

$$G, Yp, Y, X, Z, \alpha, \delta, \Gamma, \mu, \beta \geq 0 \quad \text{(t)}$$

4.8.2 Selection of Energy-Economic Policies by the Government

Selection of levels and mix of tax and subsidy will depend on the condition of whether an equation is binding or not. If an equation is binding, then policy will be to employ +T (taxes) and if an equation is not binding the policy will be to employ-T (subsidies). This is how a selection of optimum $\pm$T is made in MLP.

But the ultimate choice of $\pm$T and their optimum values will depend on the policy objective function. If an equation is binding, and the corresponding activity is preferred by the policy makers, then the selection will be +T. If +T is chosen, then other energy policies will be undertaken by the government to reduce the tightness of the constraint. Other policies will be chosen because if the constraint is binding, it will have non-zero shadow prices (defined in Chap. 6) and will attract other policy attentions.

Yp is usually exogenously determined. If Yp is endogenous in the model, it will be determined in such a way that it will control the energy resources available for economic agents so that the policy objective function attains its optimum value.

4.8.3 Conditions for Optimum Decisions of Economic Agents

In an energy system without government tax and subsidy intervention, the energy sector equilibrium conditions represent the equalities between the market costs and the imputed costs. With government intervention, equilibrium conditions change. In the latter case, the energy sector equilibrium conditions are perturbed by the government controls: ±T and Yp.

In an energy policy regime, the conditions for optimum decisions (choice of a set of optimum behavioural variables) for the economic agents are shown by the equations 4.22.n to 4.22.s. The decisions of economic agents regarding energy supply, conversion, and end-uses are guided by the following rules. Equation 4.22.n implies that market costs (fixed and variable costs) of the primary energy supplies plus net tax must be greater than or equal to the imputed value of the fixed energy resources (Ricardian rent), and to the imputed value arising from the allocation of these resources to different energy conversion technologies (users' cost). Equation B.1.o implies that the costs of secondary energy conversion technologies plus net tax must be greater than or equal to imputed costs to different conversion technologies (operation and capacity costs) less the users' cost attributed to allocation of resources to different technologies. Equation 4.22.p implies that the costs of end-use technologies plus net taxes must be greater than or equal to the imputed costs of the end-uses plus imputed costs of the end- use technologies.

Equations 4.22.q to 4.22.s imply that different forms of primary and secondary energy will be supplied and used in cases where the market costs plus net ±T and imputed costs of different forms of energy will be equal.

5 A Multi-Level Optimisation Energy Planning Model for Australia

5.1 Introduction

From the discussion in the previous chapter it is now apparent that an energy model needs to be based on the foundations of the theory of economic policy, policy system analysis and on the methodology of MLP. The model should be developed within the general framework proposed in the last chapter. Therefore, the model will be a partial equilibrium energy sectoral microeconomic planning model, explicitly based on the MLO approach.

The objective of this chapter is to develop a numerical multi-level optimisation/ multi-level energy planning model for Australia. The model set consists of two static one year models (for 1979-80 and 1989-90) and is named the Australian Energy Policy System Optimisation (AEPSOM) Model.[1]

The structure of this chapter is as follows: Section 5.2 provides a brief discussion of the Australian energy sector to prepare a background for the specification of AEPSOM. Section 5.3 presents some preliminary information about AEPSOM to provide a general context of AEPSOM. Within this energy sector conceptual and methodological context, Section 5.4 specifies the detailed structure, variables, relationships and coefficients of AEPSOM (1979-80), while the 1989-90 AEPSOM is specified in Appendix B. Section 5.5 presents a classification of the energy policy variables. Section 5.6 describes briefly the data used in the model and Section 5.7 summarises the contents of the chapter.

---

[1] Although the model is a multi-level energy planning model, it is named the Australian Energy Policy System Optimisation Model since the emphasis of this model is on the optimisation of the policy system.

5.2 The Australian Energy Sector the Context for Energy Planning and Modelling in Australia

The process of transformation of the Australian economy from predominantly agricultural towards modern manufacturing is clearly characterised by the increased importance of the energy sector in the microeconomic structure of the economy. This is explained by the fundamental and pervasive role of energy in the modern production and consumption processes in an industrialised economy. The role that the energy sector plays in the Australian economy is clearly indicated by the higher energy-GDP ratio (Folie and Ulph 1982), and by the substantial contribution of the energy sector to GDP, employment, capital expenditure, government revenue and export earnings (Department of National Development 1979; Department of Primary Industries and Energy 1988).

In the following sub-section, some aspects of the Australian energy sector such as the supply of and demand for energy resources, energy related problems in the economy, and the initiation of energy policies are discussed to justify the undertaking of an energy policy study for Australia. In view of the indispensable role of a model in energy policy studies, this discussion will also provide the background for an Australian energy model.

5.2.1 Energy Resources: Supplies and Consumption

Australia is well endowed with most fossil fuels: coal; natural gas; uranium, and oil shales. The major constraint on the Australian energy supply system is the inadequacy of oil reserves. It has a moderate hydro-electricity supply and a large biomass and solar energy potential, although its potential for other renewable energy sources such as wind, wave, ocean, and geothermal energy is considered conservatively.

In Australia, the demonstrated economic recoverable black coal reserve is 31.0 gigatonnes which, at the 1983 production rate, is expected to last for about 300 years. Australia's brown coal reserve is higher than its black coal reserve: a reserve of 37.4 gigatonnes is expected to last for about 1,000 years. Other non-renewable energy reserves are also substantial: the natural gas reserve, which is mainly located offshore, is sufficient for 55 years, and the uranium supply is good for 15.3% of the total supply of recoverable fossil fuel (Department of Resources and Energy 1983).

Australia's oil reserve can last only until 2000 A.D.- its reserve, including condensate and LPG, is only 1.0% of the total recoverable energy resources of Australia. The possible supply of fuel from biomass is about 461 petajoules, although biomass fuels such as methanol, ethanol and seed oils are found costly compared to oil products (Stewart, Nix, Gartside, Rawlines, Gifford and Siemon 1979).

Like any other country, energy consumption in Australia is shaped by its industrial, economic, demographic and geographic characteristics. Australian primary energy consumption in 1979-80 was 51.2 million tonnes of oil equivalent (MTOE) almost all of which was supplied from commercial energy sources. Total energy consumption has also grown historically to facilitate the increased development activities in the country. For example, over the period of 1977-78 to 1981-82, total energy demand increased at the annual rate of 2.1 percent (Department of Resources and Energy 1983).

The Australian economy depends heavily on liquid fuels, particularly for meeting its transport needs. Demand for different fuels in 1979-80 in MTOE was as follows: oil, 32.1 (44.40%); coal, 28.1 (38.87%); natural gas, 8.8 (12.17%); hydro-electricity, 1.2 (1.66%); and other fuels (bagasse and wood), 2.4 (3.32%) (Department of National Development and Energy 1981).

Australia is among the five net energy exporting OECD countries. Export of energy consists of black coal, uranium, coke and some petroleum products. Total export of energy in 1979-80 was 217.7 MTOE. One of the major characteristics of the Australian energy system is the dependence on imported oil. Total import of energy (crude oil and petroleum products) was 14.2 MTOE in 1979-80 which was 49.76% of the total production of domestic crude oil and 30.5% of the total oil demand in the same year (Department of National Development and Energy 1982).

5.2.2 Prospects of the Energy Sector: Justifications and Initiation of Energy Policies and Modelling in Australia

Prospects of the Energy Sector. The government forecasts for energy production and consumption was as follows (Department of National Development and Energy 1981). Total domestic energy production in 1989-90 will be 258.5 MTOE - a 256.7% increase in ten years. Total net energy consumption would be 64.1 MTOE. Australia will be a net exporter of energy. The total import of energy will be equal to 8.1 MTOE, which is lower than the total export of energy, 171.3. However, the country's oil imports are expected to increase because of its dwindling reserves of oil.[2]

In the past, Australia experienced the adverse macroeconomic effects of past events in the world energy market, in particular the three oil price shocks of 1973, 1979, and 1990 in the form of inflation, unemployment and recession (the effects of the first two price shocks are discussed in Vincent, Dixon, Parmenter, and Sams 1980).

Why Energy Policies for Australia? The survey of the Australian energy sector in the previous section highlights its salient characteristics: Australia is well endowed with major energy resources except crude oil; it is a net exporter of energy although heavily dependent on imported oil to meet the domestic need for liquid fuel, and it is expected that Australia will remain dependent on imported oil for some decades.

The question is now: Does the Australian situation warrant the formulation and implementation of energy policies? The answer to this question in general has been discussed in Chap. 1. Although the answer is not straight forward, the existence of market failures in the energy sector is the justification for government intervention in this sector. Australian writers are divided on the subject: one group believes in the infallible power of the market in solving all the problems in the energy sector (Hocking 1975; Tengrove 1986), while another

[2] The dependence of the Australian economy on oil (liquid fuel) is caused by such factors as the present transport system and non-existence of natural oil substitutes as shale oil, tar sands and oil from coal or natural gas. Since the domestic production of crude oil is not expected to increase enough to meet the domestic needs for oil, the dependency on the imported oil will remain or even increase in the future.

group advocates government intervention in the form of deliberate energy policies to solve the energy related problems and to correct for market failures (Folie and Ulph 1979; Gruen and Hillman 1981).

The justifications[3] for energy policies in Australia suggested by the second group are based on the following arguments: the Australian reserves of crude oil will be exhausted in the near future; uncertainty about the required supply of oil and its price; possible macroeconomic problems in the form of inflation, unemployment, recession and the balance of payment deficit caused by the oil supply embargoes or price increases of 1973, 1979 and 1990; the merit good character of energy, and the inefficient operation of the energy market (Folie and Ulph 1979; Gruen and Hillman 1981). The following statement may show the importance of a set of energy policies/energy management in Australia. Powell (1980) stated that 'even a lucky country cannot afford to squander the resources with which it is barely endowed' (quoted in Lloyd 1984, p. 323). Hall (1984) argued more directly and strongly for a set of energy policies for Australia.

Because of the existence of market failures and the possibility of exhaustion of oil in Australia, a certain amount of government intervention is viewed as essential; such as interventions designed to correct energy market failures, specifically to provide information and to ensure greater distribution of the income arising from the energy sector. This view is consistent with the government's attitude towards public intervention in the energy sector (Department of National Development and Energy 1979, p. 4, Department of Resources and Energy 1984, and Department of Primary Industries and Energy 1988).

The formal initiation of energy policy activities goes back as far as 1972 when the Department of Minerals and Energy was set up. There was no policy document until the publication of 'Australian Energy Policy - A Review' by the Department of National

[3] Saddler (1981) has discussed and examined in detail the views of both groups on the formulation of energy policies in the context of energy problems in Australia from their broad socio, economic and technical perspectives and suggested the formulation of energy policies for the provision, distribution and utilisation of energy resources.

Development in 1979. Since then national energy policy has become more comprehensive and integrated, although not to the desired extent.

Since Australian energy policies are still at the formative phase, some issues related to the objectives, strategies and instruments of energy policies are being debated. Such issues relate to the selection of appropriate energy policy objectives, such as the question of whether import independence should be an objective of Australian energy policies (Folie and Ulph 1979). There are other issues that relate to the choice of appropriate energy policy strategies and instruments. For example, the question of suitability of stockpiling or broader adjustment in the macroeconomy for facing any possible oil shortage has received careful consideration. These issues of Australian energy policies will be given due treatment in the appropriate places. Issues related to policy objectives are dicussed in Sect. 7.4.1, and issues related to strategies and instruments in Chap. 7.

5.2.3 Institutional Aspects

Politically, Australia is a federation with a high degree of delegation of power between the Commonwealth and State Governments.

In situ on-shore and off-shore minerals are owned by the Crown, except for uranium in the Northern Territory. The Commonwealth Government controls the price of oil and the allocation of leases for exploration of oil, coal and natural gas. Until recently, the State Governments produce and supply electricity and determine its price.

The private sector supplies or produces coal, oil, natural gas, wood, uranium and solar energy. The prices of these fuels are determined by the individual suppliers or producers except oil. Consumers make their decisions about end-uses of different fuels.

The economic agents have greater freedom in making their optimum decisions independently. Their decisions are, as is revealed from above discussions, affected by some government actions. The behaviour of economic agents is subject to the influence of the following government quantitative policies and strategies: taxes and subsidies; price control;

government expenditures for research and development, etc, and exploration, conservation and technology policy strategies.

The role of energy markets (decisions of economic agents) in Australia has been stated as follows (quoted in Department of National Development 1979, p. 4):

> Quite clearly, the Commonwealth Government's role should not be to attempt to indicate the precise future path along which energy producers and consumers should move. It is however, necessary to set the scene within which the private sector and Government instrumentalities can operate with confidence, while as far as practicable, i.e. given our other objectives, allowing the forces of the market to allocate our available resources of manpower, capital and technology.

The thrust of the Australian energy policies is stated in the following (Department of National Development, 1979 p. 4) :

> There are circumstances where market forces will not achieve the Government's objectives. The Government has used taxes and subsidies to encourage conservation, advance production of new sources of energy and intensify exploration and development of oil and gas fields.

From the above analysis, it may appear that in Australia there exists a multi-level (two-level) policy system characterised by the presence of government and economic agents in policy making processes. The major form of government intervention in the decision making of economic agents is the control of energy prices.

5.2.4 Energy Planning Modelling in Australia

It should be mentioned here that the existence of these problems and their resolution require the formulation of a set of energy policies. To undertake such policy studies, energy modelling has started in Australia.

Energy modelling activities in Australia are relatively new. An initial study in this area is the work of the National Energy Advisory Committee (NEAC) (1978). The need for, and scope of energy modelling in Australia has been discussed in NEAC (1978). Four types of models were proposed in the energy model suit: Reference Energy System (RES); the Brookhaven Energy System Optimisation Model (BESOM/ AUSTESOM); an input-output model, and a Hudson-Jorgenson type model (DRI/CRES/UNSW model).

RES was necessary to develop the data base and structure for an optimisation model-BESOM (or Australian version, AUSTESOM). But instead of a static optimisation model BESOM, a dynamic optimisation model (MARKAL) has been formulated by CSIRO (Musgrove, Stocks, Essam and Hoetzl 1983). MARKAL is a special version of DESOM.

An input-output model named MERG has also been developed by James (1984). Development of a Hudson-Jorgenson type of model named CRES/UNSW model was attempted (Folie and Ulph 1976), but was not implemented. An independent modelling work is GESOM (Schuyers 1979), which is an application of BESOM to Australia. This model has been coupled with the IMP macro-model (Brain and Schuyers 1981). Another hybrid model is MERG-MARKAL (James, Musgrove and Stocks 1986).

Strictly speaking, MARKAL and GESOM are the only two optimisation models which belong to the type of energy models considered in this study. These are mathematical programming models whose characteristics have already been discussed above.

Australian energy models belong to one or other category of the models mentioned in the model survey in Chap. 4. A classification of Australian models is as follows:

(1) Mathematical Programming Model:

- MARKAL
- GESOM

(2) Input-Output Model:

- MERG

(3) Hybrid Model

- IMP macro model + GESOM
- ORANI + MARKAL
- MERG + MARKAL

The limitations of different types of energy models discussed in Chap. 4 apply to the different types of Australian models. Since the general counterparts of the Australian models have been evaluated separately, a general statement can be made that the Australian energy models also do not satisfy the model evaluation criteria. Therefore, there is a need to developing an alternative energy model in Australia, similar to the one proposed in Chap. 4.

5.3 The Australian Energy Planning Model (AEPSOM): Some Preliminaries

5.3.1 Abstract Presentation of AEPSOM

An abstract presentation of the structure of the model[4] to be specified in this section is given here, and can be used as reference in the subsequent discussion. Two alternative specifications of the model are provided: in the first specification, budget constraints are included in the policy model (±T is not in the policy objective function), while in the second specification, ±T (budgetary implications of policies) is included in the policy objective function (budget constraints are not in the model).

Specification 1:

Min $\quad WL = wG$ (a) Policy objective function

$\{\pm T\}$

s.t.

$G = I_1 Y + I_2 X + I_3 Z$ (b) Definitional equations

$T_l \leq \pm T \leq T_p$ (c) Policy constraints

$\{(+T_1)Y + (+T_2)X + (+T_3)Z\} - \{(-T_1)Y + (-T_2)X + (-T_3)Z\} \geq 0$

(d) Budget constraints

Min $\quad C = (c_1 \pm T_1)Y + (c_2 \pm T_2)X + (c_3 \pm T_3)Z$

$\{Y, X, Z \pm T\}$ (e) Behavioural objective function

s.t. (5.1)

[4] This model is similar to the model (4.21) in Chap. 4. But this model is a price control MLP model, while the model (4.21) is a price and resources control MLP model.

$Z \geq \overline{D}$ (f) Demand constraint

$Z = aX$ (g) Intermediate energy balance constraints

$X = bY$ (h) Energy supply balance constraints

$Y \leq \overline{Y}$ (i) Resource constraints

$X \leq \overline{X}$ (j) Capacity constraints

$G, Y, X, Z \geq 0$ (k) Non-negativity constraints

where:

WL = the value of P.O.F.

w = vector of coefficients of the policy objective function (i x e)

G = vector of energy target variables (e x 1)

Y = a vector of primary energy (p x 1)

X = a vector of energy products (n x 1)

Z = a vector of end-uses of the energy products (m x 1)

D = a vector of end-uses in various sectors (q x 1)

c_1, c_2, c_3 = costs for supplying, converting and using energy {(p x 1),(n x 1),(m x 1)}

$\pm T = \{\pm T_1, \pm T_2, \pm T_3\}$ = vector of different taxes and subsidies

{Sub-vectors $\pm T_1$, $\pm T_2$, $\pm T_3$ = (p x 1), (n x 1),(m x 1)}

(+T = taxes, -T = subsidies; lower case t's are the elements)

a, b = matrices of technological coefficients {(m x n), (n x p)}

I's = identity matrices the elements of which are either 1 or 0

T_l = lower level of $\pm T$

T_p = upper level of $\pm T$

Specification 2:

$$\underset{\{\pm T\}}{\text{Min}}\ WL = wG - [\{(+T_1)Y + (+T_2)X + (+T_3)Z\} - \{(-T_1)Y + (-T_2)X + (-T_3)Z\}]$$

(a) Policy Objective Function (P.O.F.2)

s.t.

$G = I_1Y + I_2X + I_3Z$ (b) Definitional equations

$T_l \leq \pm T \leq T_p$ (c) Policy constraints

(5.2)

$$\underset{\{Y,X,Z \mid \pm T\}}{\text{Min}}\ C = (c_1 \pm T_1)Y + (c_2 \pm T_2)X + (c_3 \pm T_3)Z$$

(d) Behavioural objective function

s.t.

$Z \geq \overline{D}$ (e) Demand constraint

$Z = aX$ (f) Intermediate energy balance constraint

$X = bY$ (g) Energy supply balance constraints

$Y \leq \overline{Y}$ (h) Resource constraints

$X \leq \overline{X}$ (i) Capacity constraints

$G, Y, X, Z \geq 0$ (j) Non-negativity constraints

5.3.2 A Discussion of the Model

Model 5.1 is a price control MLP in which the policy makers at the upper level of the hierarchical structure intervene in the behaviour of the energy producers and consumers by taxes and subsidies (±T).[5] Policy makers are only interested in the policy target and instrument variables (G and ±T). The policy optimisation problem involves the minimisation of the policy objective function consisting of target variables such as energy import, total energy use, etc. subject to such constraints as policy constraints and budget constraints. The policy constraint imposes limits on the changes of taxes and subsidies, while the budget constraint requires that the government budget (taxes and subsidies) in the energy sector should be balanced or surplus.

The behavioural model is a cost minimisation linear programming model in which the economic agents choose variables Y, X, and Z after ±T is announced by the policy makers. The objective function of the behavioural model (5.1.e) consists of total costs for supplying, producing and using energy plus taxes minus subsidies. Marginal costs of various types of energy are constant irrespective of the levels of input and output, however relative prices influence resource allocation in the energy sector since in the model, price is equal to cost ± taxes/subsidies which is endogenous in the model (see 5.1.e). The equations 5.1.f to 5.1.j (relationships, variables and technical coefficients (a and b)) represent the characteristics of the underlying energy system, modelled as different types of constraints on the demand for energy, maximum possible energy supply and capacity utilisation, etc.

The primary inputs in the production processes are the primary fuels which are either converted into secondary energy or are transported to the end-users for final uses. Activities in the model represent the flows of energy from the stage of supply of primary energy to the end uses. The energy inputs and outputs are perfectly divisible. The quantities of inputs and

[5] The government indirectly influences the economy. Decisions in the energy sector are indirectly controlled by the government through taxes and subsidies (±T), prices, government expenditures, education and propaganda, and the supply of technical information.

outputs in case of conversion activities are in fixed proportions. Substitutability among primary energy, energy products, and end-uses of energy (inter-fuel substitution) exists. The linear production function of the multi-input, multi-activity and multi-output type (Naylor and Vernon 1969, Chap. 8) exists in the energy sector. The production function embedded may be written as Q(Z,X,Y) = 0, where Z, X, Y = vectors of energy end-uses, energy products and primary energy.

Capital and labour inputs are not endogenous variables in the model. Therefore, the inter-factor substitution possibility is not specified in the model.[6] Only capital supply is constrained. The supply of labour is not constrained (due to availability of sufficient labour to supply the required amount of energy). Demand for energy in each sector of the economy is given exogenously. As the demand for energy and the supply of inputs are exogenous in the model, this is a partial equilibrium energy sector model.

In summation, the MLP model (5.1) (or (5.2)) is a mathematical definition of the constituent components of the multi-level decision making system in the form of two objective functions and two sets of constraints. The programming problem embedded in the model is to determine the optimum values of the decision variables of both levels of decision makers.

[6] The inter-factor (labour, capital, energy and raw materials) substitutability has been a major focus of the econometric studies on the aggregate relationships between macroeconomic activity and energy use (Julius 1981 contains a survey). Different degrees of substitutability are assumed and specified in different types of production functions [for example Cobb-Douglas, CES and translog production functions (Berndt and Wood 1979)]. Findings of these studies have been used to predict the aggregate energy use or other energy macroeconomic relationships in the economy. It may, however, be mentioned that in mathematical programming energy models, the emphasis has been on the inter-fuel (coal, natural gas, oil etc), substitutability. This is so because most of the mathematical programming energy models are developed to capture the technical details and processes of the energy sector in which case inter-fuel substitution appears to be more important than inter-factor substitution. Relative merits and demerits of mathematical and econometric models were discussed in Chap. 4. (It was stressed that the method adopted in a study depends on the objective, nature and uses of the model.) Approaches and assumptions made in this study to undertake a specific type of energy planning study require the adaptation of an MLP model in which inter-fuel substitution appears to be a dominating issue.

5.3.3 Foundations

(1) The above model is a price control non-linear MLP (price control bi-level programming) model. The model consists of two optimisation problems, the policy optimisation problem and the energy systems optimisation problem, which are as follows:

Specification 1:

Policy Optimisation Problem:

$\text{Min WL} = wG$ (a) Policy objective function

$\{\pm T\}$

s.t. (5.3.a)

$G = I_1Y + I_2X + I_3Z$ (b) Definitional equations

$T_l \leq \pm T \leq T_P$ (c) Policy constraints

$\{(+T_1)Y + (+T_2)X + (+T_3)Z\} - \{(-T_1)Y + (-T_2)X + (-T_3)Z\} \geq 0$

(d) Budget constraints

$G, Y, X, Z \geq 0$ (e) Non-negativity constraints

Energy Systems Optimisation Problem:

$\text{Min} \quad C = (c_1)Y + (c_2)X + (c_3)Z$

$\{Y, X, Z\}$ (a) Behavioural objective function

s.t. (5.3.b)

$Z \geq \overline{D}$ (b) Demand constraint

$Z = aX$ (c) Intermediate energy balance constraints

$X = bY$ (d) Energy supply balance constraints

$Y \leq \overline{Y}$ (e) Resource constraints

$X \leq \overline{X}$ (f) Capacity constraints

$Y, X, Z \geq 0$ (g) Non-negativity constraints

(2) The model has the three elements of the theory of economic policy: (a) a policy objective function (equation 5.1a); (b) a set of constraints to represent the energy technology, policy and economic systems under study, and (c) a classification of the variables:

G = the target variables

±T = the instrument variables

Y,X,Z = the behavioural variables.

(3) AEPSOM is specified within the conceptual framework of policy systems analysis. There are several goals (G) that the policy makers (such as energy conservation) and economic agents (such as cost minimisation) try to achieve. Goals of the two level decision makers are interdependent. The existing policy system has a hierarchical character, i.e. the upper level decision makers (policy makers) influence the behaviour of economic agents by indirect intervention (±T). This two-level decision problem is interactive- *simultaneously interdependent*. The attainment of economic agents' objective is dependent on the selection of taxes and subsidies by the government. The fulfillment of the government objective is also dependent on the outcome of economic agents' behaviour: the attainment of the optimum value of the policy objective function is determined by the choice of energy activities by the economic agents.

Therefore, the model contains the characteristics of a multi-goal (G), multi-level (two), and hierarchical policy system.

5.4 AEPSOM: Model Specification

The elements of AEPSOM will be specified as follows: the policy objective function in Section 5.4.1, and the constraints in Section 5.4.2.

5.4.1 A Policy Objective Function (P.O.F.)

The policy objective function[7] AEPSOM represents the value judgments of Australian policy makers about the allocation of energy resources. So it provides the criteria for the evaluation of policy alternatives.

Specification of Policy Objective Function. The specification of a policy objective function is partly a political exercise. The political philosophy of the policy makers will largely determine the nature of the policy objective function. Economic conditions also influence the specification of a policy objective function.

A policy objective function in an energy sector planning model should contain the existing energy policy objectives and preferences regarding the allocation of resources and the distribution of income. It should be mentioned here that the policy objective function may take the form of what an economist or a planner thinks it should be on the basis of his own arguments and preferences. Alternatively, it may manifest only the preferences of the current policy makers. In the present study, the latter approach has been followed.

To establish a policy objective function, the following information is necessary:

(1) the functional form;

(2) the variables appearing in the function;

[7] In spite of the Arrow impossibility theorem (Arrow 1951), which rules out the possibility of specifying a social welfare function without violating one or more of the five acceptable axioms of social preferences, economists' endeavor to construct and analyse social welfare functions has proceeded steadily. One development in the mechanism of the specification of the social welfare function has been suggested by Downs (1957). In this approach it is assumed that the social preference is revealed through the political process of voting i.e. the individuals' preferences are signalled to the government policy makers by their vote in favour of the party elected. Therefore, the policy objective function is used as a proxy for the social welfare function. This is how Tinbergen viewed the social welfare function (Tinbergen 1952).

(3) the weights attached to each variable; and

(4) the units of measurement of the variables.

Alternative Methods of specifying the Policy Objective Function. The alternative approaches for revealing the preferences of policy makers are: direct interview; indirect interview; imaginary interview; inference from planning documents, and the revealed preference method (discussed in Johansen 1974). Because of the problems associated with the interview methods such as the non-availability of enough appropriate information to specify analytically and numerically a policy objective function (by either of the first three methods), an approach that consists of some elements of the last two methods has been adopted. Thus the adopted method of establishing the policy objective function requires one to study the policy documents and to make inferences from the actions of policy makers.

Functional Form. The methods for establishing the policy objective function stated above have been applied to specify the functional form of the policy objective function. Frisch has adopted the direct interview method (Johansen 1974), van Eijk and Sandee (1959) adopted an imaginary interview method, while Fox, Sengupta and Thorbecke (1973, Chap. 15) used the methods of inferences drawn from published documents and revealed preferences to specify the functional form of the policy objective function in their studies. For the reasons stated above, the methods of inferences from the policy documents and revealed preferences were used in the present study.

A policy objective function can take many economically acceptable functional forms (Frish 1976) such as: linear, quadratic, cubic, log, log-inverse, etc. Quadratic and linear forms are most commonly used in macroeconomic and sectoral policy studies (Fox, Sengupta and Thorbecke 1973).

For example, in Theil's (1956) macroeconometric studies of optimum policy formulation in which some desirable values of the targets and instruments can be identified, a quadratic policy objective function involving the squared deviations of the desired and actual values is specified. An alternative approach is what is termed as the multi-target policy objective function (linear or non-linear). In van Eijk and Sandee's (1959) approach to the multi-target policy objective function, no macroeconomic fixed targets were identified: a linear function involving macro target variables such as GDP, employment, inflation and the balance of payment was found to be appropriate.

In most of the MLP literature so far, relatively simpler policy objective functions have been specified because of the computational problem of an MLP model. In all large or medium scale real applications of MLP models, a linear policy objective function has been specified (see Candler and Norton 1977; Bisschop et al. 1982; Fortuny-Amat 1979). For example Candler and Norton (1977) have specified a linear policy objective function involving the following agricultural sector policy target variables: employment, farm income, the level of wheat production and the size of government budget. The policy objective function was maximised by the programming problem.

Relative superiority of different functional forms has been disputed by economists (Yotopoulas and Nugent 1976), without any definite agreement.

Theil's quadratic (1970) welfare function has gained wide application in macroeconomic policy studies. The justifications for adopting Theil's quadratic function have been stated as follows

> It is not necessary to believe that the preference functions of policy makers are necessarily and precisely quadratic forms; we may simply use quadratic forms as reasonable approximations to the true preference functions over limited ranges on either side of the desired values of the instrument variables. The justification for using quadratic preference functions, says Theil, is analogous to that for using minimum-variance estimation in statistics and mean-square error minimisation in engineering, which derived their popularity mainly from considerations of mathematical convenience. A more profound argument in favour of quadratic preference functions is that this form allows us to have decreasing 'marginal rates of substitution' between the various instrument variables and non-controlled variables. (Fox, Sengupta and Thorbecke 1973, p. 192)

Theil's quadratic function has several disadvantages. Since in this approach the specified objective is to minimise the sum of the weighted squares of deviations of instruments and targets from a desired level (the fixed target variables), it is necessary to implement this approach to determine some fixed values of the target variables. One problem of the determination of the fixed values of targets by an analyst is that it may be arbitrary, unless these values are determined by the policy makers.

In Australia, no effort has so far been devoted to determine the target values of energy conservation, oil use, oil import, etc., by either academics or government. Therefore, the specification of Theil's quadratic welfare function will be arbitrary because of the arbitrary character of the targets to be determined.

Another drawback of Theil's approach has been stated by Yotopoulas and Nugent (1976 p. 423) as: 'Moreover, this specification has the unfortunate characteristics of treating as equally undesirable positive and negative deviations from the fixed targets'.

Finally, although Theil's approach has mathematical convenience (for which it has gained wider application in macroeconomic policy studies), a linear multi-target policy objective function also has mathematical and computational convenience in mathematical programming models.

For all these reasons, a multi-target policy objective function (linear or non-linear) is being advocated here. A multi-target policy objective function approach is a flexible and commonly accepted approach (Yotopoulas and Nugent 1976; Fox, Sengupta and Thorbecke 1973). This has been argued by Yotopoulas and Nugent (1976, p. 423) as follows:

> Some of the shortcomings of Theil's quadratic objective function can be overcome by specifying a somewhat more general objective function, that is, a complete multi-target social welfare function, each different goal being weighted by its relative importance from the point of view of the decision makers.

The conclusion is that a multi-target (linear or non-linear) policy objective function may be considered as a suitable functional form for energy policy planning studies, particularly in a study where an MLP or mathematical programming model is used.

Therefore, a multi-target policy objective function of the following form is specified:

$$W = F(w_1 x_1, w_2 x_2, \dots, w_n x_n) \qquad (5.4)$$

where: w's are the weights of the policy target variables

x's are the policy target variables.

This is a general presentation of the policy objective function. Specific presentations of the two specifications of policy objective functions will be given in (5.5) and (5.18).

Variables in the Objective Function. The Objectives of the Australian Energy Policies were considered to specify the variables in the policy objective functions. The study method involving (a) the study of the energy policy documents and (b) inferences from the revealed preferences of the policy makers has been adopted in order to identify the relevant variables appearing in the policy objective function (the policy target variables).

Many governments adopted energy policies before the Australian government did so. Australia did not initiate any formal energy policies until the establishment of the Department of Energy in 1972. Since that time several government energy policy statements and documents have been published to highlight the salient features of Australian energy policies.

It was stated before that in the absence of any market failures, a perfectly competitive economy can attain an optimum allocation of resources in the energy sector. But because of the occurrence of market failures, manifested in several energy problems (stated in Chap. 1), government policies have been designed to correct these market failures and to solve these energy problems. All these policies are aimed at the efficient use of the energy resources, the determination of efficient prices, and the provision of some social goods (research and development). Furthermore energy policy objectives also embrace the need for an equitable distribution of benefits accruing in the energy sector. In 1977, the objectives of the Australian energy policies were as follows (Anthony 1977):

> ...to move crude oil prices in the direction of international levels; for the average rate of growth of energy consumption, particularly in liquid fuels, to be restrained; the highest degree of self-sufficiency in liquid fuels consistent with the broadly economic utilisation of energy reserves; that economic oil and gas reserves be developed; to encourage individual major energy projects to meet overseas demand for energy minerals where those projects are economical and will provide an adequate return to Australia; and that energy research and development (R&D) be substantially increased.

The emphasis of Australian energy policy has remained unchanged since 1977. For example in 1979 (ESCAP 1979), the policy objectives were stated as follows: to reduce energy consumption, specially in liquid fuels, attain the highest degree of self-sufficiency, increase energy reserves, encourage exports, and increase research and development. In 1986, Tengrove stated that in general government policies are designed 'to increase security of supply, to encourage industrial development, to alter distribution of income and to reduce the rate at which resources are depleted.' Similar objectives are also stated in Department of Resources and Energy (undated, probably 1984) and Department of Primary Industries and Energy (1988).[8]

Therefore, it can be stated that in spite of the changes in the government in power and changes in the energy sector, both locally and globally, the following energy policy objectives have been common to all the above energy policy development initiatives: (a) security of energy supply; (b) conservation of energy; (c) conservation of oil; (d) efficiency in energy supply; production and uses; (e) the development of the export energy sector, and (f) equity in the opportunities generated in the sector.

The above emphasis of the energy policy is not restricted to Australia. Countries of similar economic and energy sectoral backgrounds have pursued the same types of energy policy objectives (International Energy Agency 1986). Generally, Australia and other western industrialised countries have a common set of energy policies designed to achieve the objectives specified.

The citation of the historical and cross-country energy policy experiences alone is not enough to justify the identification of a set of energy policies for a country. An analysis of the energy sector problems and the prospects for its local and global developments in the context of the overall macroeconomy is necessary to justify the individual energy policy objectives relevant for a country. Such an analysis is provided below.

(1) The Security of Supply/Import Independence: The Arab oil embargoes have created a world wide sense of oil supply insecurity due to the expected non-availability of oil that may be caused by any further embargoes in the future. The problem has several interpretations (Griffin and Steele 1980). The most common one is that the non-secured oil supply is a national security problem. Oil embargoes are motivated by nationalistic policies and, therefore, oil exporting countries may prohibit oil exports for political reasons. This creates a political dependency of the oil importing countries, and may threaten their national

[8] For an account of the evolution of the Australian energy policies, see Marks (1986).

sovereignty. Another interpretation of the problem is that though the non-secured oil supply problem may not appear to threaten national security of the oil importing countries, it may however, create serious macroeconomic problems in the form of unemployment, inflation, the balance of payment deficit, and recession due to oil supply shortages or oil price hikes, and may threaten the country's economic welfare.

Whatever the exact interpretation of the problem may be, the situation certainly created a market failure - the market can not internalise the expected cost of an oil supply embargo. Therefore, a deliberate policy response from the government is necessary to deal with this problem.

At this stage a clear statement about what is meant by the terms 'the security of energy supplies' is necessary for the subsequent discussion on the topic. The Department of Primary Industries and Energy (1988) defines it as follows: '... it is more a concept of relative assurance and dependability of overall energy supplies in foreseeable circumstances ...'

As it has already been discussed in Section 5.2.1 although Australia has vast reserves of coal, natural gas and uranium, making it a net exporter of energy, the country's indigenous reserves of crude oil and condensate will decline over the coming decade. This, together with the fact that no major discoveries have been made in recent years, will make Australia dependent on imported oil, in spite of the recent downward trend in the use of oil in Australia. 'Hence a principal concern in energy security is to maintain a satisfactory supply of liquid fuels in the longer term' (Department of Primary Industries and Energy 1988).

Therefore, the concept of 'the security of energy supply' has been interpreted in the Australian context in the form of the security of supply of liquid fuels (oil) (Folie and Ulph 1979).

The conceptual difficulty with the phrase 'the security of supply of oil' is that it is subject to different interpretations, since the security of the oil supply can be achieved by pursuing several strategies such as: the reduction in oil import, self-sufficiency of indigenous oil supply through increased supply of domestic oil, general adjustments in the macroeconomy to increase the level of self-sufficiency in oil (through oil conservation, macroeconomic policy adjustments, etc.), stock piling, and diversification of energy supply and increase in the supply of oil substitutes (Folie and Ulph 1979, Department of Primary Industries and Energy 1988).

Because of the uncertainty in the possibility of increased domestic oil production in Australia in the near future, and of the possible non-effectiveness of other options in the short term, and due to the possible problems associated with the dependency of the importation of oil (inflation, embargo, etc.), the emphasis of the issue of the security of liquid fuel supply in Australia has been on the reduction of oil import, as an interpretation of the issue as well as as a policy response or objective. Therefore, a reduction in the importation of oil has become an explicit energy policy objective in Australia.

The issue is also related to the conservation of oil (Department of Primary Industries and Energy 1988). This is discussed below.

(2) Conservation of Energy: The principal concern of developed countries is the security of an adequate energy (oil) supply. This cannot adequately be addressed by only limiting oil imports, complementary strategies are also necessary. Because of the expected ultimate global exhaustion of fossil fuel, concern for inter-generational equity in the distribution of depletable energy resources, uncertainty about the future viable backstop technology and pollution from the energy industries, it is now increasingly felt that energy conservation should be specified as an energy policy objective, at least as a by-product of the concern for the security of an adequate energy supply. The Department of Primary Industries and Energy (1988, p. 4) states it in the following form: '...energy security in the broadest sense will be best served by pursuing, within a realistic economic framework, an adaptive strategy incorporating...energy conservation'.

Energy conservation is defined as an acceptable or feasible reduction in the present consumption of energy (Griffin and Steele 1980). Since the past history of economic development shows that there is a positive correlation between energy use and economic development, the rationale for energy conservation has been debated. The advocates of energy conservation base their arguments on (1) what is called the energy theory of value (Webb and Ricketts 1980) (which implies that only energy has value), and (2) external consumption and production diseconomies (pollution, etc.). However, the other position has aptly been summarised by Griffin and Steele (1980, p. 226) as follows:

> ... even though energy conservation is feasible, its desirability, when couched in terms of aggregate energy, is not obvious. Arbitrarily minimising energy/GNP values will lead to much higher production costs and a loss in economic welfare ...

This leads us to interpret energy conservation in terms of control of wastage, increased process (single or combined) efficiencies and fuel specific energy conservation through inter-fuel substitution. In this sense, the conservation of specific fuels may lead to welfare gains caused by supply security, reduction in pollutions, and the efficient allocation of energy resources.

In Australia, energy conservation has been adopted as an explicit energy policy objective, in a similar manner as in other OECD countries (Endersbee, Baxter, Butters, Corbett, Dembecki 1980; Folie and Ulph 1982; ESCAP 1979; Department of Primary Industries and Energy 1988; Department of National Development and Energy 1979). Regard has also been paid to the welfare and economic growth issues in the formulation of the Australian energy conservation policy. It was clearly stated in government policy documents. For example ESCAP (1979, p. 70) states that:

> An important constraint upon the Government's energy conservation programme was that it should not detract from the attainment of socially desirable objectives such as economic growth and the welfare of the population.

Therefore, energy conservation strategies in Australia consist of minimising the use of energy in the economy by eliminating energy waste, by improving the efficiency of energy supply, production and end-use methods, and through the development of an efficient energy system (mix of various energy forms).

(3) Conservation of Oil: The case for fuel specific energy conservation is strong. It is argued that because of (i) market failures due to externalities, and government intervention creating differences between social and market costs and benefits, and (ii) national security

considerations, fuel specific energy conservation would increase social welfare (Griffin and Steele 1980). As a result of this argument, conservation of oil, the fuel with a high national security risk, has been the major fuel specific energy conservation policy strategy in many OECD countries as well as in Australia (International Energy Agency 1986).

In terms of the proven energy reserves and future energy demand, Australia is in a better position than many other OECD countries. However, its domestic oil reserve is low. Since the energy supply is very dependent on liquid fuels, it is forecasted that the country's dependency on oil, specially imported oil, will increase over time. This situation has resulted in a serious concern for consuming oil. In some cases, the conservation of oil is seen as a separate policy objective. For example in the Department of Primary Industries and Energy (1988, p. 66) an objective of the Australian energy policy is stated as follows: 'Putting more effort into conservation/efficient use of petroleum products'.

In some other cases, the objective of conservation of oil has been specified as part of the general conservation strategy. In ESCAP (1979, p. 68) it is mentioned that one of the government energy policy objectives would be: 'To restrain the average rate of growth of energy consumption, particularly in liquid fuel'.

Therefore, one of the Australian energy policy objectives is to minimise the use of oil in the economy.

(4) Efficient Utilisation of Energy Resources: Efficient utilisation of energy resources involves the minimum cost supply of the energy demand in the economy. Efficiency can be achieved by adopting cost minimising production, transportation and end-use processes and by avoiding waste. An appropriate energy price structure is fundamental in this process of efficiently allocating resources. As efficient allocation and utilisation of energy resources are more imperative than that of any other resources because of the limited supply of the major energy fuels, this objective has received considerable attention.

(5) Maximisation of Government Revenue: In Australia, the energy sector contributes significantly to the government budget: revenue from indirect taxes including royalties was \$4729 million in 1981-82 (Department of Primary Industries and Energy 1988). The

possibility of increased government tax earning in the energy sector has risen with the advent of large scale mining in the economy and the introduction of the import parity pricing of crude oil. The government is aware of this potential of the energy sector and a government policy has been to maximise the contribution. This is reflected in the government decision to introduce resource rent tax - a tax to siphon off the surplus rent generated in the energy sector, which should be utilised for the development of the sector and the community.

Further discussion on the justifications for the revenue maximisation objective of the government is provided below (Section: The policy Objective Function Specification 2).

(6) Development of the Export Energy Sector: Following what is called the export-led growth strategy, Australia has adopted a policy of increasing its exports, its mineral (including energy) exports, in spite of the problem indicated by Gregory (1984).[9] Because of Australia's balance of payment deficit and its international competitiveness in coal and liquid natural gas (LNG), the Australian economy can gain substantially by developing the export energy sector. To help realise this potential, one of the objectives of the Australian energy policy has been the development of the export energy sector (Department of Primary Industries and Energy 1988).

(7) Equity: Equity considerations of the energy sectoral resource allocation utilisation and development have also been dominating in Australia (Gruen and Hillman 1981; Saddler 1981; Tengrove 1986).[10] The objective has been 'to seek an equitable sharing of the benefits of energy resources development amongst the Australian Community' (Department of Resources and Energy 1984, p. 47).

Since an optimum allocation of resources can be determined for every given distribution of income and wealth, and because of the problem of the incorporation of the efficiency and

---

[9] Gregory thesis states that exports of minerals in a primary commodity exporting country may de-industrialise the country instead of industrialising it.

[10] Scepticism in the market determined equity in income and property in the energy/resources sector has been an important issue in Post-Keynesian economics (Eichner 1979).

equity objectives in one model, it is generally argued that in policy studies these two objectives should be studied separately (Griffin and Steele 1980).

The present study is primarily concerned with the allocative implications of energy policies. Therefore, the equity objective has not been included in this model.

Quantification and Incorporation of the Energy Policy Objectives in the Model/Policy Objective Function. The international trade sector will not be explicitly specified in the model, thus the objective of the development of the export energy sector can not be specified in variable form in the policy objective function. However, constraints will be specified in the energy sector model to ensure that the given foreign demand for Australian energy is satisfied by the domestic production of energy (see equation 5.8).

The objective of the efficient utilisation of energy resources will betaken care of by the energy sectoral behavioural model since the energy sector behavioural model will be specified as a cost minimising linear programming model.

The remaining objectives of Australian energy policy namely reduction of oil imports, reduction in the use of oil, conservation of energy and the maximisation of net revenue will be incorporated in the policy objective function. These objectives will be represented by the following target variables (quantities): oil import (Ie_1); total use of oil ($CNo = R_2 + Ie_1$); total use of energy ($TCe = R_1 + ... + R_6 + Ie_1$) (p. 102), and $\{(+T) - (-T)\}$.

In the first type of specification the first three target variables will be included. In the second type of specification, all the four target variables will be included.

(1) The Weights of the Policy Target Variables: The mechanism for the specification of the weights of the policy target variable is discussed below. Specification of weights of policy target variables (the coefficient of the policy objective function) from the quantitative information obtained through the revelation of the preferences of policy makers is a difficult task, since hardly any information is available for this purpose (Fox, Sengupta, and Thorbecke 1973). Two approaches are usually adopted to specify the weights of the target variables. The first approach is to derive the weights as accurately as possible through one or

several methods for the specification of the preferences of policy makers (Johansen 1974). The second approach involves the derivation of a set of weights as a working set from the quantitative information gathered from published documents and announcements of policy makers, and later evaluating the sensitivity of the optimum solution of the policy model to changes in the coefficients of the policy objective function, in order to determine the robustness of the weights used in the initial specification. In AEPSOM, the second approach has been adopted.

(2) Past Examples: Several past efforts for determining the weights of the policy objective function are worth mentioning here.

(a) In Theil's quadratic welfare function approach (1970), a quadratic function of the deviation between the desired and the actual values of the target and instrument variables is minimised. Therefore there is no need for specifying the weights of the target variables.

(b) Frisch (1976) used a method based on direct interview of the policy makers to extract enough quantitative information about the coefficients in the policy objective function.

(c) Another approach involves the determination of weights of the policy objective function from studies of the underlying policy environment (for example van Eijk and Sandee 1959). In this approach, an analysis of policy statements, actions, and published documents provide information on the initial specification of weights, although the weights are subsequently changed to study the sensitivity of the optimum solution to these changes. If the optimum solution is not very sensitive to the alternative sets of weights, then the initial set of weights can be considered to be appropriate.

(d) In some policy studies, the coefficients of the policy objective function can be obtained from the economic system under study. For example, if the policy objective function is in a form that represents the social surplus (consumer's surplus plus producer's surplus) the coefficients of the policy objective function can be obtained from the model under study.

(e) In the MLP policy studies, the issue of the selection of appropriate weights has not received any serious attention, probably because of the fact that attention has mainly been paid to the computational problems and other fundamental problems associated with the mathematical properties of MLP such as existence, uniqueness and global optimality of the MLP solution (Candler and Norton 1977, Chap. 4).

Candler and Norton 1977 have adopted a method similar to van Eijk and Sandee 1959. In that study the selection of the weights of the variables in the policy objective function was somehow arbitrary, although some motivation for the initial specifications was given. A sensitivity analysis was conducted to study the effects of the changes of the coefficient in the policy objective function on the optimum solution. In other MLP studies, either there is no need for specifying weights because of the nature of the policy objective function (for example, maximisation of net benefit) as in Sparrow et al. (1979) or in some other studies (Fortuny-Amat 1979) the weights have been purely arbitrary.

(3) Weights in AEPSOM: No quantitative information about the relative importance of the various Australian energy policy objectives is available from the government or from academic publications in this area. Therefore, the specification of the weights in the policy objective function in the present study is mainly based on past experience in this area, professional judgment, and partly on the revealed preferences of the policy makers.

Of the three policy objectives to be included in the policy objective function (1), reduction in oil import may appear to be more important than the other two objectives because of its direct implications in terms of national security. But the objective of reduction of oil import may lose some weight if oil can be imported from a friendly country or oil use can be reduced by diversifying the domestic energy sector. The other two policy objectives may appear to be of equal weight i.e. conservation of oil and conservation of total energy are of equal concern.

Because of the apparent equal importance of the three policy objectives and since no information about the relative weights of different policy objectives is available, it is maintained that these three target variables will have equal weight in the policy objective function. This means that one unit reduction in the import of oil is equally important to the policy makers as one unit reduction in the total use of energy or oil. However, one unit reduction in oil import will be three times more important than one unit reduction in the use, say, of natural gas, since oil import is appearing three times in the three target variables. Similarly the reduction in oil use will get two times more weight than the reduction in the use of natural gas.

Attaching equal weights to all target variables may appear as a simplification of the exercise of the specification of the policy objective function. However, as it was stated above, literature in this area in energy economics has not yet developed unlike macroeconomics where relative prioritisation of target variables is merely a duplication exercise (Fox, Sengupta and Thorbecke 1973). The problems of relative prioritisation of targets have been discussed by Griffin and Steele (1980, p. 342) and they have expressed their concern as follows: 'How, then, does one assess the success or failure of an energy policy - weighting all goals as equal and computing a batting average?'

Also, as it was mentioned above, in existing MLP literature, weights of the policy objective function have, so far, been simple (Chap. 1).

Sensitivity analysis will, however, be conducted to study effects of the changes in weights on the optimum solution to the model to test the robustness of the initial specification of the weights (Chap. 6).

The specification of the weights of the policy objective function 2 will be discussed in Section 5.4.1.9.

Units of Measurements. The policy target variables (physical variables) in Specification 1 are measured in petajoules, while in Specification 2 the variables (physical and monetary variables) are measured in petajoules and million Australian dollars, respectively.

The Policy Objective Function: Specification 1. In Specification 1, a linear policy objective function has been adopted. A linear policy objective function is based on the assumption of separatibility and additivity of the target variables. The specification of a linear policy objective in economic policy studies (macroeconomic, planning, and sectoral) is an established practice specially in development and sectoral planning (see Fox, Sengupta and Thorbecke 1973, Chapters 7, 13, and 15). Although the linear policy objective function has the characteristics of separability and adaptivity, these characteristics do not yet appear to be inconsistent with the nature of policy preferences in the energy sector. For example, energy policy targets such as the reduction of energy imports and conservation are not highly interdependent.

The policy objective function 1 of AEPSOM is specified (in the AES symbols discussed below) as:

$$\text{P.O.F.(1): } WL = wG = Ie_1 + CNo + TCe \tag{5.5}$$

where WL = the value of the policy objective function .

The policy objective function which shows the level of the values of all the target variables is the policy criterion in the Australian energy sector.

The Policy Objective Function: Specification 2. It has been mentioned that at the present level of development, most large or medium scale MLP models have linear policy objective functions (Candler and Norton 1977). An alternative form of the policy objective function is also specified in AEPSOM to test the model solution's sensitivity to a more complex and, probably, more realistic policy objective function. In Specification 2 a multi-criteria approach (Gal 1979) to the policy objective function is adopted.

Cherniavsky (1981, p. 399) has summarised the essence of energy modelling incorporating a multi-criteria objective function as: the purpose of multi-objective analysis is to identify and quantify the trade-offs between different social objectives, and to aid policy makers in formulating decisions which achieve the best possible compromise between conflicting goals.

In this approach, several conflicting or incompatible goals are specified, some of these goals may be measured in different units (petajoules, money, environmental damage, etc.).

There are three methods which are generally adopted for specifying or solving a multi-criteria model: a) generating techniques, b) utility function approach, and c) interactive methods. In the first method, the objective functions are ordered according to some decreasing preference by the modeller. In the utility function approach, all objective functions are collapsed to form a single function by giving different weights to different objectives. In the third method, information about the preference ordering is obtained interactively from policy makers. Chernviasky (1981) has reported the experimental results of trying the three above mentioned solution techniques in the Brookhaven model. It was not possible to establish the superiority of any method in any absolute sense. The conclusion was that the choice of solution technique should depend, to a large extent, on 'the suitability of the method to the structure of the problem' (Cherniavsky 1981, p. 416).

Cherniavsky (1981) has provided a survey of multi-criteria modelling of the energy sector. In energy planning, the Brookhaven Model (BESOM) is one good example of adopting multi-criteria policy objective functions (Kydes 1978, Chap. 2). In BESOM the following objective functions (in alternative combinations) were adopted: total annual energy system cost, investment requirements, total crude oil use, oil import, total energy use, environmental effect index, and total use of nuclear fuel.

The solution technique adopted in the PPS algorithm is the utility function method. In this method various objective functions are collapsed into a single objective function by relating those functions by some weights attached to each of them. Following the utility function method approach, the policy objective function 2 of AEPSOM is specified as follows (a general presentation): P.O.F.2: a (Part 1) + b (Part 2).

For specifying weights firstly, both a and b were set equal to 1, and secondly, the values of a and b were varied subject to a + b = 1 (five other alternative sets were adopted) (Gal 1979).

The specification of the parts/policy goals in AEPSOM has been similar to that of the Brookhaven model. The alternative policy objective function has two parts: the first part dealing with the real variables and specified in linear form (the policy objective function (1) as in (5.5)) and the second part relating to financial variables (taxes and subsidies) and specified in non-linear form. The first part involves the minimisation of the use of oil, reduction of the import of oil and energy conservation. The second part of the policy objective function involves the minimisation of the budget deficit (maximisation of revenue) in the energy sector. The alternative policy objective function (P.O.F.(2)) is of the following form (using the AES symbols):

$$WL = a[wG] - b[\{(+T_1)Y + (+T_2)X + (+T_3)Z\} - \{(-T_1)Y + (-T_2)X + (-T_3)Z\}] \qquad (5.6)$$

where: $+T = \{+T_1, +T_2, +T_3\}$ = vector of three types of taxes, and $-T = \{-T_1, -T_2, -T_3\}$ = a vector of three types of subsidies.

In this alternative specification of the policy objective function, considerations of real and monetary or transfer effects (Harberger 1971) of government energy policies have been incorporated. This specification of a policy objective function has important economic significance in formulating public policies. The importance of such considerations has been stated by Sparrow et al. (1979, p. 181) as :

> Considerations of real versus monetary, or transfer effects have long been recognised by economists as crucial to the evaluation of all forms of public activity: their application is usually very limited because of insufficient data.

In this specification, real effects of energy policies are measured in physical units (petajoules); monetary effects are measured in million Australian dollars. The policy objective function embeds the choice that those government policies should be selected which cause minimum use of total energy, crude oil and imported oil in the economy and generate maximum revenue (minimise energy sector budget deficit) for the government.

In estimating the transfer effects of taxes and subsidies, it is assumed that the burden of taxes and subsidies is borne by those on whom they are imposed (Sparrow et al. 1979).

It may be necessary to mention here that some of the elements of the $\pm T$ vectors are zero i.e. taxes and subsidies are only applicable to energy activities which are subject to government fiscal instrument control. A specific presentation of P.O.F. (2), including the AEPSOM symbols, is given in (5.18).

The Policy Objective Function: The Economic Perspective. Recently, the optimum intertemporal use of natural resources, both exhaustible and renewable, has been a major concern in economics. This is so since it has been alleged that profit maximising multi-nationals and private enterprises are using the world's natural resources at a higher rate than they should. Also the environmental implications of the consumption and uses of resources by an exponentially increasing world population provides a pessimistic prediction. A large volume of economic literature has grown in this area to investigate the significance of natural resources in economic development, the economic implications of an ever increasing use of natural resources and to determine the optimum use, economic use or minimum use of natural resources (Howe 1979). A survey of the literature in this area is provided in Julius (1981). From this growing volume of literature on the economic utilisation of natural resources, one issue certainly does emerge: an efficient (intra- and inter-temporal) utilisation of natural resources is essential. (Chap. 7 of this study will deal with this issue in detail to highlight the economic implications of the issue and its resolution by the AEPSOM results.)

In the present specification of the policy objective function, this central issue of resource economics has played the prominent role since the physical target variables relate to the economic utilisation of energy resources (specially, the use of total energy and crude oil).

The present specification of the policy objective function has also incorporated another major economic concern of the western industrialised countries: self sufficiency in oil. The economic problems experienced by these countries due to their dependence on imported oil have been stated before. It was clear from the discussion that the dependency on imported oil has been advocated as a major cause of the macroeconomic problems experienced by these countries in the 1970s, 1980s and 1990s. Therefore, the policy objective of minimisation of import dependency has crucial economic implications for a country.

In addition, the policy objective function incorporates the implications of the monetary or budgetary implications of energy resource allocations and government policy intervention. As the resource sector has been a leading sector in the development in many resource rich countries including Australia, the policy objective of the maximisation of net revenue in the energy sector has an appropriate and wide economic perspective.

In this connection, it may be restated that these energy policy objectives are typical in the OECD countries. Energy policy studies in these countries have been undertaken with explicit recognition of these objectives (Webb and Ricketts 1980). Also in some mathematical programming energy planning models, a similar set of energy policy objectives has been incorporated. The Brookhaven models, BESOM and MARKAL (Kydes 1978), which are very widely used energy models, have incorporated a similar set of energy policy objectives (stated above) involving physical and monetary target variables or goals.

5.4.2 The Constraints of the Model

The objective of an energy planning exercise is to optimise the value of the policy objective function which is subject to some constraints. These constraints relate to the availability of resources, technological structure, consumers' choice, producers' behaviour, and institutional and political set-up of the economy.

Since there are two types of decision makers who formulate their own optimum decisions, these constraints can be classified into two types: the constraints on the optimising behaviour of policy makers and the constraints on that of economic agents: producers and consumer's of energy. The constraints on the policy makers' decision making are in the form of limits on their budget expenditures, restrictions imposed on the policy instruments by the underlying socio-political system, and the nature of response of the economic agents to the policy measures of the policy makers (represented by the behavioural model in an MLP model). The economic agents' optimum decisions are also subject to some constraints: resource availability, technological structure, habit, existing productive capacity, market size, and controls by the policy makers. In the following sections, the specification of the two sets of constraints will be discussed.

Policy Constraints. Several alternative types of policy constraints have been specified in the MLP literature. (i) Constraints on the changes of the policy instruments. In Candler and Norton (1977), the policy instruments (such as subsidies on fertiliser, water taxation, price support, etc.) were made subject to variations of a certain range (for example, subsidies on fertiliser had a range of zero to 50% of cost). In Bisschop et al. (1982), certain ranges of the policy instruments were also specified. (ii) Budget constraints: In Sparrow et al. (1979), the policy constraints were specified to make the transfer effects of policy instruments equal to zero (taxes equal subsidies). A quadratic policy constraint in the following form: government revenue - government expenditure > - K, was included in Fortuny-Amat's (1979) example of the large scale application of MLP.

While in the existing MLP literature, only one of these constraints is specified, in the present study, both the types of policy constraints are specified. The first type imposes limits on the variation of the taxes and subsidies. In the abstract model, equation (5.1.b) represents this type of constraint. A range of 0 to 20% of the cost on the variation of the taxes and subsidies is specified:

$0 \leq \pm t_j \leq 20\%$ of the cost of the respective variable $_j$.

In Australia, no literature exists dealing with this type of specification of the limits on the range of fiscal instruments.

This specification seems reasonable for Australia for a medium-term planning period of 10-15 years. The range is the maximum possible allowed variation of taxes and subsidies. An optimum policy solution may be obtained by only small changes (less than 20%) in many policy instruments and 20% changes (maximum 20%) in few policy instruments.

A second type of constraint is specified following the long established practice in economics in which economists have argued that public programmes should be self-financing - taxes should equal subsidies and other government expenditure (Harberger 1971). The constraint in the present model is specified to make the net revenue (taxes minus subsidies) of the government to be positive, so that other government expenditures can be met from the sectoral revenue (transfer effects are positive):

$$\{(+T_1)Y + (+T_2)X + (+T_3)Z\} - \{(-T_1)Y + (-T_2)X + (-T_3)Z\} \geq 0 \tag{5.7}$$

This constraint takes care of the monetary (budgetary) implications of government policies and restricts the selection of a set of policy instruments which does not cause a budget deficit in the sector.

Behavioural Constraints: The Energy System Model.[11] The other type of constraints in AEPSOM are the behavioural constraints which are represented by a behavioural model of the energy sector simulating the optimisation behaviour of the energy producers and consumers. For surveys of the behavioural model in the agricultural sector, see Norton and Schiefer (1980) and of the energy sector models, see Hoffman and Wood (1976). Chap. 4 also contains a survey of existing single level energy sectoral behavioural models.

In MLP studies, a variety of different types of behavioural models have been specified: a non-linear agriculture sector model involving the optimisation of the sum of consumers' and producers' surplus where the producers are risk averters (Candler and Norton 1977), a cost minimisation linear programming agriculture sectoral model (Bisschop et al. 1982), and a mixed-integer programming model of the iron and steel sector (Sparrow et al. 1979).

Since linear programming sectoral models replicate the optimising behaviour of economic agents in a perfectly competitive market situation (Samuelson 1952) and they are computationally easier in an MLP model, a linear programming cost minimisation energy sector model has been specified as the behavioural model in AEPSOM. However, as taxes and subsidies appear in the objective function of the linear programming behavioural model in AEPSOM, the behavioural model becomes non-linear.

The constraints of AEPSOM (equations 5.1.e to 5.1.j) form an energy system (ES) model of the Australian energy sector. So, to specify the behavioural constraints of AEPSOM, it is necessary to specify an ES model for Australia as in (5.3).

For a detailed specification of the Australian ES model first the salient features of the Australian Energy System (AES) will be described (for a discussion of the general features of

[11] An energy system model is a mathematical model consisting of the various entities, elements or parts (supplies, fuels, technologies, processes, end-uses, etc.) and their interrelationships (demand, supply, intermediate balance equations, etc.) of the energy sector. Alternatively, an energy system model is a mathematical model of the energy sector containing the sector-wide entities such as energy flows, costs, prices, conversion losses, processes, technologies, etc.

energy systems, see Meier (1984)). AES will provide the necessary information for specifying the ES model. In the analysis of AES, the variables, parameters, and coefficients which are included in the ES model will be defined.

(I) AES. Figure 5.1 shows an aggregate AES. AES presents a network of flows of primary energy to the end-uses via several steps of conversion, transportation, transmission and distribution. The different steps shown in the AES figure such as extraction, refinery, etc. are the different stages through which a particular primary energy flows until it reaches the end-users. AES is a multi-input (primary energy), multi-activity (technologies), multi-product (energy products) and multi-use (end-uses) energy production and consumption system.

Seven types of primary energy[1] are specified in AES: coal (R_1), crude oil (R_2), natural gas (R_3), hydro-electricity (R_4), biomass (R_5), solar (R_6) and uranium (R_7). These forms of energy are either converted into energy products or transported to the end-users.

At present coal is used either in electricity production (steam cycle)(E_1) or by the end-users in different sectors. There are two sources of crude oil: domestic production and imports. Crude oil is a compound of the methane group, containing carbon and hydrogen with a large number of atoms in their molecules. The refinery processes separate its components by primarily using a fractional distillation technique. Some of the other techniques used in the Australian refineries are: cracking, reformer and alkylation- for the extraction of lighter distillates and the purification of the petroleum products (naphtha, kerosene, light distillates, gasoline, cracker feedstock, LPG, motor spirit and lubricants). It is assumed that oil from these different sources is refined to produce petroleum products (x_2).That is, all the fractions of the refinery outputs have been aggregated into a broad group. Refinery loss is represented by γ.

[1] Harder (1982) provides a comprehensive discussion of the definitions and descriptions of different forms of energy - their chemical and thermodynamic principles, technologies (supply, conversion and end-uses), uses in the economy, costs, efficiency losses, etc.

Figure 5.1. Australian Energy System 1979-80

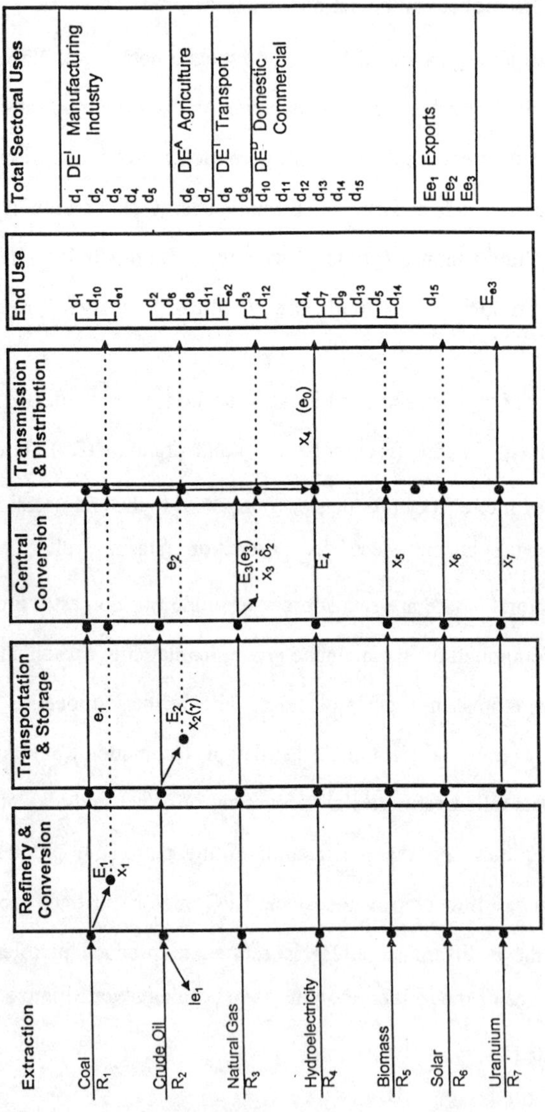

Natural gas is used for electricity generation (steam cycle and gas turbine) (E_3) and for end-uses (x_3).

The primary source of electricity is hydro electricity (R4). Other sources of electricity are: coal E_1, oil E_2 and natural gas E_3. Total electricity generation is x_4.

There are various sources of biomass (R_5) in Australia such as wood, bagasse, sugar-cane, crop residues and oil seeds, among others. Though they have the common characteristic of being composed of living matter, they differ substantially in their chemical properties, resulting in different end products, such as methanol and ethanol. In spite of this heterogeneity in the chemical properties of these fuels, here they are classified as biomass fuel (x_5) since total use of these fuels in Australia is relatively low in comparison with other fuels.

Solar energy (R_6) is considered to be feasible only in the domestic sector using water heated in solar panels. Therefore solar energy goes to the final users (x_6) instead of being supplied to the national grids.

All uranium (R_7, x_7) is exported in the form of ore and triuranium octoxide (U3O8) (E_{e3}) since there is no present domestic use.

In AES, the important conversion losses are defined. The transmission and distribution loss of electricity, distribution loss of natural gas and conversion loss of refinery are the major forms of conversion losses included in AES. These are represented by the coefficients e_o, δ and γ.

Four end-use sectors are identified in AES: manufacturing industry, agriculture (including mining), transport and domestic (including services). Not every energy product is used in every sector. A detailed listing of the uses of the fuels in all the end- use sectors isgiven below:

(a) Manufacturing Industry (DE^I):

Coal (d_1), petroleum products (d_2), natural gas (d_3), electricity (d_4), and biomass (d_5)

(b) Agriculture (DE^A):

Petroleum products (d_6), and electricity (d_7)

(c) Transport (DE^T):

Petroleum products (d_8), and electricity (d_9)

(d) Domestic (including commercial sectors) (DE^D):

Coal (d_{10}), petroleum products (d_{11}), natural gas (d_{12}), electricity (d_{13}), biomass (d_{14}), and solar (d_{15})

(e) Exports:

Coal (E_{e1}), petroleum products (E_{e2}), and uranium (E_{e3})

This background information about AES will be used to specify the constraints of the ES model.

(II) Constraints of the ES Model. There are five types of constraints in an ES the model: the demand constraints; the constraints that represent the intermediate energy balances and the supply balances (with separate specifications of the electricity and petroleum product sub-sectoral balances); and the resources and capacity constraints (for a discussion of the necessary constraints of an ES model, see Meier 1984). One feature of the present specification is that the end-uses are defined in terms of energy products, not in terms of the energy services as in Meier 1984. The symbols used in specifying these constraints are identified in Figure 5.1. Symbols with bars on them indicate their fixed quantities in 1979-80. *(1) Demand Constraints:* The demand constraints require that the energy supplies from different end-use flows must be greater than or equal to the total energy demand in each sector and exports. The following equations are formed by incorporating the sectoral flows of energy that are defined in Figure 5.1. The demand constraints of the ES model are:

$$d_1 + d_2 + d_3 + d_4 + d_5 \geq DE^I$$

$$d_6 + d_7 \geq DE^A$$

$$d_8 + d_9 \geq DE^T \tag{5.8}$$

$$d_{10} + d_{11} + d_{12} + d_{13} + d_{14} + d_{15} \geq DE^D$$

$$E_{e1} \geq \overline{E}_{e1}$$

$$E_{e2} \geq \overline{E}_{e2}$$

$$E_{e3} \geq \overline{E}_{e3}$$

The first four constraints are the demand constraints in the four sectors of the economy. The last three constraints are export constraints.

(2) Intermediate Energy Balance Equations: The constraints ensure that the uses of different energy products in the different sectors must equal the total supply of the energy products. The constraints, which are formed by the flows of end-uses and energy products defined in AES, are:

$$x_1 = d_1 + d_{10} + E_{e1}$$

$$x_2 = d_2 + d_6 + d_8 + d_{11} + E_{e2}$$

$$(1/\delta)x_3 = d_3 + d_{12}$$

$$x_4 = d_4 + d_7 + d_9 + d_{13} \tag{5.9}$$

$$x_5 = d_5 + d_{14}$$

$$x_6 = d_{15}$$

$$x_7 = E_{e3}$$

(3) Supply Balance Equations: These equations ensure that the supplies of primary energy in Australia must equal the supplies of energy products plus the conversion losses. The balance equations are:

(a) Petroleum Products Supply Balance Equation

$$E_2 + x_2 = R_2 + I_{e1} \tag{5.10}$$

(b) Electricity Supply Balance Equation

$$(1/e_o)x_4 = e_1E_1 + e_2E_2 + e_3E_3 + E_4 \tag{5.11}$$

(c) Other Supply Balance Equations

$$R_1 = x_1 + E_1$$

$$R_3 = x_3 + E_3$$

$$R_5 = x_5 \tag{5.12}$$

$$R_6 = x_6$$

$$R_7 = x_7$$

(4) Resource Constraints: In the ES model, all the primary energy supplies have been constrained to their supplies in 1979-80. The resource constraints of the model are:

$$R_1 \le \overline{R}_1$$

$$R_2 \le \overline{R}_2$$

$$R_3 \le \overline{R}_3 \tag{5.13}$$

$$R_5 \le \overline{R}_5$$

$$R_6 \le \overline{R}_6$$

$$R_7 \le \overline{R}_7$$

(5) Capacity Constraints: The capacity constraints require that the supplies of energy cannot be higher than that which can be produced by the capacity of the existing equipment, techniques and plants for mining, producing, converting, transporting and distributing, and end-uses of energy. We have specified only the constraints on electricity generation and petroleum refining since these are the major constraints.

The constraints are:

$$E_4 \leq kHe$$

$$x_4 \leq kTe \tag{5.14}$$

$$(1/\gamma)x_2 \leq RK$$

where:

He = hydro-electricity generation capacity

Te = total capacity of electricity generation

RK = total capacity of the refineries

k = capacity factors

γ = refinery losses

(6) User-Defined Constraints: It is conventional to include some 'user defined constraints' in ES models in addition to standard ones required for the normal presentation of the energy system. This is done to make the energy systems model '...reflect the real life situation where relative prices will play an important role in the choice of technologies, but other factors may also be important' (Musgrove et al. 1983, p. 15).

Some of these factors are the upper, lower or fixed bounds on the investment, capacity and market penetration or share of a technology or end-uses. In MARKAL, a large number of such constraints were specified (Musgrove 1983, p. 16).

The advantage of this type of user-defined constraints is that they make the ES model more realistic to represent the technical characteristics of the existing energy system and to forecast the short-term or medium-term energy system accurately. However, they have the disadvantage that they make the energy system model restrictive, thus leaving not much freedom to choose. In addition, this practice may not be suitable in a study designed for the formulation of optimum energy systems and policies since in such a study what is needed is not a positive forecasting of the future system, but a presentation of normative results showing the desired or optimum structure or directions of resource allocations and technological developments in the energy sector.

In AEPSOM, a 'compromise' situation was adopted as only one type of such user defined constraints was included in it. These constraints were in a form that restricted the model not to choose electricity uses in different sectors below their actual or predicted uses in 1979-80.[13] They limit the possibility of substitution of electricity by other fuels as there exists short-term technical non-substitutability in the power using industries (more discussion at the end of Sect. 6.5). The constraints on the uses of electricity are as follows:

$$d_4 \geq \bar{d}_4$$
$$d_7 \geq \bar{d}_7 \qquad (5.15)$$
$$d_9 \geq \bar{d}_9$$

(III) Behavioural Objective Function (B.O.F.). The objective function of this ES model is a cost equation. A cost equation is specified so that the behavioural model replicates the behaviour of an atomistic market consisting of cost minimising producers and end-users (Samuelson 1952). It consists of the following types of costs (net of taxes or subsidies): the cost of supplying primary energy (c_i), the cost of oil imports (c_m), the cost of conversion of primary energy to energy products (c_j), the cost of generation of electricity (c_e), and the cost of end-uses (c_k). Each type of cost consists of both fixed and variable costs (capital, labour, energy, and other operation and maintenance costs). Transportation and distribution costs of energy are included in the end-use costs.

By incorporating all the different types of costs, the cost equation can be defined as:

$$C = \sum_{i=1}^{7} c_i R_i + c_m I_e + \sum_{j=1}^{7} c_j x_j + \sum_{e=1}^{4} c_e E_e + \sum_{k=1}^{15} c_k d_k \qquad (5.16)$$

The costs are measured in terms of $ millions per petajoules of energy.

---

[13] It should be mentioned that these constraints '...affect the output from the model and this must be borne in mind when analysing the optimum solution' (Musgrove et al. 1983, p. 15). This point will be again referred to in Chap. 6. In Chap. 7, the AEPSOM results will be analysed for their policy implications, in particular, for their technological policy implications in this perspective.

In AEPSOM, the objective function of the behavioural problem contains ±T (the tax and subsidy instruments). The above presentation of the objective function of the behavioural problem does not contain the tax and subsidy instruments. To specify the tax and subsidy instrument variables, we need to discuss the existing fiscal instruments which are now being applied in Australia. This will be done in the next section. However, the following is the form of the objective function of the behavioural problem containing existing taxes and subsidies in the Australian energy sector:

$$C = \sum_{i=1}^{7} (c_i + T_i)R_i + c_m I_e + \sum_{j=1}^{7} c_j x_j + \sum_{e=1}^{4} c_e E_e + \sum_{k=1}^{15} (c_k - T_k)d_k \qquad (5.17)$$

5.5 AEPSOM Policy Variables

The following listing and classification of the policy variables in AEPSOM is based on the hierarchical, multi-goal, and multi-level energy policy system in Australia.

5.5.1 Policy Target Variables

The target variables were defined and specified in the previous section. These are reproduced here: import of oil; consumption of oil; and total consumption of energy.

5.5.2 Instruments and Strategies

Energy policy options or instruments are pursued to remove impediments of market failures to achieve the Pareto optimum resource allocation consistent with the other policy objectives in the energy sector such as the security of energy supply. A large number of policy instruments is available to the policy makers. The policy instruments set includes (1) physical controls or direct controls such as import quota, (2) technical efficient methods (determination of an intertemporal efficient energy system - fuel and technology mix), (3) determination of depletion and exploration rates, (4) fiscal instruments (taxes and subsidies), (5) direct investment, (6) price fixing, (7) expenditures and strategies related to research and development, education and information/public exhalation, and (8) other non-quantitative policies such as monopoly purchasing, (purchases by state agencies) participation (providing capital and receiving profit) (Webb and Ricketts 1980; Munasinghe and Schramm 1983; Griffin and Steele 1980). However, the task of choosing a set of policy instruments is always determined by the policy objectives to be achieved. The choice will depend on the prevailing political, economic and technological conditions in a country.

5.5.3 Existing Policy Instruments and Strategies in Australia

In 1979-80 three types of instruments were used in Australia to achieve energy policy objectives (prices, taxes and subsidies, and government expenditures) in conjunction with other policy strategies.

(1) Pricing Instrument: The price of domestic crude oil is determined by the Commonwealth Government.

(2) Taxes and Subsidies: The taxes and subsidies are: (a) Primary energy: t_1 = a levy on coal, t_2 = resource rent tax on crude oil, t_3 = resource rent tax on natural gas; and (b) End-uses: $-t_1$ = subsidy on the use of coal in the manufacturing industry sector; $-t_3$ = subsidy on the use of natural gas in the manufacturing industry sector; $-t_5$ = subsidy on the use of wood in the manufacturing industry sector; $-t_{10}$ = subsidy on the use of coal in the domestic sector; $-t_{12}$ = subsidy on the use of natural gas in the domestic sector; $-t_{14}$ = subsidy on the use of wood in the domestic sector, and $-t_{15}$ = subsidy on the use of solar energy in the domestic sector.

(3) Government Expenditure: The major heads of government expenditures in the energy sector are research and development, conservation, education and information.

(4) Energy Technological Strategy: The government announces the policy strategies related to the major forms of energy mainly for providing information to the private sector about the optimum or expected developments in the energy sector.

(5) Other Strategies: Other energy policies such as depletion policy and exploration policies are also pursued by the government.

5.6 Data

The details of the estimations of the data in AEPSOM 1979-80 and 1989-90 are given in Appendices B and C. A note on the data used in this study is necessary at this point. There were several sources of data used in this study: from both government and academic publications. Various estimates of the same data were available from these sources, specially at different dates. For example, government energy publications have produced different estimates of energy data as more accurate and up-to-date information was available. Efforts were made at the primary stage of this research to adopt a set of consistent and accurate data (available at that time) for AEPSOM; alternative data available at later stages could not be incorporated. This problem may exist in other applied modelling work which has been pointed out by Hazell and Norton (1986, p. 272) as:

> Building an applied model is a process, and the most successful models evolve through time to take account of new findings. There never is a definite version, but rather at any moment in time the model represents a kind of orderly data bank that reflects both the strengths and limitations of the available quantitative information.

As stated above, the set of data used in the present study, has been adopted partly from published sources and is partly estimated by the present author. Adaptation of the present set of data is not an indication of the refusal of the reliability or accurateness of other available data. Sources of data were selected in this study by the criteria of suitability and easy availability of the data necessary for AEPSOM.

5.7 Summary

Australian energy model AEPSOM is a set of static models for 1979-80 and 1989-90. The model is based on the framework of a price control MLP, the theory of economic policy and policy systems analysis. Justification and methods for the specification of the AEPSOM elements have been discussed in this chapter. Data for the model are either estimated from different published sources, or originally calculated by the author.

6 The Results of the Australian Energy Planning Model

6.1 Introduction

The numerical implementation of AEPSOM is supposed to provide information useful and adequate for the formulation of a multi-level energy plan. In this chapter, the AEPSOM results, which indicate the model's capability in producing useful numerical output, will be reported and discussed. The chapter is structured as follows. How AEPSOM was solved, what type of output it produced, the policy uses of these results and the alternative AEPSOM solutions - these topics are reported in Section 6.2. A general discussion of all the relevant results produced by AEPSOM is provided in Section 6.3 while the sensitivity analysis is reported in Section 6.4. Validation tests on the results of AEPSOM are stated in Section 6.6 to determine the reliability of these results for policy prescription. This discussion of the validation of results will prepare the background for the use of these results in policy formulation in the next chapter.

6.2 AEPSOM Solutions and Output

6.2.1 Model

An abstract representation of the two types of the specifications of AEPSOM from Chap. 5 is reported here to facilitate the understanding of the outputs of AEPSOM and their policy uses.

Specification 1:[1]

$$\underset{\{\pm T\}}{\text{Min}}\, WL = wG \quad \text{(a) Policy objective function (P.O.F(1))}$$

s.t.

$$G = I_1 Y + I_2 X + I_3 Z \quad \text{(b) Definitional equations}$$

$$T_l \le \pm T \le T_p \quad \text{(c) Policy constraints}$$

$$\{(+T_1)Y + (+T_2)X + (+T_3)Z\} - \{(-T_1)Y + (-T_2)X + (-T_3)Z\} \ge 0 \quad \text{(d) Budget constraints}$$

(6.1)

$$\underset{\{Y,X,Z \mid \pm T\}}{\text{Min}}\; C = (c_1 \pm T_1)Y + (c_2 \pm T_2)X + (c_3 \pm T_3)Z \quad \text{(e) Behavioural objective function}$$

s.t.

$$Z \ge \overline{D} \quad \{\alpha\} \quad \text{(f) Demand constraints}$$

$$Z = aX \quad \{\delta\} \quad \text{(g) Intermediate energy balance constraints}$$

$$X = bY \quad \{\mu\} \quad \text{(h) Energy supply balance constraints}$$

$$Y \le \overline{Y} \quad \{\Gamma\} \quad \text{(i) Resource constraints}$$

[1] This model is a reproduction of the model (5.1) in Chap. 5. Symbols used in both models are the same.

$X \leq \overline{X}$ {ß} (j) Capacity constraints

$G,Y,X,Z \geq 0$ (k)Non-negativity constraints

where: WL = value of P.O.F.

w = vector of coefficient of the policy objective function (i x e);

G = vector of energy target variables (e x 1);

Y = a vector of primary energy (p x 1);

X = a vector of energy products (n x 1);

Z = a vector of end-uses of the energy products (m x 1);

D = a vector of end-uses in different sectors (q x 1);

c_1, c_2, c_3 = costs of supplying, converting and using energy {(p x 1),(n x 1),(m x 1)};

$\pm T_1$, $\pm T_2$, $\pm T_3$ = vectors of different taxes and subsidies {(p x 1),(n x 1),(m x 1)} (lower case t's are the elements);

a, b = matrices of technological coefficients {(m x n),(n x p)};

I's = matrices elements of which are either 1 or 0;

$\overline{Y}$ = a vector of the fixed amount of available primary energy (p x 1);

$\overline{X}$ = a vector of the fixed level of capacities (n x 1);

M = {α,δ,μ,Γ,ß} = shadow prices related to different constraints.

Specification 2:

$$\text{Min } WL = wG - [\{(+T_1)Y + (+T_2)X + (+T_3)Z\} - \{(-T_1)Y + (-T_2)X + (-T_3)Z\}]$$

{±T} (a) Policy objective function (P.O.F.2)[2]

s.t.

$G = I_1Y + I_2X + I_3Z$ (b) Definitional equations

[2] This alternative specification of the policy objective function was introduced in Chap. 5, Equation (5.6).

$T_l \leq \pm T \leq T_p$ (c) Policy constraints

(6.2)

$$\text{Min} \quad C = (c_1 \pm T_1)Y + (c_2 \pm T_2)X + (c_3 \pm T_3)Z$$

$\{Y,X,Z \mid \pm T\}$ (d) Behavioural objective function

s.t.

$Z \geq \overline{D}$ (e) Demand constraints

$Z = aX$ (f) Intermediate energy balance constraints

$X = bY$ (g) Energy supply balance constraints

$Y \leq \overline{Y}$ (h) Resource constraints

$X \leq \overline{X}$ (i) Capacity constraints

$G,Y,X,Z \geq 0$ (j) Non-negativity constraints

6.2.2 Solution

The optimum solution of AEPSOM was obtained by applying the PPS algorithm developed in a previous chapter. The reader can recall that an optimal solution to an MLP involves finding the optimum basic solution to the behaviour model of AEPSOM. A solution of the above type that satisfies the constraints on the policy instruments and provides the optimum value for the policy objective function is the optimum solution for an MLP. To be able to apply the PPS algorithm, the following issues related to the techniques of solving AEPSOM as a price control MLP needed to be resolved:

(1) Development of a formula to find the units of parametric variation to solve AEPSOM; and

(2) Development of a procedure for applying AEPSOM to two types of policy studies, i.e. (a) for finding the optimum values of the existing taxes and subsidies and (b) for finding the optimum mix and optimum values of taxes and subsidies. Since these were discussed in detail in Chap. 3, only their applications to AEPSOM will be discussed in Sect. 6.2.6.

6.2.3 Optimum Solution

As AEPSOM was solved by the PPS algorithm, there was no guarantee that the global optimum was found. However, the AEPSOM results can be considered optimum for the reasons discussed in Chap. 3.

Identification of Optimum Solution:[3] Conventionally, the following two criteria are adopted to determine the optimum policy: Pareto optimality and the optimum value of the policy objective function. These two criteria were applied to identify the optimum solution of AEPSOM. The optimum solution was determined by the lowest value of the policy objective function, which is the normal mathematical criterion used for determining a minimum. The AEPSOM optimum also has economic implications. The AEPSOM optimum solution corresponds to the Pareto optimum in the energy sector in the sense that at the optimum the value of no target variable can be reduced further without increasing the values of one or more target variables in the Australian energy sector.[4]

[3] The identification and interpretation of the AEPSOM optimum solution should be made within the context of the MLP solution discussed in Chap. 3. The AEPSOM optimum is an optimum along a ray determined by parametric variations.

[4] For an analysis of the Pareto optimum implication of an MLP model solution, see Hazell and Norton (1986, p. 323).

6.2.4 Output

In the case of AEPSOM being solved using the PPS algorithm, its optimum solution generates the following results:[5]

(a) the optimum value of the policy objective function (WL);

(b) the optimum value of the behavioural objective function (C);

(c) the optimum values of taxes and subsidies ($\pm T = \pm U$);

(d) the optimum values of the activities (X, Y, Z); and

(e) a set of shadow prices or dual variables (defined below) $M = (\alpha,\delta,\mu,\Gamma,\beta)$[6] corresponding to the energy demand, conversion, supply balance, and supply and capacity constraints of the primal problem (6.1 and 6.2), and

(f) Reduced costs (Rc) (defined below) showing the amount of required cost reduction in the energy activities which will cause that activity to appear in the optimum solution.

---

[5] The unit of real and monetary variables are petajoules (PJ) and million Australian dollars.

[6] The shadow prices are the dual variables of a linear programme. For example if the general linear programming (primal) problem is as follows :

$\text{Min } C = cX_{22}$
$\{X_{22}\}$
s.t.
$A_{22}X_{22} \geq R$
$X_{22} \geq 0$

The dual problem to the above primal problem is:

$\text{Max } Z = MR$ {M is a row vector}
$\{M\}$
s.t.
$MA_{22} \leq c^T$
$M \geq 0$

There are some important primal-dual relationships (see Intriligator 1971). However, the shadow prices are the dual variables M such that $cX^*_{22} = M^*R$.

6.2.5 Uses of Results for Multi-Level Energy Planning [7]

In the previous MLP studies, model results have been used mainly to (a) determine the optimum values of existing taxes and subsidies (b) make explicit the policy - behavioural feasible region and (c) to formulate technology policies (Candler and Norton 1977; Bisschop et al. 1982; Ballenger 1984; Sparrow et al. 1979). The present MLP study has extended the scope of applications of MLP model results by undertaking the types of policy studies (specially by adopting ±T in conjunction with shadow prices and reduced cost in policy studies) discussed in this section. The uses of the AEPSOM results are discussed below.

Policy Systems Analysis. The values of the policy objective function and behavioural objective function and also the values of ±T provide insights into the characteristics of the underlying policy system.

A Multi-Level Energy Plan. (1) An Optimum Energy System: The optimum values of X, Y, Z constitute the elements of the optimum energy system.

(2) An Optimum Energy Policy Plan: The results of the model can be used to formulate a comprehensive set of energy policies. The behavioural objective function does not have any policy uses, but it is informative in the sense that the aggregate reactions of the individual economic agents to government policies can be studied from various values of the behavioural objective function.

AEPSOM results can be used for formulating the following policies:

(a) ± T for Tax and Subsidy Policy: The value of the taxes and subsidies selected by the model will be the optimum values of the tax and subsidy instruments. If an MLO model is solved by the PPS algorithm (discussed in Chap. 3), the values of the parametric variations (θ U) of the coefficients of the lower level objective function become the values of taxes and

[7] From the outset of the study, policy formulation problems in market economies have been discussed with different levels of economic controls. Therefore, it is obvious that the model will be applicable to both developed and underdeveloped market and mixed economies. An MLO model can also be applied to fully controlled economies. In these economies most of the resources are controlled and distributed by the government, but the objectives of the central policy makers and the operation level policy makers may be different. The nature of control of the activities of the operation level decision makers by the central level policy makers may also range from some tax and subsidy measures to the direct controls of price and resources. This type of policy system can also be modelled by an MLO model.

subsidies. Therefore , the optimum value of $\pm T$ is determined in the present study by $\pm\theta U$ since the PPS algorithm has been used to solve AEPSOM. Details of the meaning and the mechanism of determination of $\pm\theta U$ have been discussed in Chap. 3.[8]

(b) P for Pricing Policy: For the purpose of government pricing policy formulation (when prices are fixed by the government), the opportunity cost approach to pricing is adopted. In this approach, the price of energy should be equal to the value of the cost of the next best alternative available. In a mathematical programming energy model, shadow prices calculated by the model reflect the scarcity costs or opportunity costs of activities, and these shadow prices are adopted to formulate energy prices.

It may however be mentioned that, although the above is the normal practice, in an environment where prices are not directly fixed by the government, but are controlled by taxes or subsidies or other regulations (as in price control MLP), prices can be calculated by the formula (6.3) or (6.4) below, since these prices will be the market prices which are equal to production costs plus government taxes or minus government subsidies. Prices in this study were determined by using the following formula, shown by (6.1.e):

$$P_1 = c_1 \pm T_1,\ P_2 = c_2 \pm T_2,\ P_3 = c_3 \pm T_3 \tag{6.3}$$

where

P_1, P_2, P_3 = prices of different forms of energy

c_1, c_2, c_3 = average cost of the activities

$\pm T_1, \pm T_2, \pm T_3$ = taxes or subsidies

If the PPS algorithm is applied to solve an MLP model, prices can be calculated as follows:

$$P_1 = c_1 \pm \theta U_1,\ P_2 = c_2 \pm \theta U_2,\ P_3 = c_3 \pm \theta U_3 \tag{6.4}$$

where

P_1, P_2, P_3 = prices of different forms of energy

[8] If a resource control MLP model is solved by the PPS algorithm, the model solution will also provide the optimum values of activities which are under direct government control. These optimum values can be used to identify government investment policies in the energy sector.

θ = level of parametric variation

U_1, U_2, U_3 = unit of the parametric variations of c_1, c_2 and c_3.

However, shadow prices were used in this study to formulate other forms of energy policies (discussed below).

(c) X, Y, Z for Technology Policy: The optimum values of the activities in the energy model (energy supplies, products and end-uses) determine what may be called the optimum energy system. The optimum energy system indicates the efficient resource allocation, i.e. the optimum pattern of activities in the energy sector. A comparison of the optimum energy system with the existing energy system can provide guidelines for the formulation of energy technology policies. In an economy where government investment in the energy sector exists, these values of the activities also show the desired pattern of public sector investment. In a market economy, the values of activities are used only to formulate energy technology policies as guidelines for government energy department operations and to provide information to the private sector to help in making investment decisions.

d) X,Y,Z for Investment Policy:[9] The optimum set of energy activities shows the optimum pattern of output of energy in the economy. Incremental capital-output ratios related to energy activities can be used to calculate the levels and structure of investments necessary to attain all of these energy outputs.

(e) $\alpha, \delta, \mu, \Gamma, \beta$ for Conservation Policy, Education and Information Policy; and Research and Development Policy: Shadow prices can be used to determine priorities for the allocation of government funds for policy actions in such areas as conservation, research and development, and education and information. As shadow prices of end-use constraints indicate the effects of reduction in unit per energy consumption, these shadow prices are useful for the formulation of energy conservation policies. $\alpha = (\alpha_1, \alpha_2, ..., \alpha_n)$ shows the relative priority areas for energy conservation.

---

[9] In Australia, the state governments invest in the electricity sector. Since there is no need for a national investment policy, and as AEPSOM is not regionally segregated, no investment policy for the Australian energy sector has been formulated in this study.

The relative shares of each type of constraints of the total values of the shadow prices indicate the priorities in the allocation of funds for research and development, and education and information.

(f) Rc for Research and Development Policy: If one energy supply or technology is not viable in the market at the moment, that activity will not be in the simplex tableau of the optimum solution. The reduced cost of that activity indicates the cost reduction which will result in the penetration of the market by that activity (Bradley, Hox and Magnanti 1977). On the basis of this information government can undertake research and development policies or develop a more efficient technology or find cost-saving methods in that energy operation.

6.2.6 Types of Model Specifications, Solution and Policy Studies

The two types of AEPSOM were solved separately.

Three Types of Units of Parametric Variations. In Chap.3, three types of units of parametric variations were proposed which were applied to solve AEPSOM. These three types of units are (see symbols in models 6.1 and 6.2):

(1) $U = C = \{c_1, c_2, c_3\}$ = elements are selected to either equal c_j or 0;

(2) U = K = elements are either +1, 0 or -1; and

(3) $\pm u_j = H = -c_j \pm wI_j$; $I = \{I_1, I_2, I_3\}$; $j = 1, 2, ..., n$.

In alternative cases, AEPSOM was solved by adopting those three units of parametric variation.

Two Types of Policy Studies. It was stated in Chap. 3 (pp. 145-146) that an MLP model (AEPSOM) can be used to undertake two distinctively separate policy studies if it is solved by the PPS algorithm:

(1) to find the optimum values of the existing taxes and subsidies in an economy (existing ±T); and

(2) to find the optimum combination of taxes and subsidies and their optimum values (optimum ±T).

Methods for solving an MLP model by the PPS algorithm for these two types of policy studies were stated in Chap. 3. These methods were applied to solve AEPSOM, and to obtain results suitable for the two types of policy studies. In the next section, AEPSOM results will be reported separately for these two policy regimes. In each of the policy studies, the above mentioned three units of parametric variation were adopted to solve AEPSOM.

6.3 Presentation and Discussion of the AEPSOM Results

This section will report the major results of AEPSOM and discusses the results.[10]

The important results produced by AEPSOM which were stated before are the (optimum) values of (a) the policy objective function, (b) the behavioural policy objective function, (c) the taxes and subsidies, (d) prices (e) activities (energy supply, production and end-uses), (f) shadow prices, and (g) reduced costs. Sensitivity studies with AEPSOM also show the effects of changes in the energy sectoral variables and coefficients on the above mentioned results, especially on the policy objective function, and thus provides a comparative static framework for policy analysis.

The optimum AEPSOM solution with descriptions of the main characteristics of the model solution is given in Table 6.1. A listing of the various AEPSOM solutions is given in Appendix C.

[10] In MLP studies, numerical findings are generally used for two purposes (i) to study the characteristics of the multi-level decision making, and (ii) to analyse and/or formulate policies (for example, Candler and Norton 1977). The same approach has been adopted in this study. Comparative accounts of the findings of the present study, and previous MLP and other studies will be provided throughout the whole chapter for a relative evaluation of the findings of the present study.

Table 6.1. Optimum Model Solutions [a]

Model No.	Brief description	Type of policy	U	Policy constraints	Result
					Optimum value [b] P.O.F (PJ)
Model No. 5	AEPSOM 1979-80 data	Optimum set	U = C	$0 \leq \pm T \leq 20\%$ $B=3777.91 > 0$	6,733.70 $(\pm T \mid 0)$

[a] This model corresponds to AEPSOM in (5.1), Specification 1.
[b] P.O. F (1) $W = Ie_1 + CNo + TCo$, with the policy constraints:

(1) $0 \leq tj \leq 20\%$ of j   j = 1,2, ...37 (For 1989-90, j = 1,2, ..., 43)

(2) $B = \sum_{i=1}^{37}(+tj)xj - \sum_{j=1}^{37}(-tj)xj \geq 0$

Detailed results of all these solutions are not reported here. Only those which are significant for the present study will be reported in the tables in the next sub-sections. In those tables, several model results are reported in addition to the optimum AEPSOM solution (model solution No. 5) for comparison purposes.

6.3.1 Some Elements of the Numerical Policy System

The Policy Objective Function. The optimum values of the policy objective function in the cases of two model specifications are reported in Table 6.1.

In the case of specification 1, only Model No. 5 produced results satisfying the initial policy constraints $0 \leq \pm T \leq 20\%$. The optimum values of the policy objective function (1) are the same in the case of model solution 5 and 6 (Appendix C), although these have different upper level constraints on the policy range, while model solution 13 produces a very much lower value of the policy objective function.

To trace the relationships between the values of the policy objective function and the variations in $\pm T$ (or $\pm$ U), Table 6.2 was prepared containing the values of the policy objective function and levels of under both specifications of the policy objective function. It is evident from Table 6.2 that with the different levels of parametric variation, the values of the policy objective functions do not show any increasing or decreasing trend. This implies that the problem of finding the optimum value of ±T can not be solved by simply increasing or decreasing ±T steadily. Therefore, careful study is needed to find the optimum values of ±T.

Table 6.2. Levels of Parametric Variations and the Values of the Policy Objective Functions

Model No. 4

θ	W1[a]	W2[b]	W3[c]
0.0000	7031.66	0.00	7031.66
0.1300	7032.16	8142.39	-1110.23
0.5012	6734.20	24455.52	-17721.32
0.5900	6734.20	9202.55	-2468.35
2.2486	7037.22	26514.73	-19477.51
2.6850	7037.22	21432.75	-14395.53

Model No. 5

θ	W1[a]	W2[b]	W3[c]
0.0000	7031.66	0.00	7031.66
0.0771	6733.70	3777.91	2955.79
0.1158	6897.83	5226.25	1671.58
0.2899	6897.83	3460.04	3437.79
0.2918	7036.72	3798.89	3237.83
0.3137	7036.72	2889.04	4147.68
0.3149	7037.22	2863.57	4173.65

Model No. 6

θ	W1[a]	W2[b]	W3[c]
0.0000	7031.66	0.00	7031.66
0.0791	6733.70	3859.65	2874.05
0.1042	7110.58	4702.72	2407.86
0.1150	6898.33	5190.08	1708.25
0.2222	7773.20	2717.27	5055.93
0.2937	7912.09	3476.58	4435.51
0.3164	7912.09	2540.03	5372.06

[a] W1 = P.O.F. (1)
[b] W2 = The second part of P.O.F. (2)
[c] W3 = P.O.F. (2)

The Values of the Behavioural Objective Function. The optimum solutions to some behavioural models of AEPSOM (the single level linear programming model of the energy sector without ±T in it or when ±T = 0) are reported in Table 6.3. Optimum solutions to the same behavioural models when these models are solved as the lower level of an MLP (AEPSOM) (i.e. optimum value for the behavioural problem determined by the MLP solution) are also reported in the table.

It appears from Table 6.3 that optimum solutions to the single level behavioural model are not the same as the optimum MLP solutions to the behavioural model. In other words, the optimum value of the behavioural objective function without government intervention is different from when there is government intervention. In most of the solutions of which six are reported in Table 6.3 the former value has been lower than the latter.

Different values of the behavioural and policy objective functions are also reported in Table 6.3. It is apparent from the table that in the cases where optimum model solutions involve ±T = 0, the value of the behavioural objective function of AEPSOM is higher than the value of the behavioural objective function of the cost-minimising linear programming model of the energy sector (single level behavioural model in Model No. 7). This implies that to achieve the optimum value of policy objectives, the energy sectoral total costs have to increase. Alternatively, AEPSOM does not choose the energy sector behavioural optimum solution (without government intervention) as optimum solution for the MLP model.

These results clearly demonstrate the different and conflicting interests of the private and public sector. The public sector decision criteria select that private sector performance which is different from the private sector's own chosen optimum performance.

Table 6.3. Optimum Values of the Behavioural and Policy Objective Functions

Model number	B.O.F. (1)[a]	B.O.F. (2)[b]	P.O.F. (1)	±T
1	229336.34	229336.34	7031.68	±T=0
2	229336.34	229336.34	7031.66	±T=0
3	229336.34	229336.34	7031.40	±T=0
4	229336.34	230668.43	6734.20	±T≠0
5	229336.34	245047.03	6733.70	±T≠0
6	229336.34	251442.69	6733.70	±T≠0

[a] The value of the objective function of the single level linear programming model.
[b] The value of the objective function of the behavioural model of AEPSOM. It does not include taxes or subsidies.

This does not, however, mean that policy intervention will always raise the level of energy sector costs, as can be seen from Table 6.4. In Model Solution 13, increased value of the parametric variation has actually at some time reduced the value of the behavioural objective function. For example at = 9.118, the value of the behavioural objective function of AEPSOM is 255748.56 which is less than the value generated by the single level linear programming model.

One important aspect of the AEPSOM optimum solution should be discussed here. If the optimum values of P.O.F(1) in Model Nos 7 and 5 are compared (Table C.1 in Appendix C), it will reveal that the optimum value determined by the single level behavioral model (Model No.7): 7031.68 is higher than that of the MLP model - AEPSOM (Model No. 5).

In Figure 6.1, optimum values of different target variables generated by Model No. 5 and the single level behavioural model are shown. The bar diagrams of Iel(B), CNo.(B) and TCe(B) show the values of target variables (Iel, CNo and Tce) generated by the behavioural model which are higher than their values generated by the MLP model (Ie(M), (No(M), and TCe(M)).

Table 6.4. Different Values of θ and Three Objective Functions

Model No. 5

θ	B.O.F. (1) [a]	B.O.F. (2)	P.O.F. (1)
0.0000	229336.34	229336.34	7031.66
0.0771		245047.03	6733.70
0.1158		252385.15	6897.83
0.2899		284808.63	6897.83
0.2918		285150.94	7036.72
0.3137		289020.25	7036.72
0.3194		289237.88	7036.72

Model No. 13

θ	B.O.F. (1)	B.O.F. (2)	P.O.F. (1)
0.0000	275179.50	275179.50	8472.01
0.1000		275412.38	4680.03
0.1625		275361.06	9476.85
0.1867		275341.19	9476.85
0.5413		275048.94	9477.45
1.0000		274505.13	9477.45
1.7092		273371.75	9476.14
1.9159		272993.06	9494.46
1.9442		273904.12	9494.46
2.2645		272224.38	9494.46
9.1118		255748.56	9494.46

[a] B.O.F. (1) and B.O.F. (2) as defined before.

Figure 6.1 Values of the Target Variables.

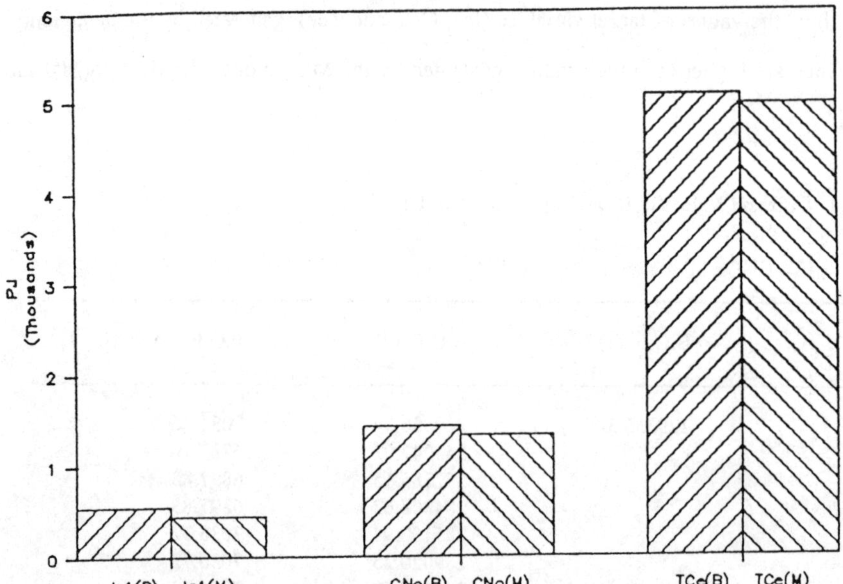

A Multi-Level Policy System Analysis. In Chap. 4 some analytical characteristics of multi-level decision making were stated. The AEPSOM results can be used to highlight some numerical characteristics of the multi-level policy system, the characteristics which exist analytically in model (4.22) in Chap. 4. The AEPSOM results demonstrate the numerical characteristics of the policy system in the Australian energy sector discussed below.

(1) Goal Interdependence: The first characteristic is goal interdependence: an indirect goal interdependence exists in the energy sector i.e. objectives of the policy makers are dependent on the objective of economic agents as well as on the energy system (which are represented by the behavioural objective function and the energy sector constraints). The optimum value of the policy objective function is the value of the (multi) goals that the policy makers sought to achieve by making a rational decision. The optimum value of economic agents' goals is reflected in the value of the behavioural objective function (Table 6.3). It is evident from Tables 6.3 and 6.4 that the achievement of goals at each level of decision making is interdependent (indirect goal interdependence): the optimum values of the policy and behavioural objective functions are interdependent. It was also found that the two level decision makers have conflicting interests (Table 6.4), and the optimum solution to the system results is a compromise situation providing the attainment of optimum goals for the decision makers at each level (saddle point, optimum solution in Table 6.4 (Model No. 5) at $\theta = 0.771$).

(2) Intervention: In the above mentioned policy system context, the adaptation of policies ($\pm$T intervention) by the policy makers results in *improved* performance of the policy system (lower level of social energy goals). This is evident from Table 6.1 since the optimum solution to AEPSOM (Model No. 5) is in the case where $\pm$T + 0 11.

In other studies, Candler and Norton (1977) and Ballenger (1984) also found that the behavioural optimum is inefficient compared with the multi-level programming optimum in the sense that 'the behavioural optimum lies ... further inside the policy-behavioural frontier' in a policy maximisation case.

This brings in the issue of the desirability of government intervention[11] in achieving the objectives of society. AEPSOM results indicate the possibility for attaining a lower level of policy goals by government policy intervention in the energy sector.

6.3.2 Appropriateness of the AEPSOM Results

It was argued in Chap. 4 that the single level (both positive or behavioural and normative or central control policy) models misrepresent the underlying multi-level decision making process. Therefore, their numerical results may generate wrong prediction or optimum policies. AEPSOM results can be used to evaluate these arguments regarding the appropriateness of single level mathematical programming models.

For that purpose, these two types of models are specified from AEPSOM as follows:

(1) Single-Level Positive or Behavioural Model:

$$\min_{\{Y,X,Z\}} C = (c_1 \pm T_1)Y + (c_2 \pm T_2)X + (c_3 \pm T_3)Z \qquad \text{(a) Behavioural objective function}$$

s.t.

$$Z \geq \overline{D} \qquad \text{(b) Demand constraint}$$

$$Z = aX \qquad \text{(c) Intermediate energy balance constraints}$$

---

[11] In the terminology of game theory (for a discussion of game theory, see Intriligator (1971), Fortuny-Amat (1979), AEPSOM results show that the policy system in the Australian energy sector is characterised by a two-person, non-zero sum, cooperative game situation. In this situation the policy makers and economic agents (two persons) are engaged in their own decision making, but the outcome of one's decision (the value of the policy objective function or behavioural objective function) does not depend only on his decision or strategy but also on the other person's decision (i.e the optimum value of the policy objective function is dependent on the optimum value of the behavioural objective function and vice versa, Table 6.3 and 6.4). Both type of decision makers mutually gain from their decisions of the game (non-zero sum game) in the sense that the optimum solution to the game results in a lower value of the policy objective function (Table 6.1). There is also the possibility of mutual cooperation. The optimum policy outcome is attained at the saddle point in the policy-behavioural feasible region ($g(G, \pm T, X, Y, Z) = 0$) in the cases of models (6.1) and (6.2).

$X = bY$ (d) Energy supply balance constraints

$Y \leq \overline{Y}$ (e) Resource constraints

$X \leq \overline{X}$ (f) Capacity constraints

$G,Y,X,Z \geq 0$ (g) Non-negativity constraints

(2) Single-Level Normative or Central Control Model:

$\underset{\{Z,Y,X\}}{\text{Min}} \quad WL = wG$ (a) Policy objective function (P.O.F.(1))

s.t.

$Z \geq \overline{D}$ (b) Demand constraint

$Z = aX$ (c) Intermediate energy balance constraints

$X = bY$ (d) Energy supply balance constraints

$Y \leq \overline{Y}$ (e) Resource constraints

$X \leq \overline{X}$ (f) Capacity constraints

$G,Y,X,Z \geq 0$ (g) Non-negativity constraints

Definitions of the symbols are the same as in model (6.1).

In Table B.1 (Appendix B), Model No. 7 and Model No. 9 are the single level energy sector positive and normative models. Model No. 7 has determined a lower level of policy goals compared to an MLO model, Model No. 5. On the other hand, Model No. 9 has determined a lower optimum policy goal level, but that can only be attained by central controls of the energy sector (not by indirect controls as in the market economy). Therefore, both the single level mathematical models (Model Nos 7 and 9) produce erroneous results for the energy sector (the optimum value of the policy objective function as well as the optimum values of other model results: prices; taxes and subsidies; shadow prices, and reduced costs). Consequently, it may be argued that an accurately specified and implemented MLO model (Model No. 5) can generate appropriate numerical results for optimum energy policy planning in a market economy.

From the evidence of past studies (Candler and Norton 1977) stated in the previous sub-section and also from the present work, it can now be concluded that an MLP model can represent the multi-level decision making system appropriately, and therefore, generates accurate energy model results (forecasts or policies).

6.3.3 Taxes and Subsidies

As it was stated before, within the structure of existing ±T, improvement in policy goals is not possible compared to a situation of market performance. Therefore, optimum values of ±T, in the cases of existing ±T, are 0.

If the policy system is allowed to choose the optimum mix and values of ±T, then the model solution finds ±T $\neq$ 0 optimum solution to AEPSOM. These values of optimum mix and optimum values of ±T are reported in Table 6.5.A.

A comparison of the optimum mix of ±T and the existing ±T reveals that the optimum mix of ±T suggested by AEPSOM is different from existing ±T (see Table 6.5.B.).

6.3.4 Prices

The calculated prices of different energy supplies, products and end-uses are reported in Tables 6.6.A. and 6.6.B. Although all these prices are reported here, not all energy prices are under government control in Australia.

Table 6.5.A. Optimum Mix and Levels of Taxes and Subsidies: 1979-80 (M$/PJ)

Energy type [a]	Model No. 5		Model No. 6		Model No. 13	
	±T on energy types [b]	% [c]	±T on energy types	% [c]	±T on energy types	% [c]
R_1	0.0000	0.0000	0.0000	0.0000	0.0280	3.8889
R_2	0.2313	4.6260	0.2373	4.7460	0.3000	6.0000
Ie_1	0.1272	2.4003	0.1305	2.4625	0.0000	0.0000
R_3	0.0000	0.0000	0.0000	0.0000	0.0120	1.5385
R_4	0.0000	0.0000	0.0000	0.0000	0.1000	0.5189
R_5	0.0000	0.0000	0.0000	0.0000	0.0000	0.0000
R_6	-0.0871	-67.0177	-0.0894	-68.7562	0.0000	0.0000
R_7	0.0000	0.0000	0.0000	0.0000	0.0000	0.0000
E_1	1.0779	7.7100	1.1058	7.9100	0.0000	0.0000
E_3	-1.7209	-7.7100	-1.7655	-7.9100	0.0000	0.0000
E_4	0.0000	0.0000	0.0000	0.0000	0.0000	0.0000
x_1	-0.0794	-7.7100	-0.0815	-7.9100	0.0000	0.0000
x_2	0.1773	12.7576	0.1819	13.0885	0.0000	0.0000
E_2	-1.4410	-7.7100	-1.4784	-7.9100	0.0000	0.0000
x_3	0.1033	7.7100	0.1060	7.9100	0.0000	0.0000
x_4	0.0000	0.0000	0.0000	0.0000	0.0000	0.0000
x_5	0.0000	0.0000	0.0000	0.0000	0.0000	0.0000
x_6	0.0000	0.0000	0.0000	0.0000	0.0000	0.0000
x_7	0.0000	0.0000	0.0000	0.0000	0.0000	0.0000
d_1	0.2120	7.7100	0.2175	7.9100	-0.2750	-10.0000
d_2	0.0000	0.0000	0.0000	0.0000	0.0000	0.0000
d_3	0.0948	7.7100	0.0973	7.9100	-0.1230	-10.0000
d_4	0.0000	0.0000	0.0000	0.0000	0.0000	0.0000
d_5	0.0000	0.0000	0.0000	0.0000	-0.0250	-10.0000
d_6	0.0000	0.0000	0.0000	0.0000	0.0000	0.0000
d_7	0.0000	0.0000	0.0000	0.0000	0.0000	0.0000
d_8	18.27270	7.6918	18.7467	7.8914	0.0000	0.0000
d_9	0.0000	0.0000	0.0000	0.0000	0.0000	0.0000
d_{10}	0.1002	7.5932	0.1028	7.7902	-0.1320	-10.0000
d_{11}	0.0000	0.0000	0.0000	0.0000	-0.3390	-34.5918
d_{12}	0.0000	0.0000	0.0000	0.0000	0.0000	0.0000
d_{13}	0.0000	0.0000	0.0000	0.0000	0.0000	0.0000
d_{14}	0.0000	0.0000	0.0000	0.0000	0.0000	0.0000
d_{15}	-0.5012	-7.4910	-0.5142	-7.6854	-0.9450	-14.1256
Ee_1	0.0000	0.0000	0.0000	0.0000	0.0000	0.0000
Ee_2	0.0000	0.0000	0.0000	0.0000	0.0000	0.0000
Ee_3	0.0000	0.0000	0.0000	0.0000	0.0000	0.0000

[a] Definitions of these energy types (both for 1979-80 and 1989-90) are given in Table 6.5.A. (Appendix below).

[b] ±T is a column of taxes and subsidies suggested by AEPSOM. The second entry in the column is tax on the second type of energy (oil). That is how T column relates to different energy forms.

[c] (i) Taxes and subsidies as percentages of costs: (T + C) X 100.
(ii) Taxes and subsidies, and costs are measured in million Australian dollars per petajoules ($M/PJ).

Table 6.5.A. (Appendix)

List of the Activities of the Behavioural Model: Energy Supplies, Production and End-uses

AEPSOM: 1979-1980 Activities/energy type	AEPSOM: 1989-1990 Activities of /energy type
A. Primary energy resources R_1 = coal R_2 = crude oil Ie_1 = imported crude oil R_3 = natural gas R_4 = hydro electricity R_5 = biomass R_6 = solar R_7 = uranium	A. Primary energy resources R_1 = coal R_2 = crude oil Ie_1 = imported crude oil R_3 = natural gas R_4 = hydro electricity R_5 = biomass R_6 = solar R_7 = uranium
B. Intermediate Energy E_1 = electricity from coal E_3 = electricity from natural gas E_4 = hydro-electricity x_1 = coal x_2 = petroleum products E_2 = electricity from petroleum products x_3 = natural gas x_4 = total electricity production x_5 = biomass x_6 = solar x_7 = uranium	B. Intermediate Energy RR_1 = synthetic oil from coal E_1 = electricity from coal E_3 = electricity from natural gas E_4 = hydro-electricity x_1 = coal x_2 = petroleum products E_2 = electricity from petroleum products x_3 = natural gas x_4 = total electricity production x_5 = biomass x_6 = methanol x_7 = solar x_8 = uranium
C. Energy end-uses i. Manufacturing industry d_1 = coal d_2 = petroleum products d_3 = natural gas d_4 = electricity d_5 = biomass ii. = Agricultural sector: d_6 = petroleum products d_7 = electricity	C. Energy end-uses i. Manufacturing industry d_1 = coal d_2 = petroleum products d_3 = natural gas d_4 = electricity d_5 = biomass ii. = Agricultural sector: d_6 = petroleum products d_7 = electricity

Table 6.5.A. (Appendix) continued

List of the Behavioural Model Activities/Energy Types

AEPSOM: 1979-1980 Activities of the behavioural model/energy type	AEPSOM: 1989-1990 Activities of the behavioural model/energy type
iii. Transport sector d_8 = petroleum products d_9 = electricity	iii. Transport sector d_8 = coal d_9 = petroleum products d_{10} = natural gas d_{11} = electricity d_{12} = methanol
iv. Domestic and other sectors d_{10} = coal d_{11} = petroleum products d_{12} = natural gas d_{13} = electricity d_{14} = biomass d_{15} = solar	iv. Domestic and other sectors d_{13} = coal d_{14} = petroleum products d_{15} = natural gas d_{16} = electricity d_{17} = biomass d_{18} = solar
v. Exports Ee_1 = coal Ee_2 = petroleum products Ee_3 = uranium	v. Exports Ee_1 = coal Ee_2 = petroleum products Ee_3 = natural gas Ee_4 = uranium

Table 6.5.B. Existing and Optimum Set of ±T

Model No. 5

Energy type	Set of existing ±T	Optimum mix of ± T
R_1	+	0
R_2	+	0
Ie_1	0	+
R_3	+	0
R_4	0	0
R_5	0	0
R_6	0	-
R_7	0	0
E_1	0	+
E_3	0	-
E_4	0	0
x_1	0	-
x_2	0	+
E_2	0	-
x_3	0	+
x_4	0	0
x_5	0	0
x_6	0	0
x_7	0	0
d_1	-	-
d_2	0	0
d_3	-	+
d_4	0	0
d_5	-	0
d_6	0	0
d_7	0	0
d_8	0	+
d_9	0	0
d_{10}	-	+
d_{11}	0	0
d_{12}	-	0
d_{13}	0	0
d_{14}	-	0
d_{15}	-	-
Ee_1	0	0
Ee_2	0	0
Ee_3	0	0

Table 6.6.A. Optimum Energy Prices in 1979-80: Model No. 5

Model No. 5

Energy type	±T	C	P (M$/PJ) [a]
R_1	0.0000	0.72	0.7200
R_2	0.2313	5.00	5.2313
I_e1	0.1217	5.30	5.4272
R_3	0.0000	0.78	0.7800
R_4	0.0000	19.27	19.2700
R_5	0.0000	1.18	1.1800
R_6	-0.0871	0.13	0.0429
R_7	0.0000	0.13	0.1300
E_1	1.0779	13.98	15.0579
E_3	-1.7209	22.32	20.5991
E_4	0.0000	0.00	0.0000
x_1	-0.0794	1.03	0.9506
x_2	0.1773	1.39	1.5673
E_2	-1.4410	18.69	17.2490
x_3	0.1033	1.34	1.4433
x_4	0.0000	6.00	6.0000
x_5	0.0000	0.00	0.0000
x_6	0.0000	0.00	0.0000
x_7	0.0000	0.00	0.0000
d_1	0.2120	2.75	2.9620
d_2	0.0000	1.42	1.4200
d_3	0.0948	1.23	1.3248
d_4	0.0000	2.30	2.3000
d_5	0.0000	0.25	0.2500
d_6	0.0000	2.00	2.0000
d_7	0.0000	0.20	0.2000
d_8	18.2727	237.56	255.8327
d_9	0.0000	228.40	228.4000
d_{10}	0.1002	1.32	1.4202
d_{11}	0.0000	0.98	0.9800
d_{12}	0.0000	3.39	3.3900
d_{13}	0.0000	6.17	6.1700
d_{14}	0.0000	0.00	0.0000
d_{15}	-0.5012	6.69	6.1889

[a] P = C ± T
C = Cost coefficient vector (cost of different forms of energy)
±T = Tax or subsidy vector (taxes or subsidies on different forms of energy)
P = Price vector (prices of different forms of energy)
Taxes, subsidies, costs and prices are measured in million Australian dollars per petajoules.

Table 6.6.B. Optimum Energy Prices in 1979-80: Model No. 6

Model No. 6

Energy type	±T	C	P (M$/PJ)*
R_1	0.0000	0.72	0.7200
R_2	0.2373	5.00	5.2373
I_e1	0.1305	5.30	5.4305
R_3	0.0000	0.78	0.7800
R_4	0.0000	19.27	19.2700
R_5	0.0000	1.18	1.1800
R_6	-0.0894	0.13	0.0406
R_7	0.0000	0.13	0.1300
E_1	1.1058	13.98	15.0858
E_3	-1.7655	22.32	20.5545
E_4	0.0000	0.00	0.0000
x_1	-0.0815	1.03	0.9485
x_2	0.1819	1.39	1.5719
E_2	-1.4784	18.69	17.2116
x_3	0.1060	1.34	1.4460
x_4	0.0000	6.00	6.0000
x_5	0.0000	0.00	0.0000
x_6	0.0000	0.00	0.0000
x_7	0.0000	0.00	0.0000
d_1	0.2175	2.75	2.9675
d_2	0.0000	1.42	1.4200
d_3	0.0973	1.23	1.3273
d_4	0.0000	2.30	2.3000
d_5	0.0000	0.25	0.2500
d_6	0.0000	2.00	2.0000
d_7	0.0000	0.20	0.2000
d_8	18.7467	237.56	255.3067
d_9	0.0000	228.40	228.4000
d_{10}	0.1028	1.32	1.4228
d_{11}	0.0000	0.98	0.9800
d_{12}	0.0000	3.39	3.3900
d_{13}	0.0000	6.17	6.1700
d_{14}	0.0000	0.00	0.0000
d_{15}	-0.5142	6.69	6.1759

* $P = C \pm T$

C = Cost coefficient vector

±T = Tax or subsidy vector

P = Price vector

6.3.5 Shadow Prices

It was mentioned before that in this study shadow prices will not be used for pricing policy purposes, but to determine the priorities in conservation programmes, research and development, and education and information policy. Shadow prices have been reported here for these uses. The proportions (%) of the shadow prices related to different types of constraints have also been reported here since these proportions indicate the relative priorities for various policy measures. Two types of shadow price proportions are calculated: (1) shadow price proportions of different sectoral end-use constraints and (2) shadow price proportions of all types of constraints in the model: energy end-uses, intermediate balance, supply balance, resource constraints and capacity constraints.

These two types of shadow prices and their proportions are reported in Tables 6.7.A and 6.7.B for Model No. 5. Proportions of sectoral end-use constraints reflect the priorities for conservation programmes, while the proportions of shadow prices related to all the constraints reflect priorities for government expenditure for research and development, and education and information policies.

6.3.6 Optimum Activities

One important result of AEPSOM is a set of optimum values of the activities in the Australian energy sector. This set of optimum activities (numerical values of the flows of primary energy, secondary energy and end-uses of energy as well as various technologies) constitutes the optimum energy system for Australia.

Table 6.7.A. Proportion of Shadow Prices: 1979-1980

Model No. 5

Constraints/symbols[a]	Shadow prices (M$/PJ)	Proportions (%)
1. Demand constraints (α) (6.1.f)	521.4165	0.6947
2. Intermediate balance (δ) (6.1.g)	177.1009	0.2359
3. Supply balance (μ) (6.1.h)	31.9612	0.0426
4. Resources constraints (Γ) (6.1.I)	6.5168	0.0087
5. Capacity constraints (β) (6.1.j)	3.6875	0.0049

[a] These constraints were specified in Model 6.1 or 6.2

Table 6.7.B. Shadow Prices Related to Different Demand Constraints

Model No. 5

Demand constraints (6.1.f)	Shadow prices (M$/PJ)	Proportions
Manufacturing industry	5.1628	0.0098
Agriculture/primary industry	9.2059	0.0177
Transport	236.0849	0.5046
Domestic and commercial	4.0107	0.0077
Electricity manufacturing	80.3937	0.1542
Electricity primary industry	74.2146	0.1423
Electricity domestic sector	85.3799	0.1637

In Table 6.8.A the optimum set of activities suggested by three model solutions along with the 1979-80 actual energy production and uses is shown. In Table 6.8.B a similar set of figures for 1989-90 is shown. When the demand and supply of energy are constrained to their actual values in 1979-80 (as in Model Nos 5 and 6) the optimum set of activities is somehow close to their actual values. However, when the constraints were relaxed by 20%, the structure of the optimum set of activities changes due to greater flexibility and substitutability among different fuels. In both cases, model results indicate different structures and values of energy activities than the 1979-80 actual figures.

In the 1989-90 energy system, the model solution suggests a set of optimum activities which is different from the 1989-90 actual figures and government projections. The differences between the 1989-90 actual energy activities and the model results (produced by an MLP model specified to determine an optimum energy policy system for Australia) clearly indicate a different profile for the energy sector growth. Some new developments in the 1989-90 AES are the uses of town gas in the domestic sector, and natural gas and coal in the mining sector (Jones , Bush, Kanakaratnam, Leonard and Gillan 1991).

Therefore, both the 1979-80 and 1989-90 model results suggest optimum energy systems for Australia different from those that have been considered to be ideal and possible by the government and the private sector.

6.3.7 Reduced Costs

The reduced costs of the 1979-80 and 1989-90 AEPSOM are reported in Table 6.9.A and 6.9.B. Although different model solutions suggest different magnitudes of reduced costs for these activities, the values of reduced costs are fairly similar in the cases of Model Nos 5 and 6. This is plausible since Model Nos 5 and 6 were specified within a given structure of the energy sector. This certainly provided a possibility for a different technological pattern and thus calculated different reduced costs which indicate that different cost savings are required for market penetration of those activities.

Table 6.8.A. Optimum Activities: 1979-1980 (PJ)[a]

Energy type	1979-80 Actual [b]	Model results		
		Model No. 5	Model No. 6	Model No. 13
R_1	2448.81	2448.8101	2448.8101	2938.5703
R_2	874.87	874.8701	874.8701	0.0000
Ie_3	435.34	453.3918	453.3918	1709.4453
R_3	364.18	364.1799	364.1799	437.0100
R_4	50.23	86.6099	86.6099	103.9300
R_5	138.14	138.1399	138.1399	165.7600
R_6	0.50	0.0000	0.0000	0.0000
R_7	586.04	586.0400	586.0400	703.2400
E_1	845.57	351.6301	351.6301	864.0101
E_3	87.91	364.1799	364.1799	0.0000
E_4	50.23	86.6103	86.6103	103.9304
x_1	493.95	2097.1797	2097.1797	2074.5601
x_2	1188.82	1063.2300	1063.2300	1275.9099
E_2	50.23	265.0317	265.0317	433.5352
x_3	251.16	0.0000	0.0000	437.0100
x_4	293.02	288.8400	288.8400	346.6000
x_5	138.14	138.1399	138.1399	165.7600
x_6	0.50	0.0000	0.0000	0.0000
x_7	586.04	586.0400	586.0400	703.2400
d_1	83.72	590.2200	590.2200	271.2700
d_2	192.56	0.0000	0.0000	0.0000
d_3	175.81	0.0000	0.0000	437.0100
d_4	108.84	108.8400	108.8400	130.6000
d_5	71.16	138.1399	138.1399	165.7600
d_6	96.28	117.2000	117.2000	140.6800
d_7	25.12	25.1200	25.1200	30.1000
d_8	807.90	812.0798	812.0798	974.4897
d_9	4.19	0.0000	0.0000	0.0000
d_{10}	4.19	234.4200	234.4200	281.2600
d_{11}	87.91	0.0000	0.0000	0.0000
d_{12}	58.60	0.0000	0.0000	0.0000
d_{13}	154.88	154.8800	154.8800	185.9000
d_{14}	66.98	0.0000	0.0000	0.0000
d_{15}	0.50	0.0000	0.0000	0.0000
Ee_1	1272.54	1272.5400	1272.5400	1522.0300
Ee_2	133.95	133.9500	133.9500	160.7400
Ee_3	581.85	586.0400	586.0400	703.2400

[a] Energy is measured in Petajoules (PJ) in Table 5.8.A and 5.8.B.

[b] Source: Department of National Development and Energy (1983).

Table 6.8.B. Optimum Activities: 1979-1980 (PJ)

Energy type	1989-90 Actual[a]	Forecast[b]	Model solution	
			Existing ±T model solution No. 19	Optimum ±T model solution No. 23
R_1	4688.0	4198.56	4198.5596	4198.5596
R_2	1182.6	1159.52	0.0000	649.5796
Ie_1	449.0	326.51	648.8518	0.0000
R_3	797.7	933.48	933.4800	933.4800
R_4	53.2	58.60	86.6100	86.6100
R_5	176.3	171.63	171.6301	171.6301
R_6	3.0	1.00	1.0000	0.0000
R_7	4291.4	4299.02	4299.0195	4299.0195
RR_1	0.0	0.00	0.0000	0.0000
E_1	1291.8	1272.54	769.2666	768.2666
E_3	160.0	133.95	0.0000	0.0000
E_4	53.2	58.60	86.6100	86.6100
x_1	193.0	594.42	3429.2935	3430.2935
x_2	1316.3	1172.08	360.0001	360.0002
E_2	37.0	8.37	288.8523	289.5797
x_3	497.0	523.25	933.4800	933.4800
x_4	475.0	447.90	330.2300	330.2300
x_5	176.3	171.63	171.6301	129.7701
x_6	0.0	0.00	0.0000	41.8600
x_7	3.0	1.00	1.0000	0.0000
x_8	1921.4	4299.02	4299.0195	4299.0195
d_1	175.3	125.61	909.3228	910.3228
d_2	150.9	96.28	0.0000	0.0000
d_3	296.8	318.14	698.5671	697.5671
d_4	182.6	171.63	100.0000	100.0000
d_5	101.5	104.65	0.0000	0.0000
d_6	89.6	123.58	255.3500	255.3500
d_7	42.0	41.86	0.0000	0.0000
d_8	3.5	4.19	0.0000	0.0000
d_9	995.3	891.62	0.0000	0.0000
d_{10}	0.4	0.00	41.8599	0.0000
d_{11}	6.6	4.19	0.0000	0.0000
d_{12}	0.0	0.00	0.0000	41.8600
d_{13}	4.0	4.19	0.0000	0.0000
d_{14}	27.0	66.98	0.0000	0.0000
d_{15}	97.0	125.58	95.4399	138.2999
d_{16}	233.7	230.23	230.2300	230.2300
d_{17}	77.0	66.98	171.6301	129.7701
d_{18}	3.0	0.00	1.0000	0.0000
Ee_1	2982.5	2519.97	2519.9702	2519.9702
Ee_2	159.0	104.65	104.6500	104.6500
Ee_3	109.6	246.97	246.9700	246.9700
Ee_4	1749.8	4299.02	4299.0200	4299.0200

[a] Source: Jones et al. (1991)
[b] Source: Department of National Development and Energy (1993)

Table 6.9.A. Reduced Costs ($M): 1979-1980

Energy type	Model No. 5 (Rc)	Model No. 6 (Rc)	Model No. 13 (Rc)
R_1	0.0000	0.0000	0.0000
R_2	0.0000	0.0000	0.0000
Ie_1	0.0000	0.0000	0.0000
R_3	0.0000	0.0000	0.0000
R_4	0.0000	0.0000	0.0000
R_5	0.0000	0.0000	0.0000
R_6	0.1200	0.0406	0.1300
R_7	0.0000	0.0000	0.0000
RR_1	0.0000	0.0000	0.0000
E_1	0.0000	0.0000	2.8553
E_3	0.0000	0.0000	0.0000
E_4	0.0000	0.0000	0.0000
x_1	0.0000	0.0000	0.0000
x_2	0.0000	0.0000	0.0000
E_2	0.0000	0.0000	0.0000
x_3	0.0000	0.0000	0.0000
x_4	0.0000	0.0000	0.0000
x_5	0.0000	0.0000	0.0000
x_6	0.0000	0.0000	0.0000
x_7	0.0000	0.0000	0.0000
x_8	3.4991	3.3794	1.1377
d_1	0.0000	0.0000	0.0000
d_2	0.0000	0.0000	0.0000
d_3	0.0000	0.0000	0.0000
d_4	0.0000	0.0000	0.0000
d_5	0.0000	0.0000	0.0000
d_6	0.0000	0.0000	0.0000
d_7	48.5300	47.3786	70.8436
d_8	0.0000	0.0000	0.0000
d_9	4.1752	4.0473	1.9847
d_{10}	3.1813	3.1706	3.2310
d_{11}	0.0000	0.0000	0.0000
d_{12}	0.8661	0.8579	0.9620
d_{13}	2.1635	2.4224	0.3357

Table 6.9.B. Reduced Costs ($M): 1989-1990

Energy type	Model No. 19 (Rc)	Model No. 23 (Rc)
R_1	0.0000	0.0000
R_2	981.8075	0.0000
Ie_1	0.0000	0.6192
R_3	0.0000	0.0000
R_4	0.0000	0.0000
R_5	0.0000	0.0000
R_6	0.0000	0.0802
R_7	0.0000	0.0000
RR_1	13.3173	10.9377
E_1	0.0000	0.0000
E_3	3.1608	3.1876
E_4	0.0000	0.0000
x_1	0.0000	0.0000
x_2	0.0000	0.0000
E_2	0.0000	0.0000
x_3	0.0000	0.0000
x_4	0.0000	0.0000
x_5	0.0000	0.0000
x_6	11.0793	0.0000
x_7	0.0000	0.0000
x_8	0.0000	0.0000
d_1	0.0000	0.0000
d_2	2.1473	2.7005
d_3	0.0000	0.0000
d_4	0.0000	0.0000
d_5	0.3742	0.4948
d_6	0.0000	0.0000
d_7	82.5036	78.0598
d_8	51.7197	42.2602
d_9	37.6223	29.4883
d_{10}	0.0000	2.9175
d_{11}	109.0059	96.4279
d_{12}	0.0000	0.0000
d_{13}	55.3883	11.0223
d_{14}	0.0000	0.0000

6.4 Sensitivity Analysis

To test the robustness of the results of AEPSOM, the sensitivities of model solutions to changes in some crucial variables, parameters and policies were tested. These variables, parameters and policies were chosen for sensitivity analysis because of either their strategic importance in the energy sector or uncertainty regarding them.

A complete list of the model solutions reflecting the changes in the policies and parameters of the Australian energy sector, effects of which have been studied, is given in Table C.1. More or less the same changes are assumed in the models in the cases of existing taxes and subsidies and optimum mix of taxes and subsidies. These changes and the models in which these changes were incorporated are as follows:

(1) Introduction of taxes on imported oil (Model No.12);

(2) Relaxation of constraints (demand and supply) by 20% and 100% respectively (Models No.13, and No.14);

(3) Limiting petroleum import (import quota) (Model No.15);

(4) Introduction of some new technologies in the 1979-80 Australian energy system (1979-80 AEPSOM) (coal conversion technologies, methanol production, electric railway, etc. (Model No.16));

(5) Administering import parity prices of all domestic crude oil (Model No.17);

(6) A doubling of the 1979-80 supply of energy resources while the demand level of 1979-80 remains the same (Model No.18);

(7) Development and solution of AEPSOM for 1989-90 (Models No.19 and No.23) and Appendix C);

(8) Different weights attached to the two components of policy objective functions (P.O.F.(2)) (Table 6.10); and

(9) Different weights attached to the three policy target variables in policy objective function P.O.F.(1) (Table 6.11). It should be noted here that none of the sensitivity studies has generated an optimum solution satisfying policy constraints.

However, these sensitivity studies are reported here to study the effects of these changes on the policy objectives.

6.4.1 Sensitivity Study (1) and (3)

The issue of energy security has dominated policy discussions in Australia for a decade. Consequently, one of the energy policy objectives has been the security of energy supply. It was stated in Chap. 5 that because of the heavy dependence of Australia on imported oil, security of energy supply has synonymously been used with self-sufficiency in oil. In Australia, the objective of the security of energy supply or self-sufficiency of oil has been pursued by adopting policies such as diversification of energy supplies and energy conservation, specially oil (Department of Primary Industries and Energy 1988).

However, the diversification of energy sources and energy conservation are only two policy options from a host of other policy strategies. These are: direct control of oil imports; suitable oil contracts; reserve standby capacity; international sharing arrangements among friendly countries; oil storage and fiscal and monetary policies designed for overall restructuring of the economy (Griffin and Steele 1980). Considerable controversies have developed regarding the relative efficacy and desirability of import controls and import tariffs[12]. Because of the superior allocative effects of import tariffs over import controls, tariffs on imported oil have been considered to be an effective policy instrument for achieving oil self-sufficiency.

Therefore, tax on the importation of oil has been introduced into the set of policy options to study the effects of this policy instrument (Sensitivity Study 1). It may be mentioned that in Australia, tax is not imposed on the importation of oil. So this sensitivity study was

[12] A discussion on the alternative instruments of commercial policy and their relative effects in the domestic economy is covered in Ethier (1988). A political economic perspective on this topic is provided in Ethier (1988) and in Todaro (1981). In this study, only two instruments, import control and import tariff are covered since these are the widely used instruments applied to the importation of energy in the developed market economics.

considered as crucial since it should reveal the implications of introducing a tax on the importation of petroleum.

The alternative policy instrument, direct control of oil imports, was also introduced into the Australian optimum policy system to compare the effects of this instrument (Sensitivity Study 3).

Effects: In the case of Sensitivity Study (1), the model solution suggests $\pm T \neq O$ (Model solution 12). Compared to the base solution, this sensitivity study also shows an improvement in the optimum level. The policy objective function (2) had a lower value compared to the policy objective function (1). However, when a limit of the 1979-80 import level was imposed on the energy system (Sensitivity Study 3), a feasible solution to AEPSOM did not exist.

6.4.2 Sensitivity Study (2) and (6)

As optimum energy system and policy are clearly dependent on the relative and absolute scarcity of different energy resources (reflected in AEPSOM in the resource constraints), relaxation of the constraints of AEPSOM were introduced in various solutions. This was aimed at studying the effects of the constraints on both optimum energy system and policy. In one type of sensitivity studies, the demand and supply constraints were relaxed by 20% and 100% of the 1979-80 supplies respectively (Sensitivity Study 2). In another study, the demand RHS's was at the 1979-80 level, and supplies were increased by 100% of the 1979-80 level (Sensitivity Study 6).

Effects: In the case of Sensitivity Study 2, the optimum $\pm T \neq 0$, while $\pm T = 0$ in the case of Sensitivity Study 6. This implies that a goal improvement is possible in the situations reflected in Sensitivity Study 2, but not in the case of Sensitivity Study 6. It is worth mentioning that out of all the model solutions, model solution 13 which is a study of Sensitivity Study 2, generated the lowest value for the policy objective function.

6.4.3 Sensitivity Study 4

Developments in energy technologies, particularly in new and renewable technologies, which will result in reduced energy costs and increased energy supplies, make the energy industry competitive, diversify the sources of supplies, while increased technological efficiencies are considered to be an effective way to achieve the energy policy objectives, i.e. to solve energy problems. In view of this, some new technologies (stated before) were introduced in the 1979-80 AEPSOM to study how these new technologies affect the Australian energy system and policies.

Effects: The introduction of new technologies in the 1979-80 energy system has predicted an improved level of social goals. The optimum $\pm T \neq 0$ implies the desirability of government intervention in the economy.

6.4.4 Sensitivity Study 5

Controversies have circulated regarding the introduction of import parity pricing of domestic crude oil in Australia, particularly in its scope and time phasing. As efficient resource allocation is considered to be a problem of efficient pricing of resources (Griffin and Steele 1980), should it be either in terms of domestic market mechanism or measured in international prices (a controversy to be discussed shortly), the effects of import parity pricing of domestic crude oil need to be understood. The Australian government followed a policy of phasing the introduction of import parity pricing by segregating off-shore and onshore oil. The study of the energy system and policy implications of the import parity pricing of all domestic oil has been the objective of this sensitivity analysis.

Effects: The introduction of the import parity pricing of crude oil did not provide any improvement in the optimum solution; the optimum $\pm T = 0$. Actually the values of the policy objective functions (1) and (2) in this case were higher than the base model solution under existing $\pm T$.

6.4.5 Sensitivity Study 7

The base year AEPSOM was specified for 1979-80 (i.e. 1979-80 data were used). Since AEPSOM is a static model, AEPSOM was also specified for 1989-90 (for existing ±T, Model No. 19; for optimum ±T, Model No. 23). The algebraic description of the 1989-90 AEPSOM and the data used in it are reported in Appendix B.

The purpose of developing the 1989-90 AEPSOM was to study the future directions of the Australian energy sector and policies, and to compare the implications and prescriptions of the 1979-80 AEPSOM results with its results. This would, of course, provide some time dimensions in the analysis and formulations of optimum energy policies and can be regarded as safeguard against myopic suggestions of a static model.

Effects: The 1989-90 specification of AEPSOM shows also an improvement in the optimum solution through government intervention: ±T (i.e. optimum ±T $\neq$ 0).

6.4.6 Sensitivity Study 8

Different weights were given to the two components of policy objective function (2).

It was stated in Chap. 5 that one of the alternatives for attaching weights to different components of a multi-criteria objective function is to make the sum of the weights equal to 1 and to vary the weights within this restriction. In this study this approach was used. In the initial specification as well as in the results reported so far in Table 6.1 for policy objective function (2), the weights of the two components of the policy objective function were 1 and 1 (see note (b) in Table 6.1). However, in Sensitivity Study 8 the weights were changed keeping the sum of weights equal to 1 and results were calculated for the policy objective function (2) (Table 6.10); solution Nos 2 to 6).

Effects: The results of these models including different weights showed that these alternative weights did not change the optimum solution to AEPSOM.

Table 6.10. Different Weights to the Two Parts of P.O.F. (2)

Model No. 5

Solution No.	Weights		Optimum solution	
	Part 1	Part 2	θ Level	P.O.F. (2)
1	1.00	1.00	0.115	1671.58
2	0.20	0.80	0.115	4473.01
3	0.30	0.70	0.115	3260.61
4	0.40	0.60	0.115	2048.20
5	0.60	0.40	0.115	-376.62
6	0.70	0.30	0.115	-1589.03

6.4.7 Sensitivity Study 9

In this study different weights were attached to the three policy target variables in policy objective function (1). Initial weights were 1,1, and 1 for three variables of the policy objective function: import of energy (Ie1), consumption of oil (CNo) and total consumption of energy (TCe). Two other sets of weights were also specified (2,1, and 1 ; 3,2, and 1) for determining the sensitivity of the model solution to the weights of the policy objective function. The results are reported in Table 6.11. It is evident from the table that for all these types of weights, optimum solution was found at the same level of the parametric variation. In other words, different weights did not change the optimum solution to AEPSOM (optimum values of taxes, subsidies, prices, activities, etc.). However, the optimum value of the policy objective function has changed in different cases because of different weights given to different variables. This leads to conclude that the optimum solution to AEPSOM is not sensitive to different weights specified in AEPSOM and therefore the initially specified weight set can be considered acceptable.

Table 6.11. Sensitivity of the Optimum Solution to Different Weights in the Policy Objective Function

Model No. 5

Solution No.	Weights - (P.O.F. (1))			Optimum solution	
	Iel	CNo	TCe	Level of θ	Values of P.O.F. (1) (PJ)
1	1	1	1	0.077	6733.70
2	2	1	1	0.077	7187.09
3	3	2	1	0.077	8968.74

6.5 Reliability of the Results: Model Validation

In this section, the reliability of the results of the AEPSOM, and thus the reliability of the policies will be tested. For this purpose, the usual model validation criteria will be adopted.

It was stated in Chap. 3 that model validation is one of the important steps of an optimisation study. It refers to the correspondence of the model to the underlying processes or systems that are being modelled (Labys 1982) or to the reliability of the model.

Hazell and Norton (1986, p. 269) have described model validation and its purposes as :

> Validation of model is a process that leads to (1) a numerical report of the models fidelity to the historical data, (2) improvements of the model as a consequence of imperfect validation, (3) a qualitative judgment on how reliable the model is for its stated purposes, and (4) a conclusion (preferably explicit) for the kinds of uses it should not be used for.

Several criteria are used to test the validation of a model (Labys 1982; Taha 1976; Hazell and Norton 1986). In Chap. 4 it was stated that there are three levels of validation tests: descriptive, analytical and experimental; and there are three types of validation criteria which are applied to these three levels of validation tests (Kresge 1980). The first type of criteria includes: (A.1) the attainment of the objectives of the model; (A.2) the appropriateness of the model structure (relates the first model evaluation criteria discussed in Chap. 2); and (A.3) the plausibility of results (corresponds to criterion 3 in Chap. 2). The second type of criteria applied to the analytical level includes (B.1) the characteristics of the model solution, and (B.2) the robustness of the results. The third type of criteria is related to the usability of the model and includes the following: (C.1) methodological tests related to; (C.1.a) model documentation; (C.1.b) cost and efficiency in model transfer and extension; and (C.2) tests related to model execution such as: (C.2.a) accuracy and efficiency of the execution; (C.2.b) cost of and efficiency in the software transfer and extension.

The above list contains almost a complete set of model validation criteria which can be used in modelling studies. It may, however, be mentioned that hardly ever all these criteria are used in a modelling study. Hazell and Norton (1986, p. 269) have stated the range of applications of these tests in the following form:

> Validation begins with a series of comparisons of model results with the reported actual values of the variables. Most often, simple comparisons are made...However, more complete tests are possible and have been done.

It should, however be noted that the validation tests, specially the statistical tests, of macroeconometric systems models (for examples of such models see Powell 1980) and mathematical programming systems models are not exactly same (Labys 1982).

In this study, a set of tests will be done, though not the complete set of tests. A discussion on the applications of these model validation criteria to AEPSOM is provided below.

(A.1) Attainment of the Objectives of the Model. Greenberger and Richels (1979, p.486) state: 'The validity of a model is most meaningfully examined in the context of purpose for which the model was constructed or to be used'.

A judgment about the uses (of the results) of the model (to obtain enough information) to attain the stated modelling objectives is, therefore, necessary. AEPSOM has provided the information (see Chaps. 6 and 7), necessary for studying the characteristics of the underlying policy and energy systems, and the formulation of a comprehensive multi-level energy plan.

(A.2) Appropriateness of Model Structure: Priori Justification About the Model Structure. By this criterion, a judgment is made on how good the model is in representing the underlying system to solve a problem or to meet the purposes for which the model is developed. In Chap. 4, it was argued that an MLP energy planning model is appropriate for multi-level energy planning. AEPSOM is formulated within the desired framework. Therefore, the results of the AEPSOM could be considered appropriate on *a priori* grounds.

(A.3) Plausibility of Results. The accuracy of the results of a model need to be checked. In this process, the relevance of the optimal solution provided by the model to the expected results or the reported actual values or the historical data set is verified. Several methods can be used for this purpose: (a) intuitive judgment; (b) comparison of results; (i) with some past data; (ii) the ability to predict the future performance of the system; or (iii) with similar studies; (c) statistical tests such as the mean absolute percentage error or the mean squared error (Labys 1982, p. 165); and (d) self auditing, third party auditing, etc.

The statistical methods of auditing were not applied in this study. The tests A.3.b.i and A.3.b.iii were not considered suitable for this study since these tests are not appropriate for normative models (like AEPSOM) of 'new' or significantly altered systems and major structural changes (Greenberger and Richels 1979, p. 486). A third party auditing could not be undertaken since only the author (first party) was involved in this study. The statistical tests (A.3.c) were not conducted as the differences between the actual and optimum values were not judged to be useful for validating AEPSOM for the reasons stated above. However, Criteria A.3.a and A.3.b were applied.

(a) Intuitive Judgment: The results of AEPSOM reported in this chapter seem to be in the expected directions. What AEPSOM has suggested is an ideal/optimum system/result. Policies are formulated to move the existing system as close as possible to the ideal system. From that point of view, AEPSOM results reflect the optimum situation in the energy sector which can only be attained by full implementation of the policies suggested by the model and to the extent that the real life energy sector characteristics are close to the ones assumed in AEPSOM and they remain unchanged as they were assumed in AEPSOM.

A note on the results of optimum activities is specially needed here which will put the AEPSOM results in proper perspective for energy planning studies. AEPSOM has selected some technologies from the available alternatives on the basis of the relative costs and prices of different technologies within the framework as determined by (i) the technical characteristics and constraints of the energy sector, and (ii) the underlying policy system in the energy sector as reflected in the energy policy objectives and instruments. The forms of these elements of energy sector technical and policy systems have influenced the AEPSOM solution.

The reasons for which some end-uses appeared to be zero are (1) the aggregated character of the model (see Appendix A), and (2) the non-inclusion of the non-zero lower bounds ($Z \geq \overline{Z}$) on most of the end-uses of fuels in various sectors. It was discussed in Chap. 5 that in linear programming energy sector models, some user defined constraints of the above form are specified to impose lower limits below which end-uses are restricted not to drop in the optimum solution. These limits reflect the underlying technical non-substitutability among different fuels at the end-use level (Julius 1981; Hall 1983) (some fuels in some sectors cannot be completely substituted by alternative fuels). This was done in MARKAL. The present author was informed by a MARKAL author (Musgrove 1987) that many user defined constraints, specifically fuel margins were specified in MARKAL to reduce this type of zero corner solutions to the end-uses.

In AEPSOM, constraints on the electricity uses in the different sectors to meet certain minimum electricity demands were specified (Section 5.4.2). But inter-fuel substitution up to a high degree among other fuels (perfect substitutability in the neo-classical form) was allowed to meet the total energy demand in each sector. This might have produced a zero-corner type of optimum solution results for end-uses. This type of zero-corner solutions could be reduced by imposing more lower bounds on the end-uses of fuels in various sectors. Greater possibility of inter-fuel substitution was allowed in AEPSOM to determine the eventual optimum end-use pattern indicating the directions of increases or decreases in the uses of energy resources compared to their present pattern in the economy, should sufficient time and perfect technical substitutability be allowed and exist. Again, this was for evolving an ideal (optimum) technological pattern, probably at the cost of some realism. Justification for this effort was discussed in Chap. 5, Sect. 5.4.2. It was also stated there that an energy model output should specially be discussed keeping the user-defined constraints in mind.

Since a compromise between the immediate/existing technical non-substitutability and the long-run potential of inter-fuel substitutability was made in AEPSOM, the AEPSOM optimum end-use pattern should be viewed as the long term desired broad directions in the allocation of resources and technological developments in the energy sector.

Therefore, a normative view of the reported model results will be taken to formulate energy technology policies, as the optimum values and other AEPSOM results were generated for normative uses rather than positive/forecasting purposes.

(b) Comparison of Results: The criterion 3.b.iii is stated by Kresge (1980, p. 185) as: '... the plausibility of the results will be judged through comparison with the results produced by other related pieces of analysis.'

The problem in applying this criterion in the present study is that no other MLP energy model exists in Australia. Therefore, comparison of the results of the present model with the results of another similar model is not possible. But it can be stated that the results in this study are not unrealistic or non-operational in the context of the Australian energy sector. Since AEPSOM is a systems optimisation study, the AEPSOM results indicate optimum systems (energy and energy policy systems). These optimum systems have been found to be different, at least partly, from the existing systems. This does not imply that model results are not plausible. It means that existing systems are not the optimum systems due to the market imperfections which prevent the existing system to attain the optimum system specified in the model (Norton and Schiefer 1980).

However, the following test of the accuracy of results was undertaken in the present study. Accuracy of an MLP model can be tested by comparing the values of policy objective functions of the following three models:

(A) A Central Control Policy (Models No. 9 and No. 10)

(B) A behavioural model of the energy sector (Models No. 7 and No. 8)

(C) An MLO model of the energy sector (Models No. 5 and No. 27)

The closer the results of (B) and (C) are to the result of (A), the more accurate the results of (B) and (C) can be considered to be.

To demonstrate the efficiency of MLP results in the present study, the optimum values of the policy objective function of AEPSOM (opt. ±T) in the above three formulations have been reported in Table 6.12.

Table 6.12. Comparison of Different Model Solutions

Model type > & No. >	A (9)	B (7)	C (5)	Difference between A and B in % of A	Difference between A and C in % of A
Value of P.O.F. (1)	5101.51	7031.68	6733.20	37.80	31.90

The values of the policy objective functions in Table 6.12 clearly demonstrate a higher value of the policy objective function suggested by the behavioural model. Compared with the central control (single level) policy model (Solution A) the multi-level programming and single level behavioural model solutions (Model C and Model B) show a deviation of 31.9% and 37.80% respectively. Other MLP models results (for example Model No. 13) are even less deviated. The P.O.F.(1) value of Model No. 13 is 4,680.03 which gives a deviation of only 8.2% from Model A. Therefore, the multi-level programming (C) model provides accurate (close to solution (A)) results.[13]

An existing multi-level programming publication (Candler & Townsley 1982, p. 27) shows that a multi-level programming policy model provides better results than a single level mathematical programming model. It was found in that study that the value of the policy

[13] By increasing the number of iterations, it is possible to find a solution very close to the global/true optimum solution (See the section 3.10).

objective function calculated in the above procedure is deviated 31% from the expected 'optimum value'.

The true value of the policy objective function in a decentralised market economy with indirect government control provided by model C will be between the levels of value determined by models (A) and (B). As this is the case in the present study and since the optimum of the policy objective function of AEPSOM (Model C) is deviated by 31.9 % from the Central Control Policy Model, it may be concluded that AEPSOM has produced (approximate) optimum results for the Australian energy sector.

6.5.1 Mathematical Properties of the Model Solutions

In Chap. 3 it was stated that the PPS algorithm would provide an optimum solution to an MLP, although there would be no guarantee that the solution would be a unique global optimum. It was also mentioned that any plan (solution) improvements over base or original plan can be considered acceptable. As it has been observed that AEPSOM (±T) has generated results and plans which are an improvement over the single-level model results or existing ±T case results, we may be content with the AEPSOM results (see Candler and Norton (1977) for justifications of such an argument).

In heuristic search methods like the PPS algorithm, the possibility of finding a global optimum increases if the number of searches is increased. Three units of parametric variations used in solving AEPSOM extended the search by the algorithm. More units could be tried. Since AEPSOM optimum results were found satisfactory, as discussed in the previous section, and further searches would have proved to be expensive (in terms of time and resources) without any definite possibility of obtaining better results (closer to the central control policy model results), no more searches were undertaken.

6.5.2 (B.2) Robustness of the Results

Results of the sensitivity analysis of AEPSOM (the optimum mix of ±T case) are reported in Table C.1. From Table C.1, it is revealed that the model solutions were not very sensitive to small changes such as the changes in the form of the introduction of tax on imported oil (Model No. 12), import parity pricing (Model No. 18) and in the coefficient of the policy objective function (Table 6.10 and 6.11).

6.5.3 Methodological Tests

With regard to the criteria (C.1), the relevant information about AEPSOM has been reported in Chap. 5. From the presentation of the AEPSOM set there, it can be argued that AEPSOM can easily be transferred and extended.

6.5.4 Model Execution Related Tests

The criteria (C.2) were discussed in Chap. 3. It was found that the PPS algorithm satisfied the relevant criteria.

To summarise, the tests A.3.b.i and A.3.b.ii were not considered suitable for this study[14] since such tests were not appropriate for normative models, like AEPSOM, of 'new' or significantly altered systems (Greenberger and Richels 1979, p. 486). Since these tests were not suitable for the present study, more emphasis was given to other criteria such as A.1, A.2, A.3.a. Justification for an emphasis on these tests have been stated as (Greenberger and Richels 1979, pp. 486-487) follows:

> In general, historical validation is inappropriate for models of 'new' or significantly altered systems, or for proposed major structural changes. A more suitable form of validation in these cases is face (or content) validation, where the assessors subjectively evaluate the degree to which the models elements and structure correspond to their perceptions about the actual phenomena that the model is meant to represent.

All other criteria: B.1, B.2, C.1 and C.2 were, however, applied.

6.6 Conclusion

This chapter has presented the results of AEPSOM. The major reported results include optimum values of the policy and behavioural objective functions, some elements of the

[14] Non-availability of historical data and time constraints sometimes prohibit the undertaking of any validation tests of models (for example, Jaforullah 1988).

energy policy system and energy system, taxes and subsidies, market prices, shadow prices and reduced costs.

These results have established some analytical aspects of the multi-level decision making process at the sectoral level in a market economy such as the need for the determination of the optimum level of policy intervention (±T), the possibility of the formulation of an improved plan by the government, and the conflicting interests of the government and private sector economic agents.

This chapter has also examined the credibility of the sector programming model by applying a standard set of model validation criteria. In spite of the difficulties in applying these validation tests to an applied model and although no consensus on the exact procedures for validating has yet been reached in the profession (Hazell and Norton 1986, p. 266), a wide range of tests were performed to validate AEPSOM.

7 An Australian Optimum Multi-Level Energy Plan

7.1 Introduction

Effects of the events in the international energy market have been considerable in Australia. Consequently, several energy policy problem areas have generated in the Australian economy. Some of these energy problem areas are: self-sufficiency in energy; appropriate pricing of energy; choice of a set of fiscal instruments; equitable distribution of the benefits created in the energy sector; conservation of energy; specially fossil fuels; finding measures appropriate for dealing with supply disturbances; optimum depletion of fossil fuels, and determination of the exact boundary of energy policies.

To deal with these energy policy issues, there are several options available to the government for each type of issue. This necessitates the formulation of an energy plan by the Australian Government so that the relevant issues and options are considered simultaneously and a resolution of these issues and options is possible. Formulation and implementation of such an energy plan will help solve the energy problems of Australia.

These factors had provided the motivation of this study: the formulation of a comprehensive multi-level energy plan[1] consisting of (a) an optimum energy system and (b) a set of energy policy instruments. This chapter deals with that essential task of the study, although within a framework which has the following limitations.

[1] Solution to AEPSOM has provided values of energy policy instruments as taxes and subsidies, prices, expenditure priorities for conservation, research and development, and education and information. The results also included values of the activities and reduced costs which gave the necessary information to formulate energy depletion, exploration and development, and technology policies. In this chapter, the policy implications of the AEPSOM results will be studied to suggest a multi-level energy plan for Australia. Various energy policy problem areas will be discussed separately. Issues and options in each problem area will be high lighted and how AEPSOM results can resolve those issues will be discussed.

The structure of this chapter is as follows. The optimum Australian energy system specified by the AEPSOM results is reported and discussed in Section 7.2. Section 7.3 presents the integration of the various types of policies needed to formulate a comprehensive set of policies for the energy sector. An integrated comprehensive set of Australian energy policies is formulated in Section 7.4, while the conclusions are stated in Section 7.5.

7.2 An Optimum Energy System Plan

Different model solutions provided various numerical optimum energy systems for Australia. Numerical values of the flows of primary energy, secondary energy and end-uses of energy as well as various technologies, which are the components of the optimum energy systems, were shown in Table 6.8. The major characteristics of the technological pattern of AES implied by the AEPSOM results are discussed below. Intuitive justifications of these results were discussed in Section 6.5.

On the energy supply side, imported crude oil (Ie_1) appears more attractive than domestic crude oil (R_2). Solar energy (R_7) was not found viable in 1979-80 although it appears viable in 1989-90.

In the area of energy conversion technologies, natural gas (x_3) for end-uses was not found viable in Model Solutions 5 and 6 although its use for electricity production (E_1) was justified. Natural gas appears in Model No. 13. For 1989-90, natural gas (x_3) use increased substantially to an amount of PJ 933.48 - which is much higher than the actual (PJ 437.0) for 1989-90.

The following end-uses were not chosen by AEPSOM Solution 5 for 1979-80: petroleum products (d_2) and natural gas (d_3) in the manufacturing industry sector, electricity (d_9) in the transport sector, and petroleum products (d_{11}), natural gas (d_{12}), biomass and solar energy (d_{13}) in the domestic and commercial sector. Results are the same in Model No. 6 while in Model No. 13 natural gas use in the manufacturing industry sector appears viable.

For 1989-90, the situation changes substantially. Some of the technologies which were not viable in the 1979-80 model solutions appear viable in the 1989-90 models, while some other 1979-80 viable technologies were not found viable in the 1989-90 models. For example, solar energy was not viable in 1979-80, however it was viable in 1989-90. In 1989-90, relatively, more use of natural gas was suggested by the Model unlike for 1979-80 when more coal use was evident. Biomass was not in the 1979-80 model solution, while it appeared in the 1989-90 solution.

Different combinations of end-uses of energy have been selected by different models depending on the assumptions made about the policy interventions, costs, technological and resources conditions and availability, time horizon etc. Table 6.8.A and 6.8.B for the years 1979-80 and 1989-90 reveal that the following end-uses were not selected by any of the five models:

(1) petroleum products in the manufacturing industry sector;

(2) electricity in the transport sector; and

(3) petroleum products in the 'domestic and other sectors'.

For the intuitive justifications of these end-use results of AEPSOM the following points may be noted (other points were discussed in Chap. 6):

(1) Regarding end-uses in the manufacturing sector, as progressive reduction of the use of oil has been a major objective of Australian energy policy, substitution of petroleum products in different sectors by alternative fuels is a desirable policy outcome. These findings have also been established by the MARKAL model (Musgrove et al. 1983, pp. 82-83). A cost saving of $3.49 M/PJ through any improvement in technical efficiency can make the use of petroleum in the manufacturing sector viable. The major competing fuels in the manufacturing sector will be different forms of coal (fluidised bed and conventional boilers), natural gas (conventional boiler) and wood and bagasse (boiler).

(2) Electricity use in the transport sector has not been chosen by AEPSOM. One possible justification is that the relative technical convenience and economy of alternative fuels such

as methanol and coal (Musgrove et al. 1983, pp. 82-83) have made electricity use in the transport sector a non-viable technology.

This result is consistent with MARKAL (Musgrove et al. 1983, pp. 82 -83) forecasts for electricity use in the transport sector. The following transport sector's electricity uses (in petajoules) were predicted by MARKAL: 2.6 in 1980, and 3.5 in 1990. These figures were quite insignificant compared to the total energy-uses in the transport sector which were (in petajoules) 799.1 in 1980 and 894.4 in 1990. If the transport sector was disaggregated in different transport modes (such as road, rail, etc.) in AEPSOM, then the model would probably have selected some use of electricity (for further discussion on the aggregation issue in this study, see Section A.3. in Appendix A).

Technical improvements in the transport sector, specially in rail transports, which can reduce cost $48.53 M/PJ (Table 6.9.A) will make the use of electricity in the transport sector viable.

(3) MARKAL predicted an oil-use of 55.5 (PJ) in the domestic and commercial sector in 1980, while this figure was predicted by MARKAL to be reduced to only 8.00 (PJ) in 1990.

7.3 Optimum Energy Policies[2]

Although the implications of all the reported model solutions were considered while formulating the set of policies, the results of Model No. 5 were mainly adopted and analysed for the following policy studies.

7.3.1 Taxes and Subsidies

In a market economy like that of Australia the major forms of government instruments to control the energy sector are the fiscal instruments (taxes and subsidies). Per unit taxes and subsidies may be imposed to correct market failures due to external effects in production,

[2] This section demonstrates the policy steering aspect of AEPSOM.

conversion and end-uses and the presence of monopoly, so that the economic agents observe the desired marginal conditions for the efficient allocation of resources. Lump sum taxes and subsidies are effective in bringing about a desired income distribution (Musgrave 1959; Henderson and Quandt 1980).

The specific objectives for which taxes and subsidies have been applied in the Australian energy sector are: conservation of energy; promotion of exploration; optimum depletion of energy; inter-fuel substitution and equity in income (Smith 1979; Groenewegen 1984).

Various forms of taxes which are generally used are *ad valorem* taxes, severance taxes, property taxes, company resource rent tax and capital gain tax (Webb and Ricketts 1980). In Australia, a combination of these taxes in various degrees is in existence.

Several forms of subsidies either to the producers or to the consumers are also in existence: considering capital cost as a current cost for tax purposes; accelerated depreciation allowance; depletion allowance; exploration expenditure allowance, and *ad valorem* sales subsidy (Webb and Ricketts 1980; Groenewegen 1984).

The issues that have been discussed to formulate an efficient set of fiscal instruments in the Australian energy sector (Smith 1979; Lloyd 1984; Branon 1975; Gruen and Hillman 1981) are (A) the determination of the appropriate mix and rates of different taxes and subsidies, and (B) the suitability of the resource rent tax (defined below). The last issue has received serious academic and government considerations (Groenewegen 1984) for several reasons: the need for the diffusion of windfall gains from energy explorations over the whole community; existence of several types of taxes and charges imposed by both Commonwealth and State Governments creating fiscal system management problems; and probably, over-taxation of mining energy. While the first issue is still being discussed, the government introduced resource rent tax, first by introducing it only to the off-shore oil industry in 1983, then progressively to the whole oil industry. Implications of the AEPSOM results in the context of these issues are discussed below.

(1) Regarding the first issue, AEPSOM results can be used to address adequately the issue. The optimum mix of taxes and subsidies[3] suggested by AEPSOM[4] is reported in Table 6.5.A. Table 6.5.B shows a comparison of the existing taxes and subsidies and the optimum mix of taxes and subsidies.

The supply side intervention by taxation is usually used as an instrument to change market prices so that they reflect the opportunity costs of various energy forms (for example, by internalising external costs), and to bring about an efficient allocation of primary energy resources, and optimum intertemporal allocations of energy resources (optimum depletion of exhaustible resources) and encouragement for exploration activities. As noted before AEPSOM results have suggested the following supply side taxes and subsidies: taxes on domestic crude oil; imported crude oil; and subsidy on solar energy.

Demand side taxes (excise taxes) and subsidies are justified because of the existence of merit want market failures (Musgrave 1959). This type of market failure is caused by the 'irrational' or short sighted preference of consumers. In the energy market, merit want appears since it is argued that consumers are variational because they waste this scarce resource. Also, in the situation that a possibility of a trade embargo exists, excise taxes on various forms of energy, which are subject to a potential trade embargo, can accommodate contingencies of such an embargo in the consumers' behaviour. Moreover, excise taxes on energy end-uses may cause inter-fuel substitution, and thus may help the development of cheap new and renewable energy.

AEPSOM results have suggested the following excise taxes or subsidies: taxes on coal and electricity in the manufacturing industry sector; on electricity in the transport sector; on coal in the domestic and commercial sector; and subsidies on none.

---

[3] It should be mentioned that the choice of ±T in this study has been determined by the criteria of attainment of the energy policy objectives and efficient allocation of (minimum cost) energy resources. Other criteria for determining a good tax system were not applied. Such criteria include equity in the distribution of income and tax burden, suitability for achieving economic stabilisation objectives, easy administrability and understandability, imposition of minimum excess burden (Musgrave and Musgrave 1984, p. 225).

[4] The plausibility of the suggested taxes and subsidies in the context of energy policy objective will be discussed in Section 7.4.

In addition, the model results have implied the following taxes or subsidies on energy conversion technologies: taxes on coal-burnt electricity, petroleum products and natural gas; subsidies on petroleum products and natural gas-burnt electricity,[5] and coal (distribution).

(2) An important issue in energy economics is the determination of an appropriate taxation scheme for taxing economic rent (resource rent) generated in the energy sector because of the limited supplies of fossil fuels (excluding normal profit).

There are several alternative measures for taxing economic rent in the energy sector, such as company income taxes, competitive bidding and royalties, and progressive resource rent tax. Every taxing scheme has its merits and demerits and in many cases a combination of schemes is suggested for taxing economic rent (Webb and Ricketts 1980; Marks 1986).

However, resource rent tax (Smith 1979) has often been advocated because of its neutral effect on supply decisions and its effects on equity. The possible problems of the determination of the exact economic rent or surplus, and the adverse effects of the resource rent tax on exploration activities, have limited its application.

AEPSOM results have indicated taxes on various energy supplies, without any indication of what type of tax would be appropriate in these cases. The issue remains what would be the appropriate form of tax in these cases.

Since the selection of the right type of taxation to extract economic rent from producers depends on many economic and non-economic considerations, a combination of several taxes, probably of severance taxes (specific or ad valorem), royalties and resource rent tax, that would move the post-tax energy prices to the levels demonstrated in Table 6.6.A is suggested.

[5] In 1989-90, a subsidy on electricity production from petroleum is suggested by the model. This result is the outcome of the existence of many factors in the energy sector (Chap. 5). To meet the demand for electricity there was a need for more electricity production from oil compared to 1979-80 production, since the uses of coal in the manufacturing and domestic sectors were comparatively more attractive than the use of coal in electricity production (Table 6.6.A and 6.6.B). The supply of the increased electricity in the market would have been possible only through a subsidisation of petroleum in electricity production. However, model results suggest that the amount of subsidy to petroleum in electricity production is smaller than the government revenue from the possible tax (suggested by the model) on the use of coal in the domestic sector, a technological alternative which required the subsidisation of electricity from oil.

7.3.2 Pricing Policy

Price is used here as the quantity of money to be paid for exchanging one unit (PJ) of energy.[6]

Determination of energy prices has been a crucial issue in energy policy analysis because of the influence of prices in efficient allocation of energy resources, public ownership of many energy industries, and the effect of prices on the depletion rate of exhaustible energy resources.

A general rule which is followed in the determination of the price of a particular good is that the price will cover (or will be based on) cost. But controversies exist regarding the concept of cost that should be used for pricing purposes. The two concepts of cost are: opportunity cost (opportunities or alternatives forgone in order to achieve something) and outlays (total money expenditure).

An example for determining energy prices in Australia on the basis of opportunity cost is the import parity pricing of domestic crude oil (i.e. setting the price of domestic oil equal to its next alternative - the price of imported oil). Arguments for determining the energy price equal to its international price (import price or export price) follow from the economic principle that efficiency in domestic production will be achieved when marginal cost of domestic production equals its international price (Little and Mirrlees 1974). In spite of doubt about the rationale of this principle on the ground that the economic structure of a foreign country is different from the domestic country (which implies different relative price structures in the two countries), setting the price to its international price has been advocated in Australia not only for oil, but also for other forms of energy including coal, natural gas, and even electricity (Saddler 1981; Treasury 1984).

---

[6] There are, however, other connotations of price such as an accounting unit and a measure of absolute value (Blaug 1985). Price has been interpreted here as relative price, and therefore, other issues related to the definition and function of price have not been considered in formulating pricing policies.

Pricing of energy on the basis of outlays has two main principles: average cost pricing and marginal cost pricing. In the average cost pricing method, which is primarily an accounting method, the price is set equal to the average cost of production.

The marginal cost pricing method, although the most powerful method and increasingly being practiced, yet the most often criticised, can be formalised by adopting the following welfare maximising model:

$$\text{Max} \int_0^T NB \,.\, \exp(-rt) \,.\, dt$$

s.t. (6.1)

$$K(t) \geq q(t) \geq 0$$

$$I(t) \geq i\,(t) \geq 0$$

and $i(t) = K\,(t) + \delta K(t)$

where

$$NB = \int_0^q p(q,t) \,.\, dq - c(q,k,t) - i(t)$$

T = time

p = consumers' willingness to pay for energy

q = energy output

c = production cost

K = capacity level

r = discount rate

i = investment rate

I = rate of capital depreciation

By applying Pontryagin's maximum principle, the following optimum price can be determined (see Munasinghe and Schramm 1983, pp. 142-143, for its derivation):

$\tilde{\tilde{P}}(t) = (\delta c/\delta q) - m_1 + m_2$

where m_1 and m_2 are the new capacity and resources supply costs.

It is argued that marginal cost pricing can yield a welfare optimum since under this rule net social surplus will be maximised. Of course, this argument is valid in a perfectly competitive market situation and in the absence of significant externalities (economies or diseconomies).

The arguments against marginal cost pricing are also very powerful. The arguments are as follows:

(1) In the case of increasing returns to scale, marginal cost pricing will result in loss to the firm or industry.

(2) The marginal cost has no unique definition (Lewis 1949) since marginal cost will depend on the level of output. Therefore it cannot be used as a basis for pricing.

(3) Administration of marginal cost pricing rule is comparatively difficult (compared to accounting cost method).

(4) There may be multiple energy pricing policy objectives such as equity (interpersonal and interregional), and industrial development, in addition to the objective of efficient allocation of energy resources. In that case, marginal cost pricing will not be appropriate.

(5) If the marginal cost pricing principle is not met in all industries, practicing this rule in an industry may result in welfare loss rather than welfare gain (the second best theory,[7] Lipsey and Lancaster 1956-57).

Inspite of the above objections, the marginal cost pricing principle has gained wide acceptance. However, a compromised principle is practiced in real life, which may be stated as follows:

(a) Set price equal to marginal cost; and

---

[7] In spite of this objection from the theory of second best this study has adopted a partial equilibrium analysis of the energy sector for the reasons discussed in Chap. 2. Consequently, the principle of marginal cost pricing will be used for formulating energy pricing policy.

(b) Make adjustment for equity, industrial development and other social-political considerations.

In Australia, the Commonwealth Government controls oil price. Electricity prices in the states are set by the State Governments while prices of natural gas, and coal are determined by the providing industries. Several issues have dominated this area: whether the government should control energy prices in Australia or not; if government control is permitted, what are the prices which should be controlled by the government; and what principles would be followed in determining energy prices.

Several justifications have been put forward for government control of energy prices, particularly of oil prices, such as: prices can be used to take advantage of any monopoly position in the world energy market; prices should be fixed so that they will earn revenue for the government; and the users will pay for the infrastructure development and ensure self-sufficiency in energy, specially in oil (Edwards 1983; Marks 1986).

While the marginal cost principle is adopted in determining electricity prices by the state governments, setting energy prices (oil, natural gas, electricity, coal) at their world levels has been advocated (Treasury 1984) and implemented (see Marks 1986). Pricing on the basis of the shadow prices of an energy sector programming model has also been advocated and illustrated (Musgrove et al. 1983). Therefore, different approaches to energy pricing are adopted for pricing different types of energy in Australia.[8]

The guidelines AEPSOM results provide in resolving the above three energy pricing issues are discussed below.

(1) The present study has demonstrated the desirability of government intervention in the energy sector to achieve the energy policy objectives. These interventions include the imposition of taxes and subsidies implying the indirect control of energy prices.

(2) Taxes and subsidies influence prices, the energy prices government influence are shown in Table 6.6. The model results suggest that, at the supply level, the prices of crude oil and

[8] The same practice will be followed in this study.

imported oil, at the secondary energy level, those of coal burnt electricity, petroleum products, and natural gas, and at the end-use level, those of coal and electricity in the manufacturing sector, electricity in the transport sector, coal in the domestic and commercial sector, should increase in the market. The model results also suggest that the prices of solar energy, natural gas burnt electricity, coal, and electricity from petroleum products should decrease.

(3) Following the dominating view that the energy price should reflect the opportunity cost to ensure efficient allocation of energy resources in an economy, it can be argued that prices of domestic energy, specially the energy forms which are traded, should be equal to their international prices. This suggests that the energy prices should be controlled or influenced by the government to move these prices to their international levels, in the case that domestic market prices are different from the international prices - either by direct price control or by imposing taxes or subsidies.

The model results, however, support indirect control of energy prices through taxes and subsidies (deregulation of prices) rather than direct control of them. This is preferred, even above the administration of import parity pricing of crude oil by the government. This is evident from the Sensitivity Study 5, which demonstrated that the introduction of import parity price in the model did not improve the value of the policy objective function, instead it diminished that level. But, if energy price is deregulated there may be a reduction in government revenue (Marks 1986) and it would be difficult to ensure that resource rents accrue to Australians which is an important motivation for price control in Australia, as the government may have to resort to some type of crude oil levy. What is needed is a policy package which would result in deregulation and at the same time ensure accruing resource rents to Australians.

It is important to note that the optimum market price for domestic crude oil (1979-80), suggested by the model, is \$5.23 M/PJ which is close to its import parity price of \$5.30 M/PJ. These results suggest that the energy policy objectives including efficiency in the energy resource allocation in Australia can be achieved by choosing an appropriate or politically acceptable form of energy taxation (alternatives are discussed above). This also implies that the administration of an import parity pricing policy by the government may not be necessary. A relevant tax can be imposed on the domestic crude oil and the market be left to adjust its price to somewhere close or equal to its import parity price.

The outcomes of this strategy would be the determination of the price of domestic crude oil equal or close to its import parity price (through the market by imposing tax without direct control by the government), and the guarantee that all resources rents accrue to Australians. This strategy has the advantage that this would help achieve the objectives of price control such as the earning of government revenue etc. mentioned above, in addition to the equity effects of such a policy.

The possible justification for this approach to oil pricing may be derived from the arguments that when there is the possibility of an oil embargo or supply uncertainty, this external cost is not internalised in the discretionary behaviour of economic agents. In the situation of such a trade embargo, there will be costs contingent in the supplies of energy. The policy implication of this situation has been stated by Gruen and Hillman (1981, p. 114) to be:

> As the adjustment costs are associated with the need to change the composition of domestic output, the theory of optimal policy indicates the form of intervention should aim directly at the product, that is, a producer tax or subsidy.

Also as one of the energy policy objectives in Australia has been the reduction of the use of oil (due to any anticipated trade embargo), raising the price of domestic crude oil somewhere close to its international level through intervention in the product market by taxation can be the optimal policy for Australia.

For similar reasons (i.e. in the context of energy problems and energy policy objectives) electricity prices in 1979-80 suggested by the model solution ($6.00 M/PJ) can be considered optimum prices for electricity.

7.3.3 Depletion Policy

Depletion policy relates to the issue of optimum resource use over time (the rate at which resources should be depleted). This is a problem of intertemporal allocation of exhaustible resources.

This policy issue is very important in view of the finite stock of exhaustible energy resources and because of the fact that any use today will leave less for future generations (the question of equity in intergenerational distribution of natural resources).

In Australia, this issue of optimum depletion policy has been discussed (Saddler 1981; Gruen and Hillman 1981). However, no definite optimum depletion rate has been prescribed, neither has the present depletion rate(s) been evaluated.

Desirability of a depletion policy in the Australian context has been discussed by referring to the existing market form in the energy supply sector (Gruen and Hillman 1981) i.e. by relating to the question whether the Australian energy suppliers are competitive or monopolistic. The argument is that if the energy supply market is monopolistic, then government policy is desirable, since a monopolistic market does not deplete resources at a social optimum rate. It may, of course, be necessary to mention that such a straight forward generalisation of monopolistic elements in the market and depletion policy intervention is not possible, since competitive and monopolistic firms appear to be over conservationist or under conservationist depletors, depending on demand, price, and supply related conditions (Howe 1979).

The AEPSOM does not directly address the issue of optimum depletion rate, but the result of the model can be used to provide some guidelines for an energy depletion policy in Australia. A comparison of the required energy supplies in 1979-80 and 1989-90 suggested by the model can be an indication of the rate of depletion of various types of energy.

If the 1979-80 actual supplies of coal, crude oil and natural gas are compared with their optimum values chosen by Model Solution 13 (in this case there was the possibility of flexibility in the supply of these energy forms), then it appears that the optimum result suggests more supplies (depletion) of coal and natural gas and less supplies of crude oil than their actual uses in 1979-80. These results are consistent with the reserve position of these fossil fuels in Australia.

7.3.4 Exploration Policy

Exploration plays a significant role in the allocation of exhaustible resources over time. A finite stock of resources can be extended by supplementing the stock through exploration activities.

AEPSOM structure implies that if the resource supply constraints in AEPSOM are binding, that will be an indication for positive shadow prices. And if these supply constraints are relaxed, it would result in reduced energy system cost. Numerically the Model Solution 13 where the supply constraints are relaxed by 20%, has provided the minimum value of the policy objective function from all the solutions (Table 6.1). The results show the importance of an increased energy supply in the Australian energy system. Increased energy supply on a sustained basis is possible through further exploration activities.

To accelerate exploration activities, a government can follow several strategies:

(1) Subsidise exploration activities by accelerated tax allowances for exploration expenditure, immediate or accelerated exploration expenditure write off etc.; and

(2) Direct involvement in exploration, possibly through an exploration company. Because of moral issues related to providing subsidies to the private sector companies and because of the common property nature of exploration activities, sometimes government participation in the exploration activities is suggested (Saddler 1981). However, as such a policy is not consistent with the political strategies of current governments in power, the policy can not be implemented.

Therefore, the encouragement of exploration activities of the private sector through various fiscal, pricing and legislative measures is recommended.

7.3.5 Conservation Policy

The objective of energy conservation has been a focal point of discussion in recent political economics (Eichner 1979). Despite the political economic implications, energy conservation has some technical dimensions.

A whole range of energy conservation instruments can be adopted to achieve the conservation objective of energy policies. The strategy of conservation programmes is to choose a level of consumption of energy and energy mixes to maximise social welfare by eliminating waste and low welfare uses.

The pricing methods are adopted to influence the consumers' and producers' decisions to allocate funds for the energy budget. The pricing methods include price fixation and control, and taxes on fuels (Btu taxes) and energy-using equipment.

The non-price methods of conservation include direct quantity rationing, instituting fuel efficiency standards such as setting minimum mileage standards for new vehicles and standards for residential insulation and energy-use efficiency, expenditure for research and development, and education and information.

In Australia, an active energy conservation programme has been pursued since the beginning of energy policy initiatives. However, due considerations have not been given to the social desirability and welfare implications of these programmes (ESCAP 1979; Department of National Development 1979; Endersbee et al. 1980; Department of Primary Industries and Energy 1988).

The Australian government has adopted the following policies to ensure energy conservation: (1) control or influence energy prices to reflect their long run costs; (2) taxes and subsidies to increase efficient and non-oil energy use; (3) increase energy use efficiency in the industry, commerce and transport sectors by improved 'housekeeping', modifications to existing operations and improved maintenance of existing energy systems, and by research and development, demonstration, advisory and legislative measures for an increasing introduction of new efficient technologies.

In this study, the proportions of shadow prices in Table 6.7.B indicate the transport sector to be the major area for conservation, followed by electricity demands in different sectors. This result is consistent with the situation in the energy sector in Australia where the transport sector is the major user of liquid fuel which is the scarcest energy resource in the economy.

This emphasis in the area of conservation indicated by shadow prices is also supported by the other AEPSOM results: pricing or taxes and subsidies. The model results (Table 6.5.B) have suggested tax on the petroleum product use in the transport sector (tax on d_8). This is consistent with the present energy pricing policy, as stated above, in which energy price influence through taxes or subsidies is suggested to reduce oil use.

Therefore, it can be argued that the conservation of oil in the transport sector by an excise tax (which will internalise the adjustment cost of oil disruption) and other technological changes and improvements (such as the use of methanol, suggested by the model) is clearly the priority area in energy conservation in Australia. Since other shadow prices were not zero, the model results also suggested conservation programmes in other sectors of the economy. Endersbee et al. (1980) has identified the major conservation measures and technologies in all sectors of the Australian economy. Measures suggested in Endersbee et al. (1980) can be adopted in Australia.

Historically, conservation programmes in Australia have passed through various phases with initial emphasis on public awareness, subsequently by awareness of the industrial and commercial users, and the transport sector (Marks 1986). The Government has realised that the conservation in the transport sector is a vital area for conservation of energy in Australia. This is also a policy strategy suggested by AEPSOM.

7.3.6 Education and Information Policy

In spite of the controversy on the effectiveness of public policies in the form of education and information in energy management, historical experiences show that these policies can be quite effective. In many national emergencies, such as war, public policies in the form of education and information may be more effective than economic policies such as taxes, subsidies, control of money supply, etc. (Griffin and Steele 1980).

In the energy sector, these policies are considered to be effective because of :

(1) The popular appeals of energy problems; and

(2) Ignorance on the part of the general public about the role they can play in solving the energy problem through better management of energy.

Education and information policies are designed to increase community-wide understanding of the energy problem so that the general public will adopt methods for better management of the energy supply, its production and its end-uses and thus conserve energy.

In Australia, an emphasis has been given to education and information policy. Programmes have been undertaken in the form of publicity campaigns, conferences, posters, etc.

AEPSOM priorities for education and information policies are indicated by the proportions of shadow prices in Table 6.7. For the obvious reason of liquid fuel security in the Australian context, the community should be made aware of this problem, specially about the possibility and methods for conservation of liquid fuel in the different sectors of the economy. This emphasis is reflected by the highest proportion of shadow prices related to the energy demand constraints in Table 6.7.A. AEPSOM results also suggest education and information priorities in the conversion technology area (the second highest proportion of shadow prices for the intermediate balance constraint).

This highest priority for education and information activities for energy conservation is consistent with the Australian energy policies. The relative priorities in education and information policies as suggested by the AEPSOM results should also be incorporated in Australian energy policies.

7.3.7 Research and Development Policy

Both basic research (without commercial objective) and applied research and development (turning research into a practical output or process) are vital to modern industrial development because of their effects on innovation, an engine of industrial development (Schumpeter 1934).

The question has frequently been debated: why should the government undertake research and development work? Since research and development work has substantial externalities i.e. one firm's findings will benefit other firms and the social rate of return for research and development is higher than its rate of return in the private sector, government undertaking of research and development is considered to be justified.

Research and development in the energy sector have been geared in the past towards an increasing energy supply and inter-fuel competitiveness through reduction in the cost of production of energy. However, a recent shift in the emphasis is noticeable with more concentration of efforts in the areas of energy conservation and increasing efficiency of new energy sources to substitute fossil fuel. In other words, the energy research and development programme is being designed to increase energy production (by finding more energy deposits and extracting existing reserves more efficiently), increase efficiency in the energy supply, its conversion and its end-uses and reduce energy use in the economy.

In Australia, there has been doubt whether Australia will pursue an energy research and development programme, substantial in size, on its own, or buy the results from other developed countries like the U.S.A., Japan and the U.K. However, the Australian governments had an active research and development programme to develop expertise in the important technologies, and to stimulate research in the technologies appropriate for Australia in terms of its resource base and export prospects. The government's research and development programme also emphasises the involvement in international research programmes and the study of the social, legal, and institutional aspects of energy sector programmes to find the appropriate strategies to develop the energy sector (Department of National Development 1979).

AEPSOM results suggest that priority for research and development for energy conservation technologies and strategies, in comparison with other areas such as supply expansion and conversion technologies, is desirable (highest shadow price proportion for the energy demand constraints in Table 6.7.A). The base model solutions and sensitivity studies indicate this emphasis in policy. These results are also consistent with existing policy strategies in Australia.

It has been mentioned above that although higher emphasis in the research and development policy was generally given in the past to energy conversion technologies such as the technologies for synthetic oil production, a shift in emphasis towards energy conservation as suggested by AEPSOM results is desirable. This is also officially being recognised. This will be evident from the shift in the government research and development policy emphasis towards conservation (Department of Resources and Energy 1985, Chap. 11). However, AEPSOM results also imply higher priorities for research and development in conversion technologies (the second highest proportion of shadow prices for the intermediate balance equations).

Research and development in the conservation area may be aimed at:

(1) Finding new technologies;[9] and

(2) Institutional development for education and information to popularise conservation programmes.

In the energy conversion area, research and development activities will be directed towards development of fuel-efficient and economic conversion technologies using less and less liquid fuels.

---

[9] Some of the areas where research and development activities can be undertaken are: increasing efficiency of single energy processes, promotion of co-generation of electricity and heat, possibility for improvement in energy husbandry, introduction of increased industrial energy recovery, etc. (Endesbee et al. 1980; Harder 1982).

7.3.8 Energy Technology Policy

A choice of an appropriate energy technology policy has several dimensions:

(1) determination of appropriate factor proportions in the energy supply, production and end-use techniques (Sen 1968);

(2) determination of the appropriate size and nature of forms of industry (centralised or decentralised/soft nature of the energy system) (Meadows, Meadows, Randers and Behrens III 1972); and

(3) selection of an efficient energy system i.e. choice of a mix of appropriate energy forms, processes or techniques (Griffin and Steele 1980) that can supply the energy required in the economy at minimum cost.

Resolution of these issues for the formulation of an appropriate energy technology policy is important. The approach adopted here to determine an optimum technology in the energy sector is that the market should determine such a system, which is subject to government interventions.

Resolution of these issues needs deliberate government policy formulation, mainly to provide information to the private sector. The purpose of providing information about energy technologies to the private sector is to influence expectations in the energy market to achieve the socially desired allocation of resources (static and intertemporal). This is so because the future energy market does not exist and the choice of appropriate energy technology policy involves the determination of adoption of some forms of energy technology which are not in the present market.

For the future sustainable energy system, the International Institute for Applied System Analysis has predicted a gradual transitionary process through various stages (Häfele 1981). First stage: from now up to 2030 - a transition from the present carbon-based energy system to a different carbon based energy system characterised by a short supply of fossil fuels but a gradual market penetration of coal gasification and liquefaction technologies and a considerable build-up of nuclear and solar power. Second stage: after 2030 - in this stage hydrogen will become the dominant energy form which will result in what is called the hydrogen economy.

Although the future is not well known, it is for sure that the energy system is in transition. The whole inventory of new and renewable energy technologies is being considered for adoption in the near future. Some of these technologies are the following: liquid and gaseous fuel conversion from coal and oil shale, nuclear energy (burner, breeder and fusion reactors), solar energy (direct use, solar cells and solar panel), wind energy, ocean energy (tidal and wave), biogas, geothermal energy, combined cycles in electric power generation (magnetohydrodynamics, thermionics and potassium turbines), and hydrogen.

In Australia, public policy has clearly recognised the fact that new and renewable technologies will be making an increasing contribution to the Australian energy sector. The government, in association with the private sector, is providing funds for research and development, and for demonstration of new and renewable energy. Relative emphasis has been given to, and optimism has been expressed about, the potential market penetration of solar energy and liquefaction and gasification of coal in the near future.

In the previous chapter, the optimum technological pattern in the Australian energy sector as reflected by the optimum selection of activities, was shown in Table 6.8. Some of the energy technology policies implied by the optimum energy system determined by AEPSOM are as follows.

(1) Increased market penetration of some renewable energy (solar energy, methanol and biomass) over time is desirable. AEPSOM results clearly support the Australian energy technological strategy of increased market penetration of new and renewable energy (such as solar, biomass and methanol). Although the synthetic fuel production is not suggested as viable, the policy implication of this result would be to direct more research and development in this area to reduce cost and develop more efficient techniques. The reduced cost (Table 6.9.B) of the activity representing synthetic oil production from coal indicates the magnitude

of cost saving necessary for penetration of the market by this technology ($11 to $13 M/PJ). Actions should be pursued to achieve this cost saving.

(2) Regarding the issue of self-sufficiency in oil today or tomorrow by suggesting a gradual adjustment in the system through inter-fuel substitution, conservation etc. is required. This will help AES for smooth transition to the post-oil era.

(3) Progressively more uses of natural gas and coal, specially in the manufacturing industry, and domestic and commercial sectors, in comparison with the use of other conventional energy are necessary.

(4) Eventual complete import independence is possible and, therefore, should be identified as a target of energy policies.

(5) Gradual reduction in the use of petroleum products, specially in the manufacturing industry sector is needed.

(6) As the production of synthetic oil from coal was not found viable, efforts should be directed to reduce the cost of this process so that the technology penetrates the market. Some strategies for cost saving would be to consider all the alternative coal liquefaction processes such as Fischer-Tropsch, SRC2, Flash Pyrolysis, Exon Donor Solvent (Musgrove et al. 1983). A reduction in coal price may also foster market viability of local liquefaction technologies.

A comparison of the prices/costs (Table 6.6.A) of the fuels and technologies suggested by the model results will reveal that the model selection of fuels and technologies has been based on their relative prices (other factors were stated in Section 6.1). The selection of the technological policy implication No. (1) above has been influenced in the model solution by the fact that prices of solar energy ($0.04 M/PJ) and biomass ($1.18 M/PJ) at the supply level are lower than other marginally competing energy forms such as domestic crude oil ($5.24 M/PJ) and hydro-electricity ($19.27 M/PJ). The policy suggestion No. (3) has been influenced by the fact that coal and natural gas are cheaper than petroleum products and electricity in the two sectors mentioned above. For justifying the policy strategy No. (5), it can be mentioned that petroleum products are certainly more expensive in the manufacturing industry, agricultural, domestic and commercial sectors compared to other fuels used in these sectors. Regarding policy suggestion No. (6), it can be argued that coal conversion technologies are still expensive. The assumed cost for the conversion of coal to oil (see Table A.3) is \$15.67 M/PJ. If the costs at the end-users' level are considered, this technology would appear to be more expensive compared to other alternatives.

The energy sector, being a dynamic and innovative sector in the economy, has experienced technological changes involving inter-fuel substitution, conservation and development of new and renewable energy technologies during the modelling period. The 1989-90 actual energy figures imply the following changes/developments (Jones et al. 1991), among others, to the 1979-80 AES: increased use of solar energy and biomass, increased use of natural gas, reduced use of petroleum products in the manufacturing industry sector, and almost the same level of oil import. A similar technological pattern has also been implied by the AEPSOM results (discussed above). The 1989-90 actual energy supply, production and end-uses figures shown in Table 6.8.B are, therefore, consistent with the technological pattern suggested by AEPSOM.

7.3.9 Sustainable Development of the Australian Energy Sector

Sustainable development has been defined as development that satisfies the needs of current and future generations (Dovers 1994, p.172). A mathematical statement of sustainable development of a sector involves finding the solution to the optimisation problem (Barbier 1989)

$$\text{Max} \int_{t=0}^{\infty} e^{-\rho t}\, U(C,X)\, dt$$

subject to $X = a\,[\,Q(X) - N(C)]$, $X(0) = X$, $X(\infty)$ free.

Sustainability of the system requires that the dynamic economy/sector ensures W = A and (R + E) = G so that the economy produces zero environmental degradation and loss in productive capacity in the economy. (Definitions of the symbols are: X = level of environmental quality, C = Consumption W = waste emitted from the economy, A= waste assimilated in the economy, R = flow of renewable resources, G = biological productivity of these resources, E = flow of exhaustible resource and a = environmental quality coefficient).

The sustainable development of the energy sector requires the determination of the magnitudes of the two effects in relation to the overall industrialisation process through the facilitation of appropriate substitution among capital, labour and non-renewable energy supplies. The other factor to consider is the scope for substitution between renewable and non-renewable energy supplies. The use of renewable energy supplies can alleviate the problem associated with finite supplies of non-renewable energy sources, and that they also produce less environmental pollutants (Dovers 1994). However, as this is not generally true for all renewable energy sources, and the scope for this substitution is limited, the issue of energy conservation arises.

Therefore, the two conditions required for a sustainable energy sectoral development are (Dovers 1994, pp.45-46) '*energy conservation* - the reduction of the amount of energy required to produce required goods and services', and '*new or alternative sources of energy* - that avoid or minimise the problems associated with the present fossil-fuel-based system'.

The energy system suggested by AEPSOM, as discussed above, is consistent with the two conditions of sustainable development. The AEPSOM results suggest energy conservation and the development of renewable energy which implies the same policies as ecologically sustainable development and consistent with the requirements for greenhouse warming reductions. In other words, if these energy policies are implemented they will consequently produce changes which are ecologically sustainable (generate less greenhouse gases) (see Islam 1996, No. 10). No extra costs to the economy may not be necessary to incur for the goal of lowering green house gas emissions if energy conservation and substitution policies are pursued.

7.4 An Energy Policy Plan for Australia

The discussion of the results in Chap. 6 regarding each energy policy separately has prepared the background for presenting a comprehensive set of integrated energy policies. In this Section such a set of energy policies for Australia will be prescribed. The details of each policy type are also reported in Islam (1994) and in his several papers (see Islam's publications in Reference)

7.4.1 Australian Energy Policy Objectives

In spite of recent formalisation of Australian energy policy activities, the objectives of Australian energy policies have taken a distinct shape. The energy policy objectives which are commonly found in most of the official government documents and academic work and the ones which were stated in Chap. 5 are as follows: security of energy supply/import independence, conservation of energy, specially oil, efficient allocation of energy resources and equity in income, and uses of resources in the energy sector.

7.4.2 A Set of Optimum Energy Policy Instruments and Strategies

Debate on the determination of a set of energy policies is getting serious, and the need for resolving the controversial issues in the Australian energy sector is becoming increasingly pressing. The following section summarises the energy policy implications of the AEPSOM by providing some empirical evidence in resolving the existing controversies in the energy sector, an area characterised by the existence of conflicts and non-compatabilities in issues and options.

(1) Pricing Policy: AEPSOM results have clearly demonstrated the need for changes in the relative price structure in the energy sector, although the model suggests deregulation of the energy market.

(2) Taxes and Subsidies: AEPSOM results also indicated the need for rearrangement of fiscal instruments in the energy sector. Taxation of 4.63% of cost of domestic crude oil is possible

by pursuing a package of fiscal instruments consisting of resource rent tax, royalties and competitive bidding. Import duty on imported crude is necessary. Some other excise taxes and subsidies will complete the energy sector fiscal instruments.

(3) Depletion Policy: Although AEPSOM results do not directly provide evidence to formulate an energy depletion policy according to the principle suggested by the optimum depletion model presented above, they do imply a higher rate of extraction of coal and natural gas and lower rate for crude oil compared to their present rates.

(4) Exploration Policy: An active government exploration policy, to be pursued through fiscal instruments, will help increase reserves of energy resources and thus will make the country more energy import independent.

(5) Conservation Policy: In view of the scarcity of liquid fuels and the problems related to their import, highest priority to the conservation activities in the transport sector followed by the priorities in the agriculture and manufacturing industry sectors will appear to be a rational prioritisation of the conservation policy in Australia.

(6) Education and Information Policy: As the lack of information is a source of market failure in the energy sector, dissemination of information about energy problems, technologies and prospects, specially about conservation measures, should be one of the strategies within the government energy policies.

(7) Research and Development Policy: As a market may fail to allocate socially desirable resources for research and development, government research and development activities directed towards energy conservation prospects can play an important role.

(8) Energy Technology Policies: In addition the need for accelerated recovery from existing non-oil fossil fuel reserves, the prospects for progressive reduction of the use of petroleum products and the market penetration of renewable energy should be stressed in the Government's energy policies. From the potential inventory of Australian energy resources and technologies, the exploration of the possibilities of cost savings in new technologies, specifically in producing liquid fuel from coal (and natural gas) should be given priority.

7.4.3 The Post 1980 Developments and the Evaluation of the Suggested Policies

The following discussion will conclude the presentation of the policy implications of AEPSOM by highlighting the effectiveness of the suggested policies to achieve the desired objectives in the context of historical developments in the energy sector.

(1) Security of Energy Supply/Self-sufficiency in Liquid Fuels. Historical energy figures show that energy self-sufficiency has increased in Australia over the period of 1979-80 to 1989-90. In 1979-80, oil import was 50% of the total domestic production of oil, while it is 38% in 1989-90, which is a 12% reduction in oil import.

In spite of various interpretations of the meaning and implications of security of energy supply, in the Australian context, it has the connotation of self-sufficiency in liquid fuels. An optimum set of policies to deal with this externality consists of: optimum pricing, taxes and subsidies, conservation of energy, specially liquid fuels, increasing the production of domestic crude oil, import control adjustments in the economy through macro-economic policies to reduce dependence on the imported fuels, and emergency measures including reserve standby capacity, oil storage, international sharing agreement's and diversification of import sources (Griffin and Steele 1980).

The policy prescriptions of AEPSOM contain a selected set of instruments and strategies, which are consistent with each other and that can achieve the objective of energy security/self-sufficiency in liquid fuels. Raising the price of domestic crude oil equal or close to its import price has made the domestic oil price competitive and thus, has reduced unnecessary wastage and uses of oil. This can also be done by including a risk premium (due to the possibility of oil embargo) with the price of domestic crude oil. Since the imported price of oil as it is in the market does not include the externality of the social cost of an oil embargo, a tariff on the imported oil, as suggested by AEPSOM, can add an adequate security premium to the market price (Griffin and Steele 1980, p. 346). AEPSOM has rejected direct import control as the sensitivity study with a constraint on the imported oil

(Sensitivity Study 3) produced a non-feasible solution. Other taxes and subsidies are also directed towards a reallocation of energy resources to reduce import dependency. Relatively slow extraction of oil will provide its future security. Conservation of oil in the transport sector, encouragement of further exploration of oil, publicity of energy information, research and development activities for oil conservation and cost savings in new technologies, and methanol use - energy policy strategies suggested by AEPSOM - will also make the economy more self-reliant in liquid fuels. As AEPSOM does not address emergency energy policy issues, the emergency measures stated before may also be adopted in conjunction with other policies implied by AEPSOM.

(2) Conervation of Energy, Specifically of Oil. From the observation of historical data it appears that although energy intensity in the Australian economy declined over the period of 1979-80 to 1985-86, it has remained almost constant for the period 1985-1986 (Jones, Bush, Kanakaratnam, Leonard and Gillan 1991). From Table 6.8 it will also appear that the actual total energy consumption in 1989-90 is more than its forecast made earlier. This means that energy has not been conserved much in recent years. Jones et. al. (1991, p. 37) have stated it as follows: 'Australian energy consumption has grown strongly in recent years, and this trend is expected to continue in the medium term'.

The possible reasons for this may be the developments in the international energy markets, especially a reduction in oil price and probably a slower response of the economy to energy conservation programmes and policies pursued by the Government during this period.

Several policy alternatives are available to achieve this energy policy objective, such as: fuel taxes and subsidies, taxes and subsidies on equipment, efficiency standard, development of fuel efficient energy supply, conversion and end-use technologies, public exhortation, influencing the rate of depletion of scarce fuels by taxes and subsidies, finding the appropriate substitutes of fuels of limited supply, and direct quantity rationing (Griffin and Steele 1980).

AEPSOM has selected a set of policies which will help achieve the conservation objective in Australia. Taxes on the fuel supplies and subsidies on non-oil equipment/end-uses are appropriate measures. The relative price structure of various fuels indicated by AEPSOM is favourable for conservation, since the model has predicted a rise in the prices of those fuels which should be conserved. AEPSOM has also suggested a specific nature of other conservation policy measures such as: slower depletion of oil, education and information policies, specially for conservation programmes, development of new technologies (solar and substitute technologies (methanol)). The adjustments in Australian energy policies implied by the above strategies will help in achieving energy conservation.

(3) Efficient Allocation and Utilisation of Energy Resources. It is often argued that the problem of efficient allocation of resources is essentially a rational pricing (static or dynamic) problem (Griffin and Steele 1980). This argument seems to have extreme neoclassical bias, and may not hold true in an economy with fixed or less flexible prices and wages (output and input prices). Therefore, supplementary policies to pricing policies are necessary.

EPSOM has formulated a set of energy prices which will reallocate energy resources in the socially desirable directions. Other policies, such as the previously mentioned taxes and subsidies, conservation programmes, and development of new technologies will also help to supplement and implement the pricing policies implied by the model. It may, however, be mentioned that the principles of pricing policy formulation in this study have been of the second-best type. It means that instead of determining the best (pricing) policy in a single fuel market, the model has determined a set of second-best energy prices by considering the externalities in all the fuel markets.

(4) Equity in the Ownership/Uses of Energy Resources. In Chap. 5, the position taken in this study regarding the equity objective was stated. Following the dominating view about the equity objective in the energy sector, this study adopted the approach that the equity policy should be studied separately from the efficiency related study after the efficiency considerations have been dealt with.[10] Therefore, the main emphasis of this study has been on the efficient (socially desirable) allocation and utilisation of energy resources.

It may, however, be mentioned that the prices, taxes and subsidies, depletion policy and technology policy formulated by AEPSOM will have equity implications. However the equity implications of the AEPSOM results may be analysed in further studies and appropriate policy instruments such as a system of income transfers and taxes, social security or minimum income schemes, inheritance laws, etc. (Groenewegen 1984; Webb and Rickets 1980, pp. 108-109) can be derived in that study. This approach is certainly different from that of Graaff (1957) who stated 'that tinkering with the price mechanism may be considered one of the more feasible and satisfactory ways of attaining what ever distribution of income and wealth is desired by the society'. Recent developments in welfare economics in the determination of optimum equity in income and wealth (Blaug 1985) may be helpful in formulating the equity policy in the energy sector.

7.5 Conclusion

The energy policy studies pursued in this chapter have demonstrated the application of an MLO model to formulate a multi-level energy plan. AEPSOM has attempted to address the problem of the determination of the optimum energy policy in Australia. As the developments in the energy sector in 1989-90 indicate that some energy policy objectives have not yet been achieved satisfactorily (Jones et al. 1991), a set of reformulated energy policies is needed. The set of optimum energy policies suggested by AEPSOM indicates the directions for the reformulation of a comprehensive integrated set of energy policies for Australia.

[10] Many government policy interventions, especially taxes and subsidies, in the economy may affect the existing pattern of ownership of wealth and factor endowments, and the supply of factors, and thus the existing pattern of distribution of wealth and income. Adjustments in the pattern of distribution of income is possible by suitably chosen tax, expenditure and income policies which may involve an efficiency loss. This fundamental contradiction in public policies in a market economy needs careful considerations in formulating an equity policy in the Australian energy sector.

8 Major Findings: Summary, Areas for Further Research, and Conclusions

8.1 Summary and Overview

To end this book on multi-level optimization which is based on Islam (1994), this chapter provides a summary and overview of the study, points out its limitations, suggests agenda for further research and draws some conclusions.

8.1.1 MLO Approach: Justification and Theoretical Formulation

Since market failures justify energy planning by the government, the energy policy system is characterised by the existence of two separate sub-problems: optimum policy formulation by the government (policy problem) and optimum production and end-use decisions of economic agents (behavioural problem). Although energy models have been developed to replicate the competitive market mechanism to reflect the decision making of individual economic agents, a clear and complete representation in these models of the policy interactions between the government and economic agents, resulting in what is called multi-level, multi-goal, hierarchical policy systems, is lacking. Consequently, existing energy models cannot provide results pertaining to the decision making process, and may not be satisfactorily applied to formulate multi-level energy planning. In addition, necessary articulation of the policy planning problem in the form of classified model variables as the target and instrument variables has not been made. Also the existing energy models can produce results adequate only for a partial set of energy policies. The mathematical programming models provide mainly energy technological policies and shadow prices, while the macroeconometric models can produce results for taxes, subsidies and other economic policies. No existing energy model can produce results adequate for the formulation of a comprehensive set of energy policies consisting of those energy technological and economic policies.

These deficiencies of existing energy models in their use in multi-level energy planning studies necessitate the adoption of an MLO approach to multi-level energy planning. In this approach, the energy planning problem is modelled to optimise a policy objective function subject to (a) the constraints on the policy options and their consequences, and on the ranges of choice and (b) the constraints imposed by the behavioural sub-model on the degrees of freedom of the policy makers. The operational technique for multi-level optimisation is called multi-level programming (MLP). An MLP model has four main components: (a) a weighted policy objective function containing the objectives of the policy makers; (b) the constraints on the choice of policy instruments; (c) the objective functions of economic agents; and (d) the constraints on the behaviour of economic agents. MLP is considered as a collection of nested optimisation problems at different levels.

The energy planning modelling approach developed in this study is also structured within the framework of Tinbergen's theory of economic policy planning since this theory of economic policy planning provides an operational framework suitable for policy planning. To understand and identify the exact characteristics of the underlying policy planning problem, an analysis of the underlying policy system and its incorporation in the policy planning model are also necessary.

Any energy planning model developed within this approach will have several advantages. (1) It represents exactly and explicitly the underlying policy planning problem (i.e. hierarchical multi-level multi-goal policy system). Therefore, this approach (a) produces improved results/plans; (b) generates some analytical results related to the underlying policy system in the form of nature of intervention and interdependence; (c) makes explicit the policy-behavioural feasible region which is implicit in other types of models, and (d) can be used to study some welfare economic implications of government intervention.

(2) It can provide a comprehensive set of energy policies consisting of energy technological and economic policies.

Considering the fact that multi-level energy planning in a market economy requires an MLO model and an integrated (technical and economic), set of energy policies, the present multi-level energy planning approach appears to be an improvement over the existing single level optimisation energy planning models.

8.1.2 The Australian Model: AEPSOM

A journey from theory to practice is always fraught with problems and difficulties, and in many cases the rigour of a theoretical model is lost in its real life applications.

To give an empirical content to the theoretical approach, an Australian energy planning model AEPSOM (for two years) was developed. AEPSOM was developed on the basis of the following specification of the Australian energy policy planning problem.

(1) Energy Policy Objectives: The major objectives of the Australian energy policy are: reduction in oil imports, reduction in the use of oil, conservation of energy, and efficient allocation of resources.

(2) Energy Policy Instruments: The possible energy policy instrument alternatives in Australia are the following: (a) Indirect Control through taxes and subsidies, and government expenditures for energy conservation, research and development, and education and information. (b) Direct Control through pricing of domestic crude oil.

(3) Energy Policy Strategies: (a) Technological strategy, (b) Depletion policy and (c) Exploration and development strategy.

AEPSOM is a price control MLP model based explicitly on the energy policy and energy systems in Australia. The policy objective function incorporates minimisation of oil imports, total oil use and total energy use as well as minimisation of the energy sectoral government budget deficit. The policy constraints of the model impose limits on the taxes and subsidies imposed by the government in the energy sector, and require the sectoral budget to be self-financing. The behavioural objective function of AEPSOM replicates the cost minimisation behaviour of the energy producers and end-users. The constraints of the behavioural model represent the structure and operation of the Australian energy system/sector.

AEPSOM is specified to capture the hierarchical multi-level (two-level) energy policy formulation process in Australia. In AEPSOM, decision making of the policy-makers and economic agents are integrated in a single model and hierarchically placed in the modelling structure. Solution to AEPSOM determines the optimum policy targets configuration in the energy sector attainable under the present political regime and the behavioural and technical constraints in the energy sector.

The base year of AEPSOM was specified for the year 1979-80 and for sensitivity studies another one for 1989-90. Some of the data were estimated by the author and others were obtained from published sources.

An energy sector MLP model can have several applications. It can be applied to a market economy, a mixed economy or a controlled economy. It can be utilised to determine the optimum values of the existing taxes and subsidies or the optimum mix and values of taxes and subsidies necessary for attaining the sectoral energy policy objectives. In addition, it provides results needed for the determination of other energy policies such as pricing policy, conservation policy, research and development policy, education and information policy, and technological policy in both the above cases.

Although MLP models have potential for wide and useful policy applications, MLP model specifications have so far been restrictive. AEPSOM is capable of including real life policy from a wider perspective and hence is applicable to different types of policy studies.

8.1.3 Solution Algorithm: The PPS Approach

The real test of an empirical model development is its numerical implementation. AEPSOM was numerically implemented by the PPS algorithm. The main difficulty with an MLP model is its implementation by an algorithm. Algorithms are either not commercially available or cannot solve large MLP models. Search for appropriate algorithms and software is still ongoing with an uncertain prospect. The present PPS algorithm solves an MLP model by solving first the behavioural model and then searching the behavioural model solution that optimises the policy objective function and satisfies the policy constraints. Optimum results produced by the PPS algorithm are close to the expected optimum results. Other criteria such as efficiency in CPU time, and cost and efficiency in extension and transfer of the algorithm were applied to test the algorithm.

8.1.4 Results: Validation Tests and Policy Implications

The main outcome of a modelling work is a set of results which can be used to provide guidelines for the formulation of policies. AEPSOM results provided a set of information for an analysis and understanding of the Australian energy policy problems. The results were capable of addressing energy policy issues in the following areas: energy taxes and subsidies; pricing; energy technology; conservation; education and information; research and development; optimum depletion of exhaustible resources; and exploration and development activities of the government.

To test the reliability of the AEPSOM results, some conventional validation tests were performed. These tests included *a priori* justifications about the relevance of the model, the underlying problems or systems, usefulness of output for achieving the objectives of the modelling study, accuracy of results, comparison of the model results with results of other studies and intuitive judgments.

AEPSOM generated a numerical policy system for the Australian energy sector which has provided some insights into the characteristics of multi-level, multi-goal hierarchical policy formulation in the energy sector.

AEPSOM results have been used to formulate a multi-level optimum energy plan for Australia. (1) AEPSOM has determined an optimum energy system for Australia. The numerical optimum energy system has been reported in Table 6.8. (2) A set of optimum energy policy instruments and strategies for Australia has been formulated. In addition to the required changes in the pricing and fiscal instruments areas, details of the desirable optimum pattern of energy supply, conversion, and end-use technologies were shown by the energy flows produced by AEPSOM. Increased production and use of coal is necessary. Progressive reduction in the use of natural crude oil is desirable. The introduction of coal conversion technologies will substitute naturally occurring crude oil, this requires improvement in its efficiency. Also, increased production and harnessing of hydro-electricity and solar energy are desirable and will reduce the use of fossil fuels, particularly crude oil, for electricity generation. Other Australian energy policy studies have suggested similar technology policy (Endersbee et al. 1980). Increased supply of primary energy and expansion of capacities will have a significant effect on Australian energy systems in the future. But currently, emphasis needs to be given to other energy policies such as an appropriate mix of ±T, conservation programmes, and appropriate technology with a long-term strategy for increasing the supply of domestic energy resources.

The result of AEPSOM in the form of energy economic and technological policies are in the lines of the no-regret policies for abating greenhouse effects and thus, in the lines of sustainable development of energy sector in Australia.

8.2 Conclusions

Although various conclusions from this study were drawn at different parts of the thesis, they can be summarised here at the end of the study as follows.

(a) Desirability of MLO Approach. The energy planning model proposed and developed in this study can represent the energy policy system of a market economy accurately. One characteristic of such a policy system revealed by the AEPSOM results i.e. the conflicting interests of the government and economic agents, reinforces the need for an MLO approach to energy planning with explicit specification of the objective functions of these decision makers.

AEPSOM has predicted an improved energy plan in the case of optimum ±T compared to a single level behavioural model and to the case of existing ±T (base or original plan[2]). If energy policies were formulated on the basis of results of a single level energy sector model (the behavioural model) the policies would be erroneous. Therefore, the MLO model can determine the value of the policy objective function and select a set of other optimum results which is different from the results of a single level model. In addition, this type of model can provide an integrated and comprehensive set of energy policies.

Also an optimum multi-level energy plan formulated by adopting an MLO approach can generate an optimum energy system plan and an optimum energy policy plan simultaneously.

In many cases, issues related to the desirability of government intervention in the energy sector, import parity pricing of energy, resource rent taxation, conservation, exploration and

---

[2] This result would seem to be of some significance in applied welfare economic study, since it provides some empirical evidence in resolving the continued controversy over the determination of an appropriate government role in energy and resource management. In Chap. 6, it was stated that this result provided evidence in justifying a point in normative economics regarding the efficiency of decentralised market behaviour in achieving societal objectives.
Views of Candler (1991) on a finding of an improved plan in an MLP study was communicated to the present author in this form: 'Provided that you have shown that you have found a better policy that the existing one, this may be enough to qualify as "a contribution to knowledge", depending on (a) the size of improvement, and (b) a clear acknowlegement that it cannot be proven to be global, and (c) some explanation that computational costs of finding the global optimum (or proving the present solution to in fact be optimal) would be excessive'.

development, and deregulation of the energy market are addressed theoretically by applying economic principles. This study has produced results which could be used to address policy issues like those mentioned above by providing empirical evidence.

Therefore, the methodological conclusion of the study is that an MLO model can provide an alternative methodology and framework for optimum multi-level energy planning.

(b) Optimistic Prospects of MLP. Existing problems in MLP were highlighted at different parts of the thesis. In specifying AEPSOM, attempts were made to improve the state of the specification and use of an MLP model. The following points have emerged from this study.

(1) An MLP can be used to undertake normative studies in the energy sector (desirability of energy policies).

(2) An MLP model can be adopted to undertake a policy system analysis to reveal numerically the characteristics of the underlying policy system.

(3) It is possible to solve a fairly large MLP model representing a sector in reasonable detail.

(4) It can produce a comprehensive integrated set of energy policies; not $\pm$T or technology policies separately.

(5) It also provides an appropriate policy modelling framework since it can explicitly be based within the framework of the theory of economic policy planning.

(6) An MLP can be used to formulate an optimum mix of $\pm$T after investigating whether the existing set of $\pm$T is desirable or not.

(7) The PPS algorithm can be used to find an optimum solution to an MLP. Although the PPS algorithm is an iterative search method, the algorithm can find an improved energy plan.

These extensions in the specification, implementation and applications of MLP models were made in the present study with the intention of generating the optimism that meaningful MLP models can be specified, numerically implemented and adopted for policy studies.

(c) Existence of Multi-Level Hierarchical Policy System. The numerical policy system analysis has demonstrated the existence of a multi-level, multi-goal, hierarchical policy system in the Australian energy sector.

(d) Possibility of Changes in AES. The Australian energy system is expected to undergo some significant changes in the long run, if the policies suggested in this study are implemented and the assumptions made remain valid.

(e) Changes in Australian Energy Policies. An EPSOM has provided the following insights, guidelines and directions in Australian energy policy planning and issues: the necessity for deregulation of energy prices, reorganisation of the existing taxes and subsidies in the energy sector, priority for conservation, education and information, and research and development policies, emphasis on the exploration and depletion policies, and the need for cost savings necessary for market penetration of new and renewable technologies.

The formulation of a comprehensive energy policy plan would, perhaps, be of some interest in the Australian energy policy context, because of the country's on-going search for a set of integrated comprehensive energy policies (Saddler 1981; Hall 1985; Marks 1986). There is a need for a comprehensive set of quantitative energy policies studied and formulated in an integrated, comprehensive, consistent and optimum set-up (by applying an optimisation model). It will, therefore, be of some use *if* the suggested policies can open new perspectives for further *dialogue* on the Australian energy policy issues.

Appendix A
AEPSOM Data: Sources and Methods of Estimation

A.1 Discussion of the General Aspects

(1) Data Need

For a numerical specification of AEPSOM, the following types of data are needed: (a) weights of the policy target variables; (b) average costs per unit of each type of energy and technologies); (c) the efficiency rates of the conversion and end-use technologies; and (d) the values of the right hand side parameters of the constraints.

(2) Units of Measurement

The energy variables and coefficients are measured in petajoules. Cost coefficients are given in 1980 million Australian dollars.

(3) Sources of Data

Sources of data are indicated in different tables. Tables/data without an indication of source are the authors' estimates based on the available information, mainly from Musgrove et al. (1983).

A.2 Data for AEPSOM

Policy Objective Function. The base case weights of the policy target variables were: Iel:1, CNo:1, and TcE:1. Sensitivity analyses were also undertaken by changing the coefficients in different combinations (Table 6.12 in Chap. 6).

Policy and Budgetary Constraints. The policy constraints were specified numerically in the text of Chap. 5. There is no need for any data to be specified in the budgetary constraints.

Behavioural Objective Function. The MARKAL estimates of costs of supply, imports, secondary energy conversion, electricity generation and end-uses for the year 1979-80 were a major source of data for the AEPSOM behavioral model. Many other complementary data were used to calculate the reported figures. These five types of costs will be discussed separately.

(1) Supply Costs. The supply and import costs of the primary energy are given in Table A.1.

Table A.1. Supply Costs of Energy

Energy	Costs ($M/PJ)
Coal (R_1)	0.72
Imported crude oil (Ie_1)	5.00
Domestic crude oil (R_2)	5.30
Natural gas (R_3)	0.78
Wood (R_6)[a]	1.18
Uranium (R_7)	0.13

[a] Source: Todd 1983.

(2) Costs of Secondary Energy Conversion and Electricity Generation. Some costs in this category relate to the secondary energy flows and some relate to individual technologies. In some cases where secondary energy is the same in primary and secondary form such as coal, natural gas and wood, no conversion costs exist, and so no secondary energy conversion costs of these types of energy have been used in the model.

Costs of the relevant secondary energy and conversion technologies are as shown in Table A.2.

Table A.2. Costs of Conversion Technologies

Conversion technologies/flows	Costs ($M/PJ)
Refinery cost (x_2)	1.39
Hydro-electricity generation (E_4)	19.27
Electricity generation from coal (E_1)	13.98
Electricity generation from petroleum products (E_2)	18.69
Electricity generation from natural gas (E_3)	22.32

These costs are sums of the investment, operating and maintenance costs of the conversion technologies or flows.

It is difficult to calculate the aggregate refinery cost of petroleum products. A modern refinery consists of many types of units to provide facilities for different types of processing of crude oil. To avoid these difficulties, total aggregated costs of all the processes was adopted to use as the average cost of refineries.

Cost of electricity generation from hydro, petroleum products and natural gas have been adopted from MARKAL. The cost of electricity generation from coal has been estimated on the basis of the weighted average of the different types of coal used in 1979-80 in electricity generation.

(3) The Costs of the End-uses. The end-use costs are based mainly on the estimates of end use costs in MARKAL. Two main types of costs have been used to estimate the average costs of the end-uses: delivery costs where appropriate, and investment, operation and maintenance costs.

(a) Delivery Cost: The delivery charges of energy have been adopted from MARKAL. The weights for estimating average delivery costs of energy in the present model are the actual quantities of fuels/energy used in different sectors, and are adopted from Department of National Development and Energy (1982).

Calculated average delivery and other costs of different forms of energy are as shown in Table A.3.

Table A.3. Delivery Costs of Energy

($M/PJ)

	Manufacturing industry	Agriculture	Transport	Domestic
Coal	0.45 (d_1)			1.32 (d_{10})
Petroleum products	0.35 (d_2)	0.35 (d_6)	1.45 (d_8)	1.40 (d_{11})
Natural gas	1.00 (d_3)			2.19 (d_{12})

(b) Investment, Operation and Maintenance Costs: Calculation of the cost of aggregated end-use technologies/flows is more difficult than aggregated cost estimates in the other cases. This is so since a substantial amount of investment, operating and maintenance costs are not involved in all end-use technologies. For example, there are different technologies in the manufacturing sector that use coal. However, not all these technologies involve substantial amounts of investment, operation and maintenance costs. Therefore, aggregation of the costs of all these technologies may not give a representative figure for aggregated end-uses. Also there was a lack of information about all these end-use technologies except for the use of coal in the industrial boiler, so that the average cost of using coal in the manufacturing sector has been adopted as typical of technology costs.

The costs of using different forms of energy to raise steam in the manufacturing sector are shown in Table A.4 and A.5.

Table A.4. Boiler Costs

Energy	Costs ($M/PJ)
Coal (d_1)	2.02
Petroleum product (d_2)	1.42
Natural gas (d_3)	1.23

Table A.5. Investment, and Operation and Maintenance Costs of Other Energy in the Manufacturing Industry Sector

Energy	Cost ($M/PJ)
Electricity (d_4)	2.30
Wood (d_6)	0.25

The cost of a heavy mobile plant has been used as the cost of end-use of energy in the agricultural sector. The cost is as shown in Table A.6.

Table A.6. Heavy Mobile Plant Costs

Energy	Costs ($M/PJ)
Petroleum products (distillate) (d_6)	71.93

Calculation of the cost of end-uses of energy in the transport sector is complicated by the fact that there are various types of end-use technologies (vehicles) which use different types of energy. The weighted average costs of the end-uses were calculated. The weights are the actual uses of the particular energy by different types of vehicles 1979-80 (source of the weights: Musgrove et al. (1983); Department of National Development and Energy 1982). Calculated investment, operation and maintenance costs of the end-use energy flows are given in Table A.7.

Table A.7. Investment, and Operation and Maintenance Costs of the End-uses of Energy in the Transport Sector

Energy	Cost ($M/PJ)	Transport type
Petroleum products (d_8)	237.56	Railway
Electricity (d_9)	220.40	Railway

The investment, and operation and maintenance costs of the energy uses in the domestic sector are given in Table A.8.

Table A.8. Investment, and Operation and Maintenance Costs of Energy Uses in the Domestic Sector

Energy	Cost ($M/PJ)
Coal (d_{10})	1.32
Petroleum products (d_{11})	0.98
Natural gas (d_{12})	3.39
Electricity (d_9)	6.17
Solar (d_{15})	6.69

A.2.1 The Behavioural Constraints

(1) Demand Constraints. Data necessary for these constraints are only the amounts of energy demanded in each of the sectors. The following figures in the Table A.9 are for the end-uses of energy in different sectors are adopted from Department of National Development and Energy (1982, p. 18).

Table A.9. Energy End-Uses: 1979-80

Sectors	Energy PJ
Manufacturing (including mining) (DE^I)	837.20
Agriculture (DE^A)	142.32
Transport (DE^T)	812.08
Domestic (DE^D)	389.30
Demand for electricity in manufacturing industry (d_4)	129.77
Demand for electricity in agriculture (d_7)	4.19
Demand for electricity in domestic sector (d_{13})	154.88
Export	
Coal (Ee_1)	1272.54
Petroleum products (Ee_2)	133.95
Uranium (Ee_3)	581.85

(2) End-use Energy Flow Constraints. These constraints define the flows of energy uses in the different sectors. It has been mentioned that the flows are gross energy uses, so the efficiency factors have not been incorporated to calculate net energy uses in these equations. There is no need for any data to be specified in these equations.

(3) Secondary Energy Supply Constraints. Efficiency factors that have been derived in AEPSOM are shown in Table A.10.

Table A.10. Efficiencies of Different Technologies

Energy	Efficiency factors
x_3	0.86
E_1	0.24
E_2	0.33
E_3	0.33
x_2	0.86
x_4	0.14

(4) The Primary Energy Balance Equations. There is no need for any data to be specified in these equations.

(5) Resource Constraints. The next set of numbers that we have adopted in our study represents the availability of resources in 1979-80. Total domestic supplies of coal, crude oil and natural gas are the upper limits on the availability of primary energy resources in the model (see Table A.11.).

Table A.11. Primary Energy Resources: 1979-80

Energy	PJ
Coal (R_1)	2448.81
Crude oil (R_2)	874.87
Natural gas (R_3)	364.18
Wood (R_6)	138.14
Solar energy (R_7)	0.50[a]
Uranium (R_8)	586.04

Source: Department of National Development and Energy 1982, p. 18.

[a] Solar energy supply level is adopted from MARKAL (MARKAL determines 0.50 PJ as the optimum level for 1979-80).

(6) Capacity Constraints. The capacities of different technologies in 1979-80 are shown in Table A.12.

Table A.12. Capacities of Different Technologies 1979-80[a]

Energy	PJ
Hydro-electricity (E_4)	86.61
Total electricity (x_4)	411.11
Petroleum products (x_2)	1586.49

Source: Department of National Development and Energy 1981, pp. 24-29.

[a] The electricity generation capacity and refinery capacity (MW and barrel/day) have been converted to PJ by the appropriate conversion factors. See Meier (1984, Chap. 8) for conversion factors that relate MW to Mwh/year.

A.3 Methods and Principles of Estimation and/or Aggregation of Data in AEPSOM

In MARKAL, almost all the possible existing and future individual energy supply, secondary and end-use conversion technologies are specified. For AES in the present work, the aggregated energy flows at different stages are mainly specified, except in some cases where a single technology has been specified. To make the MARKAL data consistent with the requirements of AEPSOM, the data have been aggregated with weights. The weights are the actual energy production and end-uses in 1979-80, adopted from Department of Resources and Energy (1982). In some cases, actual energy flows corresponding to some individual technologies were not available. In these cases, optimum values of energy determined by the MARKAL solution were adopted.

Although the aggregation of many technologies and fuel uses into a broad group of technologies and end-uses was necessary for putting numbers in the behavioural model of

AEPSOM, which was specified as a relatively small model in comparison with MARKAL due to computation problems, the problem of such aggregation should be noted. When different technologies (for example different technologies for electricity generation from oil) are disaggreted in a mathematical programming model, the model may choose some or all of the technologies in the optimum solution. It is unlikely that the model will choose no technology from all the alternative technologies. However, if all the technologies are aggregated there will be only two outcomes when the model is implemented, either the technology is feasible or not feasible. If the model does not select the technology as feasible, the model result will be biased against the technology. In the case of a small mathematical programming energy sector model this problem of aggregation resulting in corner solutions exists. From the reported results in Chap. 6, it appears that this type of corner solutions were also encountered in this study.

Appendix B
AEPSOM: 1989-90

B.1 AEPSOM: 1989-90 Model Specification

B.1.1 Preliminaries

(1) Assumptions: The assumptions made in AEPSOM: 1979-80 are also valid for AEPSOM: 1989-90.

(2) Abstract Model: The abstract representation of AEPSOM: 1989-90 is similar to AEPSOM: 1979-80.

(3) Foundations: These are the same as in AEPSOM: 1979-80.

B.1.2 Specification of AEPSOM

The principles and mechanism for the specification of AEPSOM: 1989-90 are similar to those in AEPSOM: 1979-80, therefore only a listing of AEPSOM: 1989-90 equations will be provided here.

The Policy Objective Function. This is the same as in AEPSOM: 1979-80.

The Constraint Set.

(1) The Policy and Budgetary Constraints: They are the same as in AEPSOM: 1979-80.

(2) The Behavioural Model of the Energy Sector: The behavioural constraints of AEPSOM: 1989-90 will consist of an ES model for 1989-90. Specification of the ES model: 1989-90 will be based on the Australian energy system for the year 1989-90. AES for 1989-90 is shown in Figure B.1.

The following new conversion technologies have been introduced in AES:1989-90 - coal liquefaction, and methanol production from biomass. The following new end-uses were also introduced: coal, natural gas, and methanol uses in the transport sector.

The constraints of ES model: 1989-90. These are the same as those in the ES model: 1979-80 in AEPSOM: 1979-80. So we shall not discuss in detail the specification of the constraints of the ES model: 1989-90. The following is a list of the equations of the ES model: 1989-90.

Demand Constraints (including the export constraints):

$$d_1 + d_2 + d_3 + d_4 + d_5 \geq DE$$

$$d_6 + d_7 \geq DE^A \tag{B.1}$$

$$d_8 + d_9 + d_{10} + d_{11} + d_{12} \geq DE^T$$

$$d_{13} + d_{14} + d_{15} + d_{16} + d_{17} + d_{18} \geq DE^D$$

$$E_{e1} \geq \bar{E}_{e1}$$

$$E_{e3} \geq \bar{E}_{e3}$$

$$E_{e4} \geq \bar{E}_{e4}$$

$$E_{e2} \geq \bar{E}_{e2}$$

Intermediate Energy Balance Equations.

$$x_1 = d_1 + d_8 + d_{13} + E_{e1}$$

$$x_2 = d_2 + d_6 + d_9 + d_{14} + E_{e2}$$

$$(1/\delta_2)x_3 = d_3 + d_{10} + d_{15}$$

$$x_4 = d_4 + d_7 + d_{11} + d_{16}$$

Figure B.1 Australian Energy System 1989-90

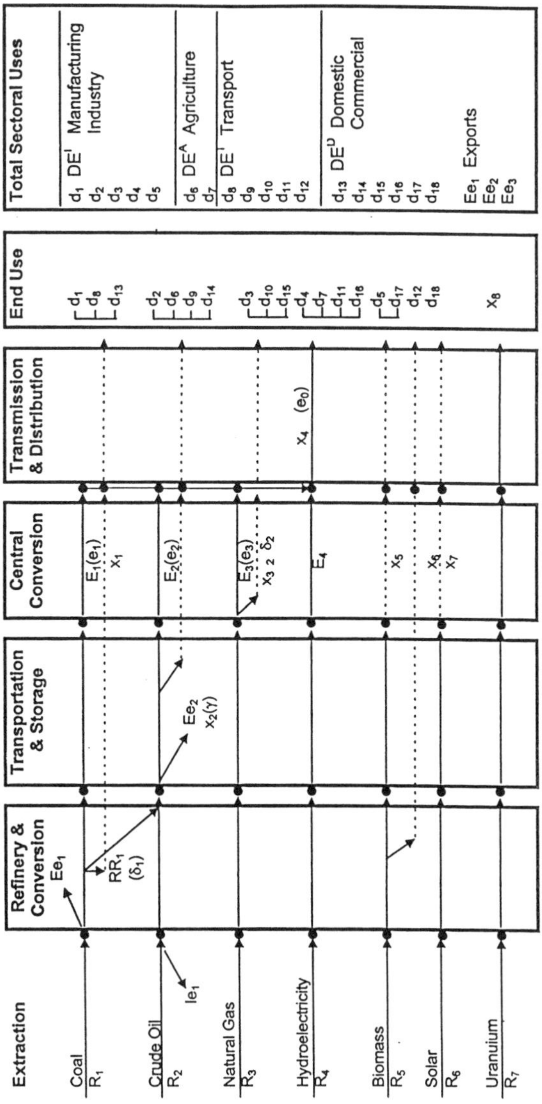

$$x_5 = d_{17} \tag{B.2}$$

$$x_6 = d_{12}$$

$$x_7 = d_{18}$$

$$x_8 = E_{e3}$$

Supply Balance Equations.

(1) Petroleum Products Supply Balance Equation:

$$E_2 + x_2 = (1/\delta_1)RR_1 + R_2 + I_{e1}B \tag{B.3}$$

(2) Electricity Supply Balance Equation:

$$(1/e_0)x_4 = e_1E_1 + e_2E_2 + e_3E_3 + E_4\,B \tag{B.4.}$$

(3) Other Supply Balance Equations:

$$R_1 = x_1 + RR_1 + E_1$$

$$R_3 = x_3 + E_3$$

$$R_5 = x_5 + x_6 \tag{B.5}$$

$$R_6 = x_7$$

$$R_7 = x_8$$

(4) Resource Constraints:

$$R_1 \le \overline{R}_1$$

$$R_2 \le \overline{R}_2$$

$$R_3 \le \overline{R}_3 \tag{B.6}$$

$R_5 \leq \overline{R}_5$

$R_6 \leq \overline{R}_6$

$R_7 \leq \overline{R}_7$

(5) Capacity Constraints:

$E_4 \leq kHe$

$x_4 \leq kTe$

$$(1/e_2)E_2 + (1/\gamma)x_2 \leq Rk \qquad \text{(B.7)}$$

(6) User-Defined Constraints:

$d_4 \geq \overline{d}_4$

$$d_7 \geq \overline{d}_7 \qquad \text{(B.8)}$$

$d_{11} \geq \overline{d}_{16}$

Objective Function. The objective function of the ES model: 1989-90 is also similar to the objective function of the ES model: 1979-80 in AEPSOM: 1979-80. However, the objective function of the ES model: 1989-90 is different in the following respects:

(1) It contains costs of some additional activities.

(2) The costs are 1989-90 costs in 1979-80 real prices.

(3) Taxes and subsidies are for the year 1989-90.

The objective function of the ES model: 1989-90 is as follows:

$$C = \sum_{i=1}^{7} (c_i + T_i)R_i + c_m I_e + \sum_{j=1}^{7} c_j x_j + \sum_{e=1}^{4} c_e E_e + \sum_{k=1}^{18} (c_k - T_k)d_k \qquad \text{(B.9)}$$

Output of AEPSOM: 1989-90. The output of AEPSOM: 1989-90 is the same as it is in AEPSOM: 1979-80.

B.2 Data for AEPSOM: 1989-90[1]

(1) The Policy Objective Function 1: The weights in AEPSOM: 1989-90 are: Ie1: 1, CNo: 2, and TCe: 1.

(2) The Policy and Budgetary Constraints: Same as in AEPSOM 1979-80.

(3) The Behavioural Objective Function: The following real rates of increases and absolute increases in the base year (1979-80) costs of fuels and new technologies were assumed (reasons are discussed below):

Table B 1. Increase in the Costs of Primary Energy

Energy	Per annum real increases % (cost $M/PJ)
Coal (R_1)	2.9
Domestic crude oil (R_2)	5.0
Imported crude oil (Ie_1)	3.0
Natural gas (R_3)	1.5
Solar energy (R_5)	0.0
Wood (R_6)	0.0
Uranium (R_7)	1.5

Table B 2. Increases in the Costs of Conversion Technologies

Conversion technologies/flow	Real increases (costs $M/PJ)
Refinery cost (x_2)	1.5
Hydro-electricity generation (E_4)	2.0
Electricity generation from coal (E_1)	1.5
Electricity generation from petroleum products (E_2)	1.5
Electricity generation from natural gas (E_3)	1.5

[1]Sources of data: Tables/data without any source are the estimates of the author.

Table B.3. Cost of New Technologies

New conversion technologies	Costs ($M/PJ)
Conversion of coal to oil (RR_1)	15.67
Conversion of wood to methanol (x_6)	43.60

Table B4. Increases in the Cost of End-use Technologies

(Costs $M/PJ)

	Manufacturing industry	Agriculture	Transport	Domestic
Petroleum products	2.00 (d_2)	2.00 (d_6)	2.00 (d_8)	2.00 (d_{11})
Electricity:		1.00		
Exports				
Coal 1.50				
Natural gas 2.00				
Uranium 1.50				

Some of the features of the cost structures of 1989-90 AES are: (a) Increases in the costs of primary fuels at different rates; (b) Increases in the cost of oil-based secondary energy conversion technologies but no increases in the costs of other secondary energy conversion technologies; and (c) Increases in the cost of oil-based end-use technologies by 5% but no increases in the cost of other end-uses.

The reasons for assuming these types of increases in future energy costs are as follows: (a) Increases in primary energy costs are based mainly on the past increases; (b) No increases in cost of the non-oil-based secondary energy conversion technologies are assumed because it is expected that subsidies will be given to the non-oil-based technologies, and that there will be improvements in the efficiencies of these technologies (see Schuyers 1979 for a detailed study of learning effects in the Australian energy sector). In contrast, oil-based technologies are expected to have no subsidies, and are predicted to have relatively fewer improvements in conversion efficiencies; thus their costs are expected to rise.

B.2.1 The Behavioural Constraints

(1) Demand Constraints. The following figures for the end-uses of energy in different sectors are adopted from the Department of National Development and Energy (1983, p. 51):

Table B.5. End-uses of Energy 1989-90

Sectors PJ	Notations energy
Manufacturing (DE^I)	1707.89
Agriculture (DE^A)	255.35
Transport (DE^T)	899.99
Domestic (DE^D)	489.76
Export	
Coal (Ee_1)	2519.97
Petroleum products (Ee_2)	104.65
Natural gas (Ee_3)	246.97
Uranium (Ee_4)	4299.02
Demand for electricity in manufacturing industry (d_4)	171.63
Demand for electricity in agriculture (d_7)	41.63
Demand for electricity in domestic sector (d_{13})	230.23

Source: Department of Natural Development and Energy (1983, p. 51).

(2) End-use Energy Flow Constraints. None needed.

(3) Secondary Energy Supply Constraints. The efficiency factors that have been derived for use are shown in Table B.6.

Table B .6. Efficiencis of Different Technologies: 1989-90

Fuel	Efficiencies
x3	0.86
RR1	0.54
E1	0.22
E2	0.31
E3	0.32
x2	0.90
X4	0.86

(4) Primary Energy Balance Equations. We do not need any data to be specified in these equations.

(5) Resource Constraints.

Table B.7. Primary Energy Resources: 1989-90

Energy	PJ
Coal (R1)	4198.60
Crudel oil (R2)	1029.76
Natural gas (R3)	933.48
Wood (R6)	171.63
Solar energy (R7)	1.00
Uranium (R80)	4299.02

(6) Capacity Constraints. The following increases in the capacities of different technologies in 1989-90 were estimated in Table B.8.

Table B.8. Capacities of Different Technologies

Energy	PJ
Hydro-electricity (E_4)	1.50
Total electricity (x_4)	5.00
Petroleum products (x_2)	4.00

Appendix C
A Complete List of AEPSOM Solutions

C.1 Model Specification and Solutions

The optimum AEPSOM specification and solution with descriptions of the main characteristics of model solutions was given in Table 6.1. A listing of the various AEPSOM solutions with necessary explanations is given in this appendix.

AEPSOM was solved for different units of parametric variations: K, C, H ; in two types of tax and subsidy policy regimes (existing mix and optimum mix); for the two types of specifications stated above; for the years of 1979-80 and 1989-90; and under varying conditions in the energy sector (sensitivity studies). In the first three solutions only existing taxes and subsidies were included in AEPSOM, while the optimum mix of taxes and subsidies were obtained and included in the next three Solutions (Solutions 4, 5, and 6). The behavioural model part of AEPSOM for 1979-80 and 1989-90 (without policy objective function, policy constraints and taxes and subsidies in the behavioural objective function) was also solved (Model No. 7 and 8). The Central Control Policy Model (Models No. 9 and 10, behavioural model with policy objective function instead of behavioural policy objective function) was also solved for these two time periods to obtain the optimum mix of taxes and subsidies (Optimum ±T) in 1979-89 and 1989-90. This type of policy problem was embedded in Model No. 4, No. 5, No. 6, and No. 11 to No. 23. For sensitivity studies, AEPSOM was solved in two different policy regimes (existing mix and optimum mix of taxes and subsidies) by incorporating the changes to be discussed in a later section on the sensitivity analysis.

Table C.1. A List of Model Specifications and Solutions - Base Solutions (Without Policy Constraints)

Model No.	Brief description	Type of policy	U[a]	Remarks: ±T= 0, ±T≠ 0	Results	
					Optimum value of P.O.F. (1)[b] (PJ)	Optimum value of P.O.F. (2)[b]
Model No. 1	AEPSOM 1979-80 data	Existing ± T	U = I	±T= 0	7031.68 (±T= 0)	7031.68 (±T= 0)
Model No. 2	AEPSOM 1979-80 data	Existing ±T	U = C	±T= 0	7031.66 (±T= 0)	7031.66 (±T= 0)
Model No. 3	AEPSOM 1979-80 data	Existing ±T	U = H	±T= 0	7031.40 (±T= 0)	7031.40 (±T= 0)
Model No. 4	AEPSOM 1979-80 data	Optimum set ±T	U = I	±T≠ 0	6734.20 (±T≠ 0)	-19477.51 (±T≠ 0)
Model No. 5	AEPSOM 1979-80 data	Optimum set ±T	U = C	±T≠ 0	6733.70 (±T≠ 0)	1 671.58 (±T≠ 0)
Model No. 6	AEPSOM 1979-80 data	Optimum set ±T	U = H	±T≠ 0	6733.70 (±T ≠ 0)	1 708.25 (±T≠ 0)

[a] U = Units of parametric variation

[b] (1) P.O.F. (1) WL = Iel + CNo + TCo (the abstract model (5.1), but the policy constraints are not included in these solutions. The policy constraints are included in model solutions in Section E of this Table. The unit of measurement is petajoules (PJ)).

(2) P.O.F. (2) $WL = Iel + Cno + Tco - \sum_{j=1}^{37} (+tj)\, x j + \sum_{j=1}^{37} (- tj)\, xj$, j = 1,2, ..., 37

This specification corresponds to the abstract model (5.2) (in the 1989-90 AEPSOM, j = 1,2, ..., 43)

Table C.2. Results: Single Level Models

Model No.	Brief description	Type of policy	U	Remarks: ±T= 0, ±T≠ 0	Results	
					Behavioural objective function (PJ)	Optimum value P.O.F. (1) (PJ)
Model No. 7	Behavioural model of AEPSOM, 1979-80 data (Single level model)	±T not included	U not included	±T = 0	225117.84	7031.68
Model No. 8	Behavioural model of AEPSOM, 1989-90 data (Single level model)	±T not included	U not included	±T= 0		10988.46
Model No. 9	Central control policy model for 1979-80 data (Single level model)	±T not included	U not included	U not included	U not included	5101.51
Model No. 10	Central control policy model for 1989-90 data (Single level model)	±T not included	U not included	No result	U not included	6,708.43

Table C.3. Results: Sensitivity Analysis: Existing ±T (Without Policy Constraints)

Model No.	Brief description	Type of Policy	U	Remarks: ±T=0, ±T≠0	Result	
					Optimum value P.O.F. (1) (PJ)	Optimum value of P.O.F. (2)
Model No. 11	AEPSOM 1979-80 data	Existing ±T and t_3	U=H	±T≠0	6811.47 (±T≠0)	6643.30 (±T≠0)
Model No. 12	AEPSOM 1979-80, introduction of t_3	Existing	U=H	±T≠0	7131.66 (±T=0)	7063.86 (±T=0)
Model No. 13	AEPSOM 1979-80, constraints relaxed by 20%	Existing	U=H	±T≠0	4680.03 (±T=0)	4839.43 (±T=0)
Model No. 14	AEPSOM 1979-80, constraints relaxed by 100%	Existing	U=H	±T≠0	14045.27 (±T=0)	9877.63 (±T≠0)
Model No. 15	AEPSOM 1979-80, constraints on petroleum import	Existing	U=H		No feasible solution	
Model No. 16	AEPSOM 1979-80, introduction new technologies, 1979-80 cost for old technologies, 1989-90 cost for new technologies	Existing	U=H	±T≠0	6027.75 (±T=0)	6020.37 (±T≠0)

Table C.4. Results: Sensitivity Analysis: Existing ±T (Without Policy Constraints)

Model No.	Brief description	Type of policy	U	Remarks: ±T=0, ±T≠0	Result	
					Optimum value P.O.F. (1) (PJ)	Optimum value of P.O.F. (2)
Model No. 17	AEPSOM 1979-80, import parity price for domestic crude oil	Existing ±T	U=H	±T=0	7131.66 (±T=0)	7131.66 (±T=0)
Model No. 18	AEPSOM 1979-80, supply double, but demand same as in 1979-80	Existing	U=H	±T=0	6258.12 (±T=0)	6258.12 (±T=0)
Model No. 19	AEPSOM 1979-80 data, new technologies	Existing	U=H	±T≠0	10988.46 (±T≠0)	9879.25 (±T≠0)

Table C. 5. Results: Sensitivity Analysis: Existing ±T (Without Policy Constraints)

Model No.	Brief description	Type of policy	U	Remarks: ±T=0, ±T≠0	Result	
					Optimum value P.O.F. (1) (PJ)	Optimum value of P.O.F. (2)
Model No. 20	AEPSOM 1979-80, constraints relaxed by 20%	Optimum	U=H	±T≠0	8069.45 (±T≠0)	-6387.54 (±T≠0)
Model No. 21	AEPSOM 1979-80 constraints relaxed by 100%	Optimum	U=H	±T≠0	13449.34 (±T≠0)	-10648.12 (±T≠0)
Model No. 22	AEPSOM 1979-80, supply double, but demand same as in 1979-80	Optimum	U=H	±T≠0	6094.15 (±T≠0)	-6003.74 (±T≠0)
Model No. 23	AEPSOM 1989-90 data, new technologies	Optimum set	U=H	±T≠0	10988.46 (±T=0)	10397.79 (±T=0)

Table C.6 Alternative Model Solutions: AEPSOM with Policy Constraints (Feasible Optimum Solution)

Model No.	Brief description	Type of policy	U	Policy Constraints	Result
					Optimum value P.O.F. (1)[a] (PJ)
Model No. 5	AEPSOM 1979-80 data	Optimum set	U=C	$0 \leq \pm T \leq 20\%$ $B = 3777.91 > 0$	6733.70 ($\pm T \neq 0$)
Model No. 6	AEPSOM 1979-80 data	Optimum set	U=H	$0 \leq \pm T \leq 54\%$ $B = 3859.65 > 0$	6733.70 ($\pm T \neq 0$)
Model No. 13[b]	AEPSOM 1979-80 data	Existing	U=H	$0 \leq \pm T \leq 61\%$ $B = -159.40 < 0$	4680.03 ($\pm T \neq 0$)
Model No.19	AEPSOM 1989-90 data	Existing	U=H	$0 \leq \pm T \leq 56\%$ $B = 587.19 > 0$	10988.46 ($\pm T \neq 0$)

[a] P.O.F. (1) W = Iel+ CNo + TCo

With the policy constraint:

(1) $0 \leq tj \leq 20\%$ of j j = 1, 2, ...37 (For 1989-90, j = 1,2, ...43)

(2) $B = \sum_{j=1}^{37} (+tj)\, x j - \sum_{j=1}^{37} (-tj)\, xj \geq 0$

These models correspond to the abstract representation of AEPSOM in (6.1), Specification 1.

[b] Though Model No. 13 does not satisfy the second policy constraint and the range of $\pm T$ is $0 \leq \pm T \leq 61\%$ of costs, its results are reported here since this model solution produced lowest value of P.O.F. (1) among all the model solutions.

C.2 Selection of the Appropriate Model Specification and Solution

It can be seen from Table C.6 that in the case of Model No.1, No. 2, and No. 3 (AEPSOM with existing $\pm T$), the optimum solution to AEPSOM was obtained when $\pm T = 0$. In other words, the behavioural optimum solution was also found to be optimum for the policy problem. This means that persuasion of existing $\pm T$ of any value does not improve the value of the policy objective function.

However, the situation changed in the case of the optimum $\pm T$ mix (Model No. 4, No. 5 and No. 6). In these solutions, optimum solution to AEPSOM was obtained with $\pm T \neq 0$. This implies that the behavioural optimum solution (with $\pm T \neq 0$) was not optimum for the policy problem and introduction of $\pm T$ influenced the allocation of resources in the economy, resulting in an improved value of the objective function.

Results of Model No. 4, No. 5 and No. 6 were preferred for discussion of the AEPSOM results since these solutions generated a lower value of the policy objective function than those of Model No. 1, No. 2 and No. 3.

Optimum solutions to AEPSOM are reported in Table C.5. These are the solutions which satisfy the policy and budget constraints and attain the optimum value for the policy objective function (feasible optimum solution). Model Nos 5, 6, 13 and 18 satisfy the policy constraints to various degrees. From all these models specifications, Model No. 5 will be mainly selected for policy studies since it produces a lower value of the policy objective function and satisfies the policy constraint ($0 \leq t_j \leq 20\%$ of the cost of the j-th activity) and the budget constraints. Other model results were also reported (Model Nos 6, 13 and 18) where necessary for comparison purposes.

It may be noticed that only Specification 1 generates optimum feasible solutions. Specification 2 did not generate an optimum feasible solution. Therefore, results for Specification 2 were not included in the optimum solution table and the results of the Specification 2 were not adopted for policy studies. Moreover Specification 1 can be considered a realistic representation of the Australian energy policy system since the policy planning problem is really to achieve the three energy policy objectives by adopting a set of instruments which are subject to some constraints.

It is also worth mentioning that in some cases two specifications of AEPSOM generated the same solution to AEPSOM (for example Model Nos 17 and 18).

C.2.1 The Effects of the Units

The effects of the units of the parametric variations on the optimum solution can be observed from Table 6.1. In Model Nos 4, 5, and 6, the three units of parametric variations produced different optimum solutions to AEPSOM. It is obvious that the effects of the units of parametric variations on the solution of AEPSOM is significant. In all the model specifications other than Model Nos 1, 2, 3, 4, 5, and 6, the units identified by H were adopted, because these units provide appropriate directions for search in the PPS algorithm. Since the PPS algorithm is an interactive method, application of different units increases the possibility of finding the true/global optimum.

C.3 The Policy Objective Function

The optimum values of the policy objective function in the cases of various model solutions are reported in Table C.1. These values are reported for two types of policy studies, base cases and sensitivity studies separately. In every solution, optimum values of the policy objective function were calculated for the two types of specifications of the policy objective function shown in Table 6.1. (P.O.F. (1), and (2)). Definitions of the two P.O.F.s were presented in Chap. 6. The justification and significance of these alternative specifications were discussed in Chap. 5.

It was mentioned in the previous section that Model Nos 1, 2, and 3 did not produce any values of the policy objective function which were different from those generated by the behavioural model. This applies to both the alternative specifications (1) and (2) of the policy objective function.

Model Nos 4, 5 and 6 produce $\pm T \neq 0$ optimum values for the policy objective function of both specifications. Optimum values for the policy objective function (1) in these three solutions are close: 6734.20, 6733.70 and 6733.70. Optimum values for the policy objective function (2) did not show the same pattern. The optimum values were numerically different from each other: 19,477.51, 1,671.58 and 1,708.25.

In the case of alternative specifications, only Model No. 5 produced results satisfying the initial policy constraints $0 \leq \pm T \leq 20\%$. Two other solutions are also reported which satisfy the upper level of policy constraints of 54% and 61%. The optimum values of the policy objective function (1) are the same in the case of Model Solution Nos. 5 and 6, although these have different upper level constraints on the policy range, while model solution 13 produces a very much lower value of the policy objective function.

One striking result is that optimum model solutions are different in two alternative specifications of the policy objective function. For example, the solution of Model No. 5 produces optimum values for the policy objective function (1) and (2) equal to 6733.70 and 1671.58 respectively while for the first component of the policy objective function (2) it is 6897.83. (First component of the policy objective function (2) is equal to the policy objective function (1)). It means that two alternative specifications of the policy objective function generate different optimum solutions to the model.

References

Al-ali, H. M. 1979, 'Input-output Analysis of Energy Requirements: An Application to the Scottish Economy in 1973', *Energy Economics*, October, pp. 211-218.

Allen, E. L. et al. 1976, *US Energy and Economic Growth*, Institute for Energy Analysis, Oak Ridge Associated Universities, Oak Ridge, Tennessee.

Amman, H. M., Kendrick, D. A. & Rust, J. 1996, *Handbook of Computational Economics*, Elsevier, Amsterdam.

Anthony, J. D. 1977, *National Energy Policy*, Commonwealth Australia, Canberra.

APEX III, *Reference Manual*, Control Data Corporation.

Arrow, K. J. 1951, *Social Choice and Individual Values*, Wiley, New York.

Arrow, K. J. & Intriligator, M. D. (eds) 1981, *Handbook of Mathematical Economics*, vol. 1. North-Holland, Amsterdam.

Asian and Pacific Development Centre 1985, *Integrated Energy Planning: A Manual*, 3 volumes, Kuala Lumpur.

Australian Bureau of Statistics 1984, *Australian National Accounts: Input-Output Tables 1978-79*, Canberra.

___ (different volumes), *Australian Year Book*, Canberra.

Australian Institute of Energy & Institute of Engineers, Australia 1983, *Energy 83: Towards an Energy Policy for Australia*, Position Papers, Sydney.

Ball, R. J. & Bowers, C. J. 1983, 'Distortions Created by Taxes which are Options on Value Creation: The Australian Resources Rent Tax Proposal', *Australian Journal of Management*, vol. 8, pp. 1-14.

Ballenger, N. S. 1984, *Agricultural Policy Analysis for Mexico: Sectoral and Macro Impacts*, Ph.D. dissertation, University of California, Daris, cited in Hazell and Norton 1986.

Bannock, G., Baxter, R.E. & Rees, R. 1984, *The Penguin Dictionary of Economics*, 3rd Edition, Penguin, New York.

Bard, J. F. 1983a, 'An Efficient Point Algorithm for a Linear Two-stage Optimisation Problem', *Operations Research*, vol. 31, no. 4.

___ 1983b, 'An Algorithm for Solving the General Bilevel Programming Problem', *Mathematics of Operation Research*, vol. 8, no. 2, pp. 260-723.

___ 1984a, 'Optimality Conditions for the Bilevel Programming Problem', *Naval Research Legistics Quarterly*, vol. 31, pp. 13-26.

___ 1984b, 'An Investigation of the Linear Three Level Programming Problem', *IEEE Trans. on Systems, Man and Cybernetics*, vol. SMC-14, no. 5, pp. 711-717.

___ 1985, 'Geometric and Algorithmic Developments for a Hierarchical Planning Problem', *European Journal of Operations Research*, vol. 19, pp. 372-83.

Bard, J. F. & Falk, J. 1982, 'An Explicit Solution to the Multi- level Programming Problem', *Computer and Operations research*, vol. 9, no. 1, pp. 77-100.

Berndt, E. R. & Wood, D. O. 1975, 'Technology, Prices, and Derieved Demand for Energy', *Review of Economics and Statistics*, vol. 57, no. 3, pp. 259-268.

Barnett, D. W. 1979, *Minerals and Energy in Australia*, Cassell, Sydney.

Barbier, E. B. 1989, *Economics, Natural- Resource Scarcity, and Development*, Earthscan Publications, London.

Basu, D. R. 1981, *Future Energy Policies for the UK: An Optimal Control Approach*, Macmillan Press, London.

Bator, F. 1958, 'The Anatomy of Market Failure', *Quarterly Journal of Economics*, vol. 72.

Baughman, L. 1972, *Dynamic Energy System Modelling: Inter-fuel Competition*, Ph.D. thesis, School of Engineering, M.I.T., Mass.

Bayraktar, et al. (eds) 1981, *Energy Policy Planning*, Plenum Press, New York.

Behling, D. J., Marcuse, W., Luckachiuski, J. & Dullien, R. 1977, 'The Long Term Economic and Environmental Consequences of Phasing Out Nuclear Electricity', in *Modelling Energy Economy Interactions: Five Approaches,* ed. C. J. Hitch, Resources for the Future, Washington D.C.

Behling, D. J., Marcuse, W., Swift, M. & Tessmer, R. 1975, 'A Two-level Iterative Model for Estimating Inter-fuel Substitution Effects', presented at Summer Computer Simulation Conference, San Francisco, California, July 21-23.

Bensousan, A. et al. 1974, *Management Applications of Modern Control Theory*, North-Holland , Amsterdam.

Bialas, W. & Karwan, M. H. 1980, *Multi-level Optimisation: A Mathematical Programming Perspective*, Dept. of Industrial Engineering, State University of New York, Buffalo.

__ 1982, 'On Two-level Optimisation', *Transactions on Automatic Control,* vol. AC-27, no. 1, pp. 211-214.

__ 1984, 'Two-level linear Programming', *Management Science*, vol. 30, no. 8, pp. 1004-1019.

Bialas, W., Karwan, M. & Shaw, J. 1980, *A Parametric Complementary Pivot Approach for Two-Level Linear Programming, Research Report*, Department of Industrial Engineering Operations Research Programme, State University of New York, Buffalo.

Bisschop, J., Candler, W., Duloy, J. H. & O'Mara, G. T. 1982, 'The Indus Basin Model: A Special Application of Two-Level Linear Programming', Mathematical Programming Study, vol. 20, pp. 30-38.

Bjerkholt, O., Olsen, O. & Vislie, J. (eds) 1990, *Recent Modelling Approaches in Applied Energy Economics*, Chapman & Hall, New York.

Black, J. (ed.) 1982, *Liquid Fuels in Australia: A Social Science Research Perspective*, Pergamon, Sydney.

Blaug, M. 1985, *Economic Theory in Retrospect*, 4th edn, Cambridge University Press, Cambridge, MA.

Bracken, J. & McGill, J. T. 1973, 'Mathematical Programmes with Optimisation Problems in the Constraints', *Operations Research*, vol. 21, pp. 37-44.

Bradley, S. P., Hox, A. C. & Magnanti, T. L. 1977, *Applied Mathematical Programming*, Addison-Wesley, Reading.

Brain, P. & Schuyers, G. 1981, *Energy and the Australian Economy*, Longman Cheshire, Sydney.

Branon, G. M. (ed.) 1975, *Studies in Energy Tax Policy*, Ballinger Press, Cambridge, MA.

Brock, H. W. & Nesbitt, D. M. 1977, *Large Scale Energy Planning Models: Methodological Analysis*, Stanford Research Institute, Menlo Park, CA.

Brosowski, B. & Deutsch, F. 1985, *Parametric Optimisation and Approximation*, Birkhauser Verlag, Boston.

Bullard, C. W. & Sebald, A. V. 1975, 'A Model for Analysing Energy Impact of Technological Change', presented at the Summer Computer Simulation Conference, San Francisco, California.

Candler, W. 1989, 1990, 1991, *Personal Communication*, World Bank, Washington D.C.

Candler, W. & Norton, R. 1977, *Multi-level Programming and Development Policy*, Bank Working Paper no. 258, World Bank, Washington D.C.

Candler, W. & Townsley, R. 1982, 'A Linear Two-level Programming Problem', *Computers and Operations Research,* vol. 9, no. 1, pp. 59-76.

Candler, W., Fortuny-Amat, J., & McCarl, B. 1981, 'The Potential Role of Multi-level Programming in Agricultural Economics', *American Journal of Agricultural Economics*, vol. 63, August, pp. 521-531.

Carey, M. et al. 1976, *The UK Energy Sector: A Cost Minimising Model with Fixed Demands*, Discussion Paper, Faculty of Commerce and Social Sciences, Birmingham University, Birmingham.

Carter, A. P. 1974, 'Energy, Environment and Economic Growth', *Bell Journal of Economy and Management Science*, vol. 5, pp. 578-592.

Cassing J. H. & Hilman. A. L. 1982, 'State-Federal Resource Rivalry: The Queensland Railway and the Federal Export Tax', *Economic Record*, vol. 58, pp. 235-241.

Centre for Applied Economic Research 1985, *Energy Modelling in Australia*, University of NSW, Sydney.

Cesar, H. S. J. 1994, *Control and Game Models of the Greenhouse Effect*, Springer-Verlag, Heidelberg.

Cherniavsky, E. A. 1981, 'Multi-objective Energy Analysis', pp. 399-420, in Bayraktar et al. (eds) 1981.

Christensen, L. R. et al. 1973, 'Transcendental Logarithmic Production Frontiers', *Review of Economics and Statistics*, vol. 55, no. 1 (February), pp. 28-45.

Christensen, L. R. et al. 1975, 'Transcendental Logarithmic Utility Functions', *American Economic Review*, vol. 65, no. 3 (June), pp. 367-383.

Clarke, R. J. et al. 1982, *Energy Pricing Issues in Victoria*, Centre Policy Studies, Monash University, Melbourne.

Common, M. 1988, *Environmental and Resource Economics: An Introduction*, Longman, New York.

Considine, D. M. 1977, *Energy Technology Handbook*, McGraw-Hill, New York.

Cook, P. L. & Surrey, A. J. 1977, *Energy Policy*, Martin Robertson.

Corbett, A. H. 1976, *Energy for Australia*, Penguin, Harmondsworth.

Crossley, D. J., Dick, J. & Mardon, J. D. 1980, 'Developing Energy Strategies for Australia', *Search,* vol. 11, no. 4, pp. 98-108.

Daellenbach, H. G., George, J. A. & McNickle, D. C. 1983, *Introduction to Operations Research Techniques,* Allyn and Bacon, London.

Daintith, J. (ed.) 1981, *Dictionary of Mathematics*, J. M. McGregor, Sydney.

Dantzig, G. B. 1974, 'On the Reduction of an Integrated Energy and Interindustry Model to a Smaller Linear Program', Technical Report SOL 74-20, System Optimisation Laboratory, Sandford University, Sandford.

Dantzig, G. B. & Wolf, P. 1961, 'The Decomposition Principle for Linear Programs', *Econometrica*, October, pp. 767-778.

Dantzig, G. B. et al. 1978, *Stanford Pilot Energy/Economic Model*, Stanford University, Palo Alto.

Debanne, J. G. 1975, 'Towards a Network Representation of Total Energy Supply-Distribution Systems', presented at the Summer Computer Simulation Conference.

Defrano, M. E. & Nugent, J. B. 1967, 'The Effects of Long-Run and Short-Run Planning Goals on Economic Policy Instruments', paper presented to the Econometric Society, Washington D.C., December 28.

Debrue, G. 1959, *The Theory of Value*, Wiley, New York.

DeLucia, R. & Jacoby, H. 1982, *Energy Planning for the Developing Countries: A Study of Bangladesh*, Johns Hopkin University Press, Baltimore.

Department of National Development 1979, *Australian Energy Policy: A Review*, AGPS, Canberra.

Department of National Development and Energy 1981, *Australian Energy Statistics*, AGPS, Canberra.

___ 1982, *Energy Demand and Supply Australia 1960-61 - 1980-81*, AGPS, Canberra.

___ 1988, *Energy 2000: A National Energy Policy Paper*, AGPS, Canberra.

__ 1983, *Forecast of Energy Demand and Supply in Australia: 1982-83 to 1991-92*, AGPS, Canberra.

__ 1984 ?, *Recent Development in Energy Policy*, AGPS, Canberra.

__ 1985, *A Modified Free Market for Indigenous Crude Oil*, Canberra.

__several issues, *Australian Energy Statistics*, AGPS, Canberra.

Derrick, S. D., McDonald, D. & Rosendale, P. 1981, 'The Development of Energy Resources in Australia: 1981 to 1990', *Australia Economic Review*, 3rd Quarter, pp. 13-55.

Diesendorf, M. O. (ed.) 1979, *Energy and People: Social Implications of Different Energy Futures*, Society for Responsible Society, Canberra.

Dirickx, Y. M. & Peter, L. 1979, *System Analysis by Multi-methods: With Application to Economics and Management*, J. Wiley, Chichester,

Dixon, L. C. W. & Szego, G. P. 1980, 'Numerical Optimisation of Dynamic Systems: A Survey', in *Numerical Optimisation of Dynamic Systems*, eds L. C. W. Dixon, & G. P. Szego, North-Holland, Amsterdam.

Dixon, P. B., Parmenter, B. R., Sutton, J. & Vincent, D. P. 1982, *ORANI: A Multi-sectoral Model of the Australian Economy*, North-Holland, Amsterdam.

Donnelly, W. A. 1984, *Energy Model for Australia*, Centre Resources Environmental Studies Working Paper no. 1984/4, CRES, Australian National University, Canberra.

Dovers, S. (ed.) 1994, *Sustainable Energy Systems: Pathways for Australian Energy Reform*, Cambridge University Press, Cambridge, MA.

Downs, A. 1957, *An Economic Theory of Democracy*, Harper and Row, New York.

Dudley, N. 1981, *Towards Optimal Decisions on Oil Stockpiling in Australia*, Centre for Applied Economic Research Paper no. 11, University of NSW, Sydney.

Edelman, D. J. 1978, 'Recent Energy Models A Review of Methodologies', *Journal of Environmental Systems*, vol. 7, no. 3, pp. 279- 292.

Edwards, G. W. 1983, 'Economic Aspects of Energy Policy', *Energy 83: Towards an Energy Policy for Australia*, Position Papers, Australian Institute of Engineers, Sydney.

Edwards, G. W. & Thorpe, M. W. 1978, 'Energy policy for Australia', *Australian Quarterly*, vol. 50, no. 2, pp. 22-38.

Eichner, A. S. 1979, *A Guide to Post-Keynesian Economics*, Macmillan, NY.

Emerson, C. & Lloyd, P. J. 1983, 'Improving Mineral Taxation in Australia', *Economic Record*, vol. 59, pp. 232-44.

Endersbee, L. A. et al. 1980, 'An Energy Policy for Australia', *Energy*, vol. 5, pp. 295-323.

Energy Victoria 1984, *Victoria Energy Plan: Progress Report on Energy Planning*, Department of Minerals Energy, Melbourne.

Enthoven, A. 1962, *Operations Research at the National Policy Level*, (Unpublished transcript of an address at the Operations Evaluation Group Biannual Conference, Washington, D.C., May), cited in *USCS and Limitations of System Analysis* (1967), C. T. Whitehead, Rand Corporation, Santa Monica, California.

Ethier, W. J. 1988, *Modern International Economics*, 2nd edn, W. W. Norton, New York.

ESCAP 1979, *Proceedings of the Working Group Meeting on Energy Planning and Programming and of the Committee on Natural Resources*, ERDS no. 20, UN, New York.

Esso Australia Ltd 1984, *Australian Energy Outlook*, Sydney.

Falk, J. 1987, *A Personal Communication*, Department of Operations Research, George Washington University, WA.

Fane, G. & Smith, B. 1986, 'Resource Rent Tax', in *Australian Energy Policies in the 80s*, eds Hocking et al. Ch. 7, pp. 209-241. Allen & Unwin, Sydney.

Fishbone, L. G. & Abilock, H. 1981, 'MARKAL - A Linear Programming Model for Energy System Analysis: Technical Description of the BNL Version', *Energy Research*, vol. 5, pp. 353-375.

Folie, G. M. & Ulph, A. M. 1976, *An Outline of an Energy Model for Australia*, CRES Working Paper R/WP5, Australian National University, Canberra.

__ 1977, *The Role of Energy Modelling in Policy Formulation*, CRES Working Paper CRE/WP7, Australian National University, Canberra.

__ 1979, 'Self-Sufficiency in Oil: An Economic Perspective on Possible Australian Policies', CAER Paper no. 6. University of New South Wales, Sydney.

__ 1982, 'Energy Policy for Australia', in *Industrial Economics: Australian Studies*, eds L. R. Webb & R. H. Allen, George Allen & Unwin, Sydney.

Forrester, T. W. 1961, *Industrial Dynamics*, John Wiley, New York.

Fortuny-Amat, J. 1979, *Multi-Level Programming*, Ph.D. Thesis, Department of Industrial Engineering, Purdue University, United States of America.

Fortuny-Amat, J. & McCarl, B. 1981, 'A Representation and Economic Interpretation of a Two-Level Programming Problem', *Journal of Operational Research Society*, vol. 32, pp. 783-792.

Fox, K. A., Sengupta, J. K. & Thorbecke, E. 1973, *The Theory of Quantitative Economic Policy with Applications to Economic Growth, Stabilisation and Planning*, North-Holland, Amsterdam.

Frisch, R. 1976, *Economic Planning Studies*, D. Reidel, Dordrecht, Holland.

Gal, T. 1979, *Postoptimal Analyses, Parametric Programming, and Related Topics*, McGraw-Hill, New York.

Galligan, B. 1983, 'National Energy Policy in Canada and Australia', *Australian Canadian Studies*, vol. 1, pp. 14-29.

Garnaut, R. & Clunies Ross, A. 1984, 'Uncertainty, Risk Aversion and the Taxing of Natural Resource Projects.', in *Mineral Economics in Australia*, ed. P.S. Lloyd, Allan and Unwin, Sydney.

Gatenby, H. 1986a, 'Two Sub-programmes for Finding Policy Optimum', University of Tasmania, Australia.

__ 1986b, 'Two Sub-programmes for Doing the Searches as is Proposed in Heaps 1986 and for Finding Policy Optimum', University of Tasmania, Australia.

Goreux, L. M. & Manne, A. S. 1973, *Multi-level Planning: Case Studies in Mexico*, North-Holland, Amsterdam.

Graaff, V. de V. 1957, *Theoretical Welfare Economics*, Cambridge University Press, London.

Graycar, A. (ed.) 1983, *Retreat from Welfare State*, Allen and Unwin, Sydney.

Gregory, R. G. 1984, 'Some Implications of the Growth of the Mineral Sector', in *Mineral Economics in Australia*, ed. P.J. Lloyd, Allen & Unwin, Sydney, pp. 285-310, first published in *Australian Journal and Agricultural Economics*, vol. 20, August 1976, pp. 71-91.

Greenberger, M. & Richels, R. 1979, 'Assessing Energy Models: Current State and Future Directions', *Annual Review of Energy*, vol. 4, pp. 467-500.

Griffin, J. M. & Steele, H. B. 1980, *Energy Economics and Policy*, Academic Press, London.

Groenewegen, P. 1984, *Public Finance in Australia*, 2nd ed., Prentice-Hall, Sydney.

Gross, P. & Smith, R. D. 1976, *Systems Analysis and Design for Management*, Dun-Donnelley.

Gruen, I. H. & Hillman, A. L. 1981, 'A Review of the Issues Pertinent to Liquid Fuel Policy', *Economic Record*, June, pp. 111- 127.

Häfele, W. 1981, *Energy in a Finite Word: Paths to Sustainable Future*, Ballinger, Cambridge, MA.

Hall, V. B. 1983, 'Some Thoughts on Energy Modelling and Policy in Australia', Department of Economics, University of Sydney, Australia.

__ 1984, 'Some Thoughts on Energy Modelling and Policy in Australia,' *Economic Papers*, vol. 3, no. 1, pp. 21-36.

Hallet, A. H. & Rees, H. 1983, *Quantitative Economic Policies and Interactive Planning: A Reconstruction of the Theory of Economic Policy*, Cambridge University Press, Cambridge, MA.

Hansen, B. 1958, *The Economic Theory of Fiscal Policy*, Harvard University Press, Cambridge, MA.

Harberger, A. 1971, 'Three Basic Postulates of Applied Welfare Analysis', *Journal of Economic Literature*, vol. 9, no. 3, pp. 785-797.

Harder, E. L. 1982, *Fundamentals of Energy Production*, Wiley, New York.

Harris, S. F. 1981, 'Energy and Equity: What is the Market's Place?', in *Proceedings of the 51st ANZAAS Congress*, Sect. 24 (Econ.), Presidential Address, Brisbane.

Hazell, P. B. R. & Norton, R. D. 1986, *Mathematical Programming for Economic Analysis in Agriculture*, Macmillan, London.

Heaps, T. 1985, *A Formula to Determine Some Alternative Combinations of the Units for Parametric Variations*. Dept. of Economics, Simon Frasher University, Canada, (personal communication).

Heliwell, J. F. 1984, 'Natural Resources and the Australian Economy', in *The Australian Economy: A View from the North*, eds R. E. Caves L. R. Krause, pp. 81-126, Washington DC.

Henderson, J. F. & Norman, P. M. 1975, 'The Equations of the RBA1/74 Model of the Australian Economy', Reserve Bank of Australia, Research Discussion Paper 7504, Sydney.

Henderson, J. M. & Quandt, R. E. 1980, *Microeconomic Theory*, 3rd ed., McGraw-Hill, London.

Hevendeen, R. A. 1974, 'Use of Input-Output Analysis to Determine the Energy Cost of Goods and Services', in *Energy Demand, Conservation and Institutional Problems*, ed. M. S. Macrakis, MIT Press, Massachusetts.

Higgins, C. I. & Fitzgerald, V. W. 1973, 'An Econometric Model of the Australian Economy', *Journal of Econometrics*, vol. 1, pp. 229-65.

Hildebrandt, T. (undated), 'Evolution and State of the Art of Energy Modelling in Europe', *System Research and Technological Development*, Nuclear Research Centre, Julich.

Hitch, C. J. (ed.) 1977, *Modelling Energy-Economy Interactions: Five Approaches*, Research Paper R. 5, Resources for the Future, Washington, D.C.

Hocking, D. M 1975, 'Do We Need a National Energy Policy?', background paper prepared for conference on Energy Resources Policy: The Australian Prospect, Sydney University Extension Board, Sydney.

Hoffman K. C. 1974, 'A Unified Framework for Energy System Planning', in *Energy Modelling, Special Issue of Energy Policy*, IPC Science and Technological Press, Surrey, U.K.

Hoffman, K. C. & Jorgenson, D. 1977, 'Economic and Technological Models for Evaluation of Energy Policy', *Bell Journal of Economics*, vol. 8, no. 2, pp. 444-446.

Hoffman, K. C. & Wood, D. O. 1976, 'Energy System Modelling and Forecasting', *Annual Review of Energy*, vol. 1, pp. 423-454.

Hogan, W. W. & Manne, A. S. 1977, 'Energy-Economy Interactions: The Fable of the Elephant and the Rabbit?', in Hitch (1977).

Hogan, W. W. & Weyant, P. 1980, 'Combined Energy Models', Energy and Environmental Policy Centre, John F. Kennedy School of Government, Harvard University, Boston, MA.

Hotelling, H. 1931, 'The Economics of Exhaustible Resources', *Journal of Political Economy*, vol. 39, pp. 137-175.

Howe, C. W. 1979, *Natural Resources Economics*, Wiley , New York.

Hudson, E. A. & Jorgenson, D.W. 1974, 'U.S. Energy Policy and Economic Growth 1975-2000', *Bell Journal of Economics and Management Science*, vol. 5, pp. 461-514.

___ 1976, 'Tax Policy and Energy Conservation', in *Econometric Studies of U.S. Energy Policy*, ed. D.W. Jorgenson, North-Holland, Amsterdam.

Hunt, V. D. 1979, *Energy Dictionary*, Van Nostrand Reinhold Company, New York.

Idrus, N. & Islam, N. 1992, 'Development Changes, Environmental Implications and Adjustments in Policy Measures in the South Pacific Economies', paper presented at the National Conference on Environmental Engineering, 'The Global Environment - Australian Implications', Institution of Engineers Australia, Gold Coast, National Conference Publication no. 92/5.

International Energy Agency 1986, *Energy Policies and Programmes of I.E.A Countries,* OECD, Paris.

International Energy Agency 1996, *World Energy Outlook,* OECD, Paris.

Intriligator, M. D. 1971, *Mathematical Optimisation and Economic Theory*, Prentice-Hall, N.J.

Islam, S. M. N. 1983, 'An Optimum Economic Policy Framework for the Energy Sector,' paper presented to the 12th Conference of Economists, 28 August - 1 September, Hobart.

__ 1991a, 'Mathematical Properties of Multi-level Programming', *PNG Journal of Mathematics,* vol. 2, no. 1, pp. 8-13.

__ 1991b, 'Resource Control Multi-level Programming: A Parametric Programming Search Algorithm', *PNG Journal of Mathematics*, vol. 2, no. 2, pp. 66-73.

__ 1994, 'AEPSOM: The Australian Energy Policy System Optimisation Model - Model Specification, solution Algorithm and Model Results', Centre for Strategic Economic Studies, Victoria University of Technology, Melbourne.

__ 1995, 'Australian Dynamic Integrated Climate Economic Model (ADICE): Model specification, Numerical Implementation, and Policy Implication', Seminar paper presented at CSES, Victoria University, Melbourne, 8 September, 1995.

__ 1995, 'The Role of Renewable Energy in the Energy System: An Issue in the Philosophy of Renewal of Natural Resources', *Energy Economics*, vol. 17, no. 2, pp. 117-124.

__ 1996 (forthcoming), 'Energy Planning and Multi-Level Optimisation: The Australian Energy Planning System Optimisation (AEPSOM) Study', in *Systems Modelling for Energy Policy*, ed. D. W. Bunn & E. Larsen, John Willey, UK.

__ 1996, 'Pricing Issues in the Energy Sector: On an Integrated Approach to Energy Pricing', *International Journal of Global Energy Issues*, vol. 6, pp. 469-475.

__ 1994-1996, some papers from the Centre for Strategic Economic Studies, Victoria University, Melbourne:

(1) Taxes and Subsidies in the Energy Sector: Can We Make a Rational Choice?

(2) The Existence of the Multi-level Policy System in the Energy Sector: An Exercise in Numerically Explicating the Characteristics of the Multi-level Policy System.

(3) Conservation of Energy: Justification and Welfare Implication.

(4) Technological Developments, the Decision Making Constrains and the Choice of Technologies in the Energy Sector.

(5) Exploration and Development Policies in the Energy Sector: An Empirical Approach

(6) Resource Depletion Policy in the Energy Sector: On the Choice of Policy in a Multi-level Policy Environment.

(7) Market Failures, Multi-level Policy System and Improved Policy Performance in a Sectoral Context.

(8) Hierarchical Decision Making and Optimum Policy Choice Under Different Market Conditions: Explanations by Adopting Multi-level Programming.

(9) Energy Planning and Multi-level Optimisation, Seminar Paper, 17 August 1995, CSES, VUT

(10) Sustainable Industry Economic Development in the Australian Energy Sector: Findings of the Australian Energy System Optimisation Model : AEPSOM.

Islam, S. M. N. & Sheehan, P. 1996, 'Research and Development Expenditure, Social Welfare and Industrial Development: An Australian Energy Economics Prospective', *Proceedings of the Joint International Institutes of Applied System Analysis/ Japan Society of Energy and Resource Workshop on Energy, Economics, and Environment*, Osaka University, June 25-27, Japan.

Jaforullah, M. 1988, 'Energy Modelling in a General Equilibrium Framework with Alternative Production Specifications', unpublished Ph.D. thesis, University of Adelaide, Adelaide.

James, D. 1983, *Integrated Energy-Economic-Environment Modelling with Special Reference to Australia*, Dept. of Home Affairs and Environment, Canberra.

___ 1987, personal communication, Macquire University, Sydney.

James, D., Musgrove, A. R. & Stocks, K. J. 1986, 'Integration of an Economic Input- Output Model and a Linear Programming Technological Model for Energy System Analysis', *Energy Economics*, April, pp. 99-112.

Johansen, L. 1960, *A Multi-Sectoral Study of Economic Growth*, North-Holland, Amsterdam.

___ 1974, 'Establishing Preference Functions for Macroeconomic Decision Models - Some Observations on Ragnar Frich's Contributions', *European Economic Review*, vol. 5, pp. 41-66.

Jones, B., Bush, S., Kanakaratnam, A., Leonard, M. & Gillan, P. 1991, *Projections of Energy Demand and Supply: Australia 1990-91 to 2004-2005*, Australian Bureau of Agricultural and Resources Economics, Canberra.

Julius, D. 1981, *Energy Pricing in the Developing Countries: A Review of Literature*, World Bank Energy Department, Paper no. 1, Washington D.C.

Just, J. E. 1974, 'Impacts of New Energy Technology Using Generalised Input-Output Analysis', ed. M.S. Macrakis, MIT Press, Massachusetts.

Kaldor, N. 1939, 'Welfare Comparisons of Economics and Interpersonal Comparisons of Utility', *Economic Journal*, vol. 49, pp. 549-552.

Karunaratne, N. D. 1981, 'An Input-Output Analysis of Australian Energy Planning Issues', *Energy Economics*, vol. 3, no. 3, pp. 159-168.

Kneese, A. V. & Sweeney, J. L. 1993, *Handbook of Natural Resources and Energy Economics*, vol. 1-3, North Holland, Amsterdam

Kornai, J. 1969, 'Man-Machine Planning', *Economics of Planning*, vol. 9, no. 3, pp. 209-234.

Kresge, D. 1980, 'An Approach to Independent Model Assessment', in *Validation and Assessment Issues of Energy Models*, ed. S.I. Gass, National Bureau of Standards Special Publication 569, Washington D.C.

Kydes, A. 1978, *The Brookhaven Energy System Optimisation Model - Its Variants and Uses*, Brookhaven National Laboratory, BNL- 50873, Upton, N.Y.

Labys, W. C. 1982, 'Measuring the Validity and Performance of Energy Models,' *Energy Economics*, July, pp. 159-168.

Lewis, A. 1949, *Overhead Cost*, London.

Lipsey, R. G. & Lancaster, K. 1956-1957, 'The General Theory of Second Best', *Review of Economic Studies*, vol. 24, no. 1, pp. 11-32.

Lloyd. P. J. (ed.) 1984, *Mineral Economics in Australia*, Allen & Unwin, Sydney.

Lotus Development Corporation, *Lotus 1-2-3*.

Malinvaud, E. 1967, 'Decentralised Procedures for Planning', in *Activity Analysis in the Theory of Growth and Planning*, eds Malinvaud and M.O.L. Bacharach, Macmillan, London.

Manne, A. S. 1977, 'ETA-MACRO A Model of Energy-Economy Interactions', in *Modelling of Energy-Economy Interactions: Five Approaches*, ed. C. J. Hitch, Resources for the Future, Washington D.C.

Manne, A. S. & Goreux, L. M. (eds) 1973, *Multi-level Planning: Case Studies in Mexico*, North Holland, Amsterdam.

Marcuse, W. & Bodin, L. 1975, 'A Dynamic Time Dependent Model for the Analysis of Alternative Energy Policies', presented at the Summer Computer Simulation Conference.

Marks, R. 1986, 'Energy Issues and Policies in Australia', *Annual Review of Energy*, vol. 11, pp. 47-75.

Marshall, A. 1920, *Principles of Economics*, Macmillan, London (originally published in 1890).

McCarl, B. A. & Spreen, T. H. 1980, 'Price Endogenous Mathematical Programming as a Tool for Sector Analysis', *American Journal of Agricultural Economics*, vol. 62, pp. 87-102.

McColl, G. D. 1982, 'Changes in the International Energy Situation and their Implications for Australia', CAER Paper no. 15, Centre for Applied Economic Research, University of New South Wales, Sydney.

Meadows, D. L. et al. 1972, *The Limits to Growth*, Universe Book, Washington D.C.

Meier, P. 1984, *Energy System Analysis in the Developing Countries*, Springer-Verlag, New York.

__ 1986, *Energy Planning in Developing Countries: An Introduction to Analytical Methods*, Westview Press, Denver.

Mendelsohn, R. 1983, *Australian Social Welfare Finance*, Allen & Unwin, Sydney.

Mesarovic, M. D., Sanders, J. L. & Sprogue, C. E. 1973, 'An Axiomatic Approach to Organisations from a General Viewpoint', in *System Analysis*, ed. S.L. Optuer, Penguin Books, Middlesex.

Mishan, E. J. 1981, *Introduction to Normative Economics*, Oxford University Press, Oxford.

Mork, K. A. (ed.) 1981, *Energy Prices, Inflation and Economic Activity*, Ballinger, Cambridge, MA.

Mubayi, V. & Meier, P. 1981, *Energy Models for Developing Countries: A Comparative Assessment*, Brookhaven National Laboratory, BNL-51446, Upton, N.Y.

Munasinghe, M. & Schramm, G. 1983, *Energy Economics, Demand Management and Conservation Policy*, Van Nostrand Reinhold, New York.

Murtagh, B. A. 1981, *Advanced Linear Programming*, McGraw-Hill, New York.

Musgrave, R. A. 1959, *The Theory of Public Finance*, McGraw-Hill, New York.

Musgrove, A. R. 1987, personal communication, CSIRO, Lucas Heights, New South Wales.

Musgrove, A. R., Stocks, J. K., Essam, P., Le, D. & Hoetzl, V. J. 1983, *Exploring Some Australian Energy Alternatives using MARKAL*, Division of Energy Technology, Technical Report TR2, CSIRO, Lucas Heights, NSW.

National Energy Advisory Committee 1978, 'Some Aspects of Energy Modelling in Australia', Canberra.

Naylor, T. H. & Vernon, J. M. 1969, *Microeconomics and Decision Models of the Firm*, Harcourt, Brace and World, New York.

Neil, R. F. 1977, *Managing the Energy Transition, A System Dynamics Search for Alternatives to Oil and Gas*, Ballinger, Mass.

Nemetaz, P. N., Vertinsky, I. B., Vertinsky, P. & Kanetkar, V. 1984, 'Threat in Opportunity and Opportunity in Threat: Energy Prospects for Australia and New Zealand', *Journal of Energy Development*, vol. 9, pp. 263-88.

Norton, R. D. & Schiefer, G. W. 1980, 'Agricultural Sector Programming Models: A Review', *The European Review of Agricultural Economics*, vol. 7, no. 3, pp. 229-264.

Nykamp, P. & Somerneyer, W. H. 1971, 'Explicating Implicit Social Preference Functions', *Economics of Planning*, vol. 11, no. 3, pp. 101-119.

Optner, S. L. (ed.) 1973, *System Analysis*, Penguin Books, Middlesex.

Oser, J. &. Brue, S.L 1988, *The Evolution of Economic Thought*, 4th ed., Harcourt Brace Jovanovich, New York.

Park, S. H. 1982, 'An Input-Output Framework for Analysing Energy Consumption', *Energy Economics*, April, pp.105-110.

Park, S. H. & Kubursi, A. A. 1983, 'The Energy Constraints and Development; Consistency and Optimality Overtime', *Energy Economics*, January, pp. 9-15.

Pearse, A. R. & Hardaker, J. B. 1984, 'A Program for Solving Linear Programming Problems', Miscellaneous Publication no. 8, Department of Agricultural Economics and Business Management, University of New England, Armidale.

Planco Inc. 1979, *Survey of the Research into Energy-Economy Interactions*, 2 Volumes, Dallas, TX.

Powell, A. A. 1974, *Empirical Analytics of Demand Systems*, Lexington Books, Mass.

___ 1980, 'The Major Streams of Economy-Wide Modelling: Is Rapprochement Possible?', in *Large Scale Econometric Models: Theory and Practice*, eds J. Kmenta & J.B. Ramsey, North-Holland, Amsterdam.

Preston, A. J. & Pegan, A. R. 1983, *The Theory of Economic Policy*, Cambridge University Press, Cambridge, MA.

Propoi, A. 1980, 'Dynamic Linear Programming', in *Numerical Optimisation of Dynamic Systems*, eds L.C.W. Dixon & G.P. Szego , North-Holland, Amsterdam.

Propoi, A. & Zimin, I. 1981, 'Dynamic Linear Programming Models of Energy Resource, and Economic Development Systems', RR-81-44, International Institute for Applied System Analysis, Laxenburg, Austria.

Rath-Nagel, S. & Voss, A. 1981, 'Energy Models for Planning and Policy Assessment', *European Journal of Operation Research*, vol. 8, pp. 99-114.

Riaz, T. 1984, *Pakistan: The Energy Sector*, Ferozsons Ltd, Lahore.

Richards, W. 1982, 'The Energy Policy Framework: A State Bargaining Approach', *Journal of Australian Political Economy*, vol. 12/13, pp. 110-28.

Richards, W. & Saddler, H. D. W. 1981, 'Petroleum Pricing: Equity Versus Efficiency', Petroleum Industry Research Project Background Paper, Centre for Resources and Environmental Studies, Australian National University, Canberra.

Rooke, Sir D., Fells, I. & Horlock J. 1995, Energy for the Future, The Royal Society, New York.

Saddler, H. D. W. 1981, *Energy in Australia: Politics and Economics*, Allen & Unwin, Sydney.

Samuelson, P. A. 1952, 'Spatial Price Equilibrium and Linear Programming', *American Economic Review*, vol. 42, pp. 283-303.

Schuyers, G. P. 1979, *New Energy Technologies in Australia*, Ph.D. thesis, University of Melbourne, Melbourne.

Sengupta, J. K. & Fox, K. A. 1969, *Economic Analysis and Operation Research Optimisation Techniques in Quantitative Economic Models*, North-Holland, Amsterdam.

Shaw, J. P. 1980, *A Parametric Complementary Pivot Approach to Multilevel Programming*, M.Sc. Thesis, State University of New York, Buffalo.

Shumway, C. R. & Chang, A. A. 1977, 'The Linear Programming versus Positively Estimated Supply Functions: An Empirical and Methodological Critique', *American Journal of Agricultural Economics*, vol. 59, pp. 344-357.

Skrapek, W. A., Korkie, B. M. & Daniel, T. E. 1976, *Mathematical Dictionary for Economics and Bussiness Administration*, Allan and Bacon, Boston.

Smith, B. (ed.) 1979, *Taxation of the Mining Industry*, CRES, Australian National University, Canberra.

Sparrow, T., Pilati, D. & Marcuse, W. 1979, 'A Programming Model for Industrial Energy Conservation Policy', *Resources and Energy*, vol. 2, pp. 179-199.

Stancescu, I. D. 1985, *Energy and Nuclear Power Planning in Developing Countries*, International Atomic Energy Agency, Viena.

Sterner, T. (ed.) 1992, *International Energy Economics*, Chapman & Hall, New York.

Stewart, G. A., Nix, H. A., Gartside, G., Rawlins, W., Gifford, R. & Siemon, J. 1979, *The Potential for Liquid Fuels from Agriculture and Forestry in Australia*, CSIRO, Canberra.

Swaine, D. J. (ed.) 1990, *Greenhouse and Energy*, CSIRO, Melbourne.

Swan, P. L. 1984, 'Resource Rent Tax: The Issues', *Economic Papers*, vol. 3, pp. 1-10.

___ 1984b, 'Real Rates of Return in Electricity Supply: New South Wales. Tasmania, and Victoria.', paper presented at Conference Economic Electric Power System, University of New South Wales, Sydney, May 2-3.

Sweeney, J. L. 1981, 'Energy and Economic Growth: A Conceptual Framework', in *Mathematical Modelling of Energy Systems*, ed. I. Kavrakoglyu, Sijthoff & Noordhoff International Publishers B.V., Netherlands.

Taha, A. H. 1976, *Operations Research: An Introduction*, 2nd ed., Macmillan, New York.

Takayama, A. 1974, *Mathematical Economics*, Holt, Rinehart & Winston, New York.

Tengrove, C. D. (ed.) 1986, *Australian Energy Policies in the 80's*, Allen and Unwin, Sydney.

Tessmer, R. G. & Hoffman, K. C 1975, 'Coupled Energy-System- Economic Models and Strategic Planning', in *Computers and Operations Research*, vol. 2. Pergamon Press, Oxford.

Theil, H. 1956, 'On the Theory of Economic Policy', *American Economic Review, Papers and Proceedings*, vol. 46, May, pp. 360-366.

__ 1970, *Economic Forecasts and Policy*, North-Holland, Amsterdam.

Tinbergen, J. 1952, *On the Theory of Economic Policy*, North- Holland, Amsterdam.

__ 1956, 'Determination of an Optimum Economic Policy', *Econometrica*, vol. 28, pp. 1-10.

Todaro, M. P. 1971, *Development Planning Models and Methods*, Oxford University Press, Nairobi.

Todd, J. 1983, 'Some Comments on Australian Fuelwood Use', keynote address, *Firewood Forum*, Institute of Foresters Australia Inc., Canberra, 29-30 April.

Treasury of Australia 1984, 'Energy Markets: Some Principles of Pricing', in *Mineral Economics in Australia*, ed. P. J. Lloyd, Allen & Unwin, Sydney.

Trehan, R. K., Leigh, J. G. & Park, W. R. 1979, *Energy and Development: A Preliminary Analysis for Less Developed Countries*. Mitre Corporation, McLean, VA.

Unlu, G. 1987, 'A Linear Bilevel Programming Algorithm Based on Bicriteria Programming', *Computers Operation Research*, vol. 14, no. 2, pp. 173-179.

Van Dugteren, T. (ed.) 1980, *Oil and Australia's Future: The Economic, Social and Political Aspects*, Hodder & Stoughton, Sydney.

van Eijk, C. J. & Sandee, J. 1959, 'Quantitative Determination of an Optimum Economic Policy', *Econometrica*, vol. 27, pp. 1-13.

Vincent, D. P. et al. 1979, *The Short-term Effect of Oil Price Increases on the Australian Economy with Special Reference to the Agricultural Sector*, paper presented to the Australian Agricultural Economics Society, 23rd Annual Conference, Canberra, (cited in Brain & Schuyers 1981).

Vincent, D. P., Dixon, P. B., Parmenter, B. R. & Sams, D. C. 1980, 'Implications of World Energy Price Increases for the Rural and Other Sectors of the Australian Economy', in *The Impact of Changes in Energy Costs on the Rural Sector of the Australian Economy*, eds K.M.W. Howers et al., Division Land Resources and Management, CSIRO, Perth.

Walras, L. 1954, *Elements of Pure Economics* (translated by W. Jaffe), Allen & Uwin, London. (Originally published in 1874).

Webb, M. G. 1967, *Pricing Policies for Public Enterprises*, Macmillan, London.

Webb, W. G. & Ricketts, M. J. 1980, *Economics of Energy*, Macmillan, London.

Wells, G. M. 1977, *Optimal Economic Policies in Australia*, Ph.D. thesis, Department of Economics, University of Tasmania.

Wen, U. 1981, *Mathematical Methods for Multi-level Programming*, Ph. D. thesis, State University of New York, New York.

Wen, U. & Bialas, W. F. 1986, 'The Hybrid Algorithm for Solving the Three-level Linear Programming Problem', *Computers and Operation Research*, vol. 13, no. 4, pp. 366-377.

Weymans-Jones, T. 1986, *The Economics of Energy Policy*, Gower,

Wright. A. W. 1978, 'The Case of the United States: Energy as a Political Good', *Journal of Comparative Economics*, vol. 2, pp. 144-70.

Index

Druck: Strauss Offsetdruck, Mörlenbach
Verarbeitung: Schäffer, Grünstadt